VEGAS® 6 REVEALED:
THE OFFICIAL GUIDE

Doug Sahlin

THOMSON
━━━━━✶━━━━━ ™
COURSE TECHNOLOGY
Professional ■ Technical ■ Reference

Publisher and General Manager, Thomson Course Technology PTR: Stacy L. Hiquet

Associate Director of Marketing: Sarah O'Donnell

Manager of Editorial Services: Heather Talbot

Marketing Manager: Heather Hurley

Executive Editor: Kevin Harreld

Senior Editor: Mark Garvey

Marketing Coordinator: Jordan Casey

Project Editor: Kezia Endsley

Technical Reviewer: Bonnie Blake

Thomson Course Technology PTR Editorial Services Coordinator: Elizabeth Furbish

Copyeditor: Kezia Endsley

Interior Layout Tech: Sue Honeywell

Cover Designer: Steve Deschene

Indexer: Kelly Talbot

Proofreader: Sean Medlock

THOMSON

COURSE TECHNOLOGY

Professional ■ Technical ■ Reference

25 Thomson Place
Boston, MA 02210
www.courseptr.com

Vegas® 6 is a registered trademark of Sony Pictures Digital, Inc.

All other trademarks are the property of their respective owners.

Important: Thomson Course Technology PTR cannot provide software support. Please contact the appropriate software manufacturer's technical support line or Web site for assistance.

Thomson Course Technology PTR and the author have attempted throughout this book to distinguish proprietary trademarks from descriptive terms by following the capitalization style used by the manufacturer.

Information contained in this book has been obtained by Thomson Course Technology PTR from sources believed to be reliable. However, because of the possibility of human or mechanical error by our sources, Thomson Course Technology PTR, or others, the Publisher does not guarantee the accuracy, adequacy, or completeness of any information and is not responsible for any errors or omissions or the results obtained from use of such information. Readers should be particularly aware of the fact that the Internet is an ever-changing entity. Some facts may have changed since this book went to press.

Educational facilities, companies, and organizations interested in multiple copies or licensing of this book should contact the publisher for quantity discount information. Training manuals, CD-ROMs, and portions of this book are also available individually or can be tailored for specific needs.

ISBN: 1-59200-971-9

Library of Congress Catalog Card Number: 2005927431

Printed in U.S.A.

06 07 08 09 PH 10 9 8 7 6 5 4 3 2

For Emily, whenever I may find her.

Acknowledgments

Without a cast of thousands, a book could not be written. And the daunting task of which members of the cast to acknowledge is always handed off to the author. I apologize in advance for anyone I may have overlooked. First and foremost I would like to thank Stacy Hiquet and Kevin Harreld for making this project possible. I'd also like to thank project editor extraordinaire Kezia Endsley for keeping this project on track and doing an incredible job of manicuring the text for this book.

Special thanks to my friend and digital video guru Bonnie Blake for doing an extraordinary job of tech editing this book. Your comments were spot on, Lucy.

Thanks to the fine folks at Sony Pictures Digital, Inc. for creating an awesome application. Vegas rocks! Two AttaBoys are awarded to Vegas Product Manager Dave Hill for promptly answering my queries.

I'd also like to thank my friends and support team. Hats off to my agent Margot Maley Hutchison. Kudos to fellow authors Bonnie Blake, Joyce Evans, and Ken Milburn for being a source of inspiration and a sounding board for ideas. Thanks to Barry Murphy and Elaine Kreston for being great musicians, world-class friends, and an endless source of creative inspiration. As always, special thanks to my friends, mentors, and family members; especially you, Karen and Ted. Warm regards to my companion of six years, a loveable calico named Niki, who thinks she's Queen of The Universe.

About the Author

DOUG SAHLIN is an author, photographer, and videographer living in Lakeland, Florida. He uses Sony Vegas to create video productions for viewing on the Web, computer monitors, and for DVDs that will be viewed with set-top DVD players. His clients include authors, actors, fashion models, manufacturers of skin care products, and Web designers.

Sahlin is the author of 15 books on graphic design, image-editing, and office applications including *Naked Vegas 5*, *Digital Photography QuickSteps*, and three editions of *How To Do Everything with Adobe Acrobat*.

In his spare time, Doug enjoys watercolor painting, music, working out, and practicing yoga.

ACKNOWLEDGMENTS/ABOUT THE AUTHOR

CONTENTS

**Chapter 4
Using Advanced Video Editing
Techniques   133**

Chapter 7
Creating Generated Media   265

Revealed Series Vision

A book with the word "Revealed" in the title suggests that the topic that is being covered contains many hidden secrets that need to be brought to light. For Vegas, this suggestion makes sense. Vegas 6 is an awesome application. However, finding out exactly how to accomplish some task can be time-consuming without some help. This book was designed to enable you to quickly find the information you need to accomplish specific tasks.

As you dive into the *Revealed* series, you'll find a book with a split personality. The main text of each lesson includes a detailed discussion of a specific topic, but alongside the topic discussions are step-by-step objectives that help you master the same topic that is being discussed. This unique "read it and do it" approach leads directly to "understand it and master it."

—The *Revealed* Series

Author Vision

While I was creating the outline for this book, I thought back to my first experiences with Vegas 4.0. I was an experienced video editor. As such, I was expecting a complicated interface with mega-windows. I was pleasantly surprised when I first launched the application. The Vegas designers did an awesome job of designing an intuitive, well thought out interface. The more I worked with the application, the more appreciative I became of the unique features of the application.

However, any new application has a learning curve. My goal while writing this book was to create content that would minimize the learning curve, revealing all of the information I gleaned while working with the Vegas 6 beta, and transferring my knowledge from previous versions of the application. The first few chapters in the book were designed to quickly get readers up to speed with the powerful features of Vegas. If you're new to video editing or Vegas, you'll find this information imperative. Experienced Vegas users may find the first few chapters useful as a refresher course.

I chose to pack all of the cool features of Vegas in the middle chapters of the book. Here you find specific tasks that show how to add pizzazz to your productions through the use of multiple tracks, video transitions, editing media clips, and so on. Sound is an important facet of any video production, so I devoted an entire chapter to the subject. I also devote a chapter to creating generated media, which are used to credit titles, credits, and backgrounds for special effects.

I use a lot of the Vegas features to create special effects for my productions. I cover these techniques in several chapters. I show you easy step-by-step methods for creating compelling intros to your productions, and how to use event panning and cropping to create moving video collages and other effects.

Producing a long video from hundreds of video clips can be a daunting task. However, Vegas does have several features you can use to manage your work. After you create a compelling production, you render the production to share it with friends, or with the rest of the world. Vegas gives you hundreds of options for creating video that is viewed on the Web, or destined to be included on a DVD that will be broadcast on a television set. The last chapter of the book cuts to the chase and shows you what you need to know to render your projects.

Along with every discussed task are several step-by-step objectives that show you a simplified example of the discussed topic. Each was created to keep the number of steps to a minimum. I've tried to add some variety here and there, but none of these examples should be overwhelming. These examples should serve as a starting point for more creative work.

Many of the objectives build on each other. I instruct you to create a new project, and then show you the steps needed to cover a specific task. I instruct you to keep the project open when it will be used in the next objective. However, if you need a break, and will not move onto the next objective, save the project to your desktop for your next reading.

Vegas is an incredible application, but it isn't overwhelming. In the pages that follow, you find most every feature is covered, providing you with a reference that you can use whenever you get stuck or to give you some creative inspiration.

—Doug Sahlin

Introduction

Welcome to *Vegas 6 Revealed: The Official Guide*. Whether you're a seasoned digital video editor or you're just getting your feet wet, Vegas 6 has all of the features you need to create a professional video production with bells and whistles such as eye-popping transitions and special effects such as video clips in motion, split-window titles, and so on. Within this book you'll find explicit instructions on how to come to terms with Vegas 6.

The first chapters of this book introduce you to Vegas 6 and show you how to edit your digital video. You learn to work within the Vegas workspace and customize the application to suit your working preferences. You also learn to create new projects, specify project settings, add media to your projects, and edit your digital video clips.

The middle part of the book deals with advanced digital video techniques. You learn to work with multiple tracks, add compelling transitions to your projects, and work with sound. Creating generated media such as titles and credits are also revealed in this part of the book. If you want to add special effects and visual eye candy to your projects, you learn to do so in Chapters 8 and 9.

The last chapter of the book shows you how to render your projects for viewing on the Web, computer monitors, or television sets. You also learn to create custom templates to suit your needs. Finally, the bonus chapter, which you can download from the book's Web site, shows you some tips and tricks you can use to simplify your workflow in Vegas.

VEGAS® 6 REVEALED
THE OFFICIAL GUIDE

chapter **1**

GETTING TO KNOW
Vegas 6

1. Explore the workspace.

2. Explore the timeline.

3. Learn the menu commands.

4. Edit with tools.

5. Save a project.

6. Customize Vegas.

7. Set Vegas preferences.

GETTING TO KNOW
Vegas 6

Sony Vegas 6 enables you to edit digital video and create compelling video productions. Sony Vegas is now in its sixth iteration and is packed with features that rival many so-called industry leaders. Since the release of Vegas 4.0 in February 2003, the application has received rave reviews and as a result is no longer the best-kept secret in nonlinear video editing software. The application has powerful features such as color correction that are normally found in applications costing three times the cost of Vegas 6. Vegas 6 is the second release of the application under Sony's tenure. With exciting new features such as the **Media Manager** and unparalleled ease of use, the application has a bright future.

Sony Vegas 6 is a flexible and easy-to-use video editing application. You edit your video clips on a sophisticated timeline and can work with multiple video and audio tracks, composite video, and much more. While you're editing a production, you can preview your work with any standard video card. If you're using Vegas with a powerful computer, you can preview your video projects that have no effects applied in real

time. Other applications require high-end video cards to preview a production in real time. Vegas 6 has an interface that might seem foreign to users of other video-editing applications. However, users of **Acid Pro**, Sony's award-winning music-creation program, will feel right at home with Vegas 6. Converts from other video editing applications quickly adapt to and favor the Vegas workspace. Instead of having to scurry through multiple menus to find the applicable commands, you can quickly access a related command by right-clicking an object and then choosing the desired command from the shortcut menu. And yes, that's a shortcut menu because Vegas 6 is a Windows-only application.

Whether you're creating, editing, and producing video for the World Wide Web, multimedia productions, or DVD projects, Sony Vegas 6 is your complete video editing solution. You can mix and match videos of different frame rates and use unlimited tracks. You can composite videos from various tracks to create special effects or apply video filters to individual video clips (known as events) or to an entire track. If necessary, you can apply one or more video filters (a single video filter is an **Event FX**, whereas multiple video filters applied to a video event are known as a **plug-in chain** in Vegas) to all videos in a production through the use of a **video bus**.

You have equal flexibility with audio tracks. You can add an unlimited number of audio tracks to a production. You apply audio filters to individual audio events, to entire audio tracks, or to audio for the entire production through the use of **audio busses**. You can also use audio busses to mix the audio tracks in your project.

In this chapter, you'll find basic information about Sony Vegas 6. You'll learn your way around the interface; learn how to begin a new project, and learn how to add media to the timeline. You'll also learn to save a project for future editing and customize Vegas to suit your working style. The material presented here will give you an idea of basic workflow in Vegas and serve as a starting point for more advanced material.

Tools You'll Use

EXPLORE THE
WORKSPACE

What You'll Do

In this lesson, you learn to launch Vegas and create a new project. After creating the project, you import a media file.

Viewing the Main Window

When you launch Vegas for the first time, you see the main window, which has a menu bar, a toolbar, a time display, and a timeline. Below the time display, you see a large window divided in two. As you build your video project, this window becomes home to the individual audio and video tracks you use to create the finished product. Below the track window, you see the **Window Docking area**. This area is where you'll find windows you use to add media to a project, generate media such as titles and backgrounds, add video transitions to your productions, and so on.

As you create your project, you'll frequently move from the timeline to the Window Docking area, and then use menu commands to edit your project. In addition to using menu commands to edit a project, you can take advantage of time-saving shortcut menus.

The Vegas design team has done a wonderful job of making the interface user friendly, and at the same time flexible. When you add video clips to a track or create a new video track, you can manipulate the view to suit your needs. Vegas video tracks feature thumbnail images of the timeline. If you need to zoom in on a particular frame of your production, you can easily do so. When you zoom in, you have a full-color thumbnail image of the frame, which makes it easy to ascertain what's happening in this part of your production. If you've worked with other nonlinear video editing applications that only show a thumbnail of the first and last frame of a clip, you know what a valuable feature this is.

Saving a Project File

When you're done editing a project for the day, you can save the project. When you save a project, you don't create a movie, you create a *VEG file that contains all the pertinent information you need to reconstruct the track timelines, as well as any transitions or video effects you've applied to the project video clips.

As you gain experience with Vegas, you'll find yourself using the same windows and menu commands on a regular basis. Although video editing can be complex, the Vegas design team has engineered a lot of flexibility into the workspace, which makes it easy for you to come to grips with the application. You can open and close windows as needed with menu commands, keyboard shortcuts, or by clicking a tab of a window currently displayed in the Window Docking area. You can also float any window, which is a handy feature when you're fine-tuning a production or setting parameters for a video clip (known as an *event* in Vegas), while previewing your production in the Video Preview window. Figure 1-1 shows the Vegas workspace as it appears after opening a previously saved project.

FIGURE 1-1

Creating a project in Vegas

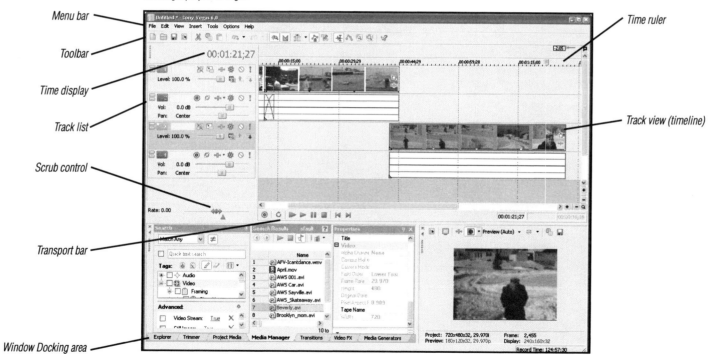

Menu bar

Toolbar

Time display

Track list

Scrub control

Transport bar

Window Docking area

Time ruler

Track view (timeline)

Launch Vegas and create a project

1. Launch Vegas from your desktop by choosing Start > All Programs > Sony > Vegas 6.0.

   ### QUICKTIP

   To create a desktop shortcut for Vegas, open Windows Explorer, navigate to the folder in which your Vegas applicant files are stored (the default installation path is C:\Program Files\Sony\Vegas 6.0), right-click the Vegas60.exe icon, and drag it to the desktop. Release the mouse button and then choose Create Shortcuts Here from the shortcut menu.

2. Choose File > New.

   Vegas displays the New dialog box. From within this dialog box, you set the parameters for the project you are creating.

3. Accept the default settings and then click OK.

4. Choose File > Import Media.

   Vegas displays the Import Media dialog box.

5. Navigate to the folder in which you've stored your video files, select a video file, and then click Open.

   Vegas imports the file and adds the clip to the Project Media window. Figure 1-2 shows several video clips in the Project Media window of the Window Docking area.

6. Keep the file open, as you'll be using it in upcoming lessons.

Explore the Window Docking area

1. Click the Explorer tab.

FIGURE 1-2

Window Docking area is divided into tabs

Close window

Expand/
Collapse
window

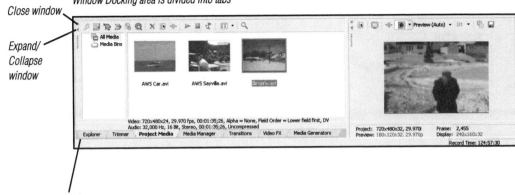

Window Docking area tabs

The Vegas Explorer is similar to Windows Explorer. You use the Vegas Explorer to navigate to directories on your hard drive and select media.

2. Navigate to the folder where you store your video files; then double-click a video file.

When you double-click a video file from the Explorer, Vegas creates a video track. If the video has embedded audio, Vegas creates an audio track and adds the file to the Project Media window.

3. Click the video clip on the timeline, right-click, and then choose Open in Trimmer from the shortcut menu.

You use the Trimmer to remove unwanted frames from video events without altering your original video clips.

4. Click the Project Media window to display the clips you've imported into your project.

The Project Media window is a visual representation of the media you've imported into your project. You can further organize the Project Media window by creating **media bins** and renaming media.

> **QUICKTIP**
>
> Click the triangle below the Close button to expand or contract the docking window.

5. Click the Media Manager tab.

The Media Manager displays all video clips you've worked with since launching Vegas 6. You use the Media Manager to add information to video clips such as your rating of the clip, copyright information, author of the media, and so on. You can also use search

features of the Media Manager to locate media you've previously imported into Vegas.

6. Click the Transitions tab.

The Transitions window of the Window Docking area is divided into two sections. The left section shows the title of each Transition group. The right section contains thumbnail previews of each transition within the selected group.

7. Click the Video Effects tab.

The Video Effects window of the Window Docking area is also divided into two sections. The left section lists the title of each Video Effects group, whereas the right section contains thumbnail previews of each effect within the selected group.

> **QUICKTIP**
>
> Click the Close button to close the currently selected tab in the Window Docking area.

8. Click the Media Generator tab.

The Media Generator window of the Window Docking area is divided into two sections. The left section contains the title of each Media group, whereas the right section contains a thumbnail preview of the media. You use the Media Generator to create backgrounds, titles, credits, and so on for your video productions.

> **QUICKTIP**
>
> Click the divider on top of the Window Docking area and drag up or down to change the height of the window. Drag the divider to the right of the window and drag right or left to change the width of the window.

EXPLORE THE TIMELINE

What You'll Do

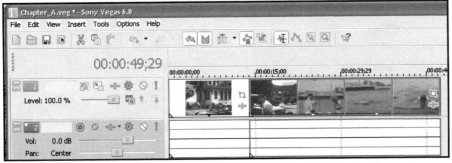

 In this lesson, you add media from the Project Media window to the timeline. You use the controls at the bottom of the main window to change your view of the timeline.

Working with the Timeline

The timeline is where it all happens. You add media to the timeline and then arrange the media to create the final production. Figure 1-3 shows a timeline with a single video and audio track to which multiple video clips have been added. Video and audio clips added to the timelines are known as *events* in Vegas. You can alter the duration of an event and apply Event FX

(which are similar to filters in image-editing applications) without altering your original clip. When you add clips to the timeline, you can overlap the events to create a transition from one event to the next. You can also apply video effects to a single event, or an entire track. For example, you might need to color correct the footage for an individual event, or brighten and enhance the contrast of a flat washed-out footage. In addition, you can apply one or

more effects (known in Vegas as a plug-in chain) to an entire track.

Working with Multiple Tracks

After adding a video clip with embedded audio to the timeline, you have two tracks with which to work. This enables you to apply video effects to the video track and audio effects to the audio track. From within Vegas, you can launch Sony Sound Forge if you have the application installed on your system and edit audio tracks.

When you create a project that has multiple video clips, you can arrange the events on a single timeline track or create additional video tracks. When you have multiple video tracks, you can composite the tracks to create special effects, as you'll learn to do in upcoming chapters. You can also use filters to create special effects, and use multiple tracks to create effects such as a video within a video and much more.

In addition, you can have multiple audio tracks in a project. When you have multiple audio tracks, you can control the volume and pan of each track to create the desired effect. You can also apply audio effects to individual audio clips on a track, or apply the desired effects to an entire audio track. You can then use the **master mixer** to mix all audio tracks before rendering the project. But before you can do all of this cool stuff, you have to know your way around the timeline. Consider this lesson your baptism by fire.

FIGURE 1-3
Multiple events on the timeline

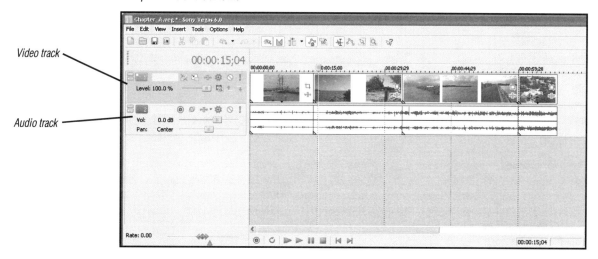

Video track

Audio track

Add media to the timeline

1. Create a new project and import four video clips, as outlined in the previous lesson.

2. Drag a video clip from the Project Media window and drop it in the main window.

Vegas creates a track for the video clip. When you insert a video clip with embedded audio, Vegas creates an audio and video track. When you add a clip to the timeline, Vegas snaps the clip to a tick mark on the time ruler, if you have snapping enabled; however, the clip is added to the timeline in the relative position where you drop it. In other words, Vegas does not snap the clip to the beginning of the timeline, or the tail of the event nearest the position where you drop the clip you are inserting.

> **QUICKTIP**
> You can also import media by clicking the Explorer tab in the docking window and navigating to the folder in which you store video clips. Click the desired file and drop it on the desired track.

3. Align the clip to the beginning of the timeline.

4. Add three more clips to the timeline, aligning the clips end to end. Your timeline should resemble Figure 1-4.

> **QUICKTIP**
> You can select a range of media clips from the Project Media window by clicking a video clip, and then Shift-clicking the last video clip you want to import. You can also import noncontiguous clips by clicking a clip, and then Ctrl-clicking additional clips you want to import.

FIGURE 1-4

The Media pool

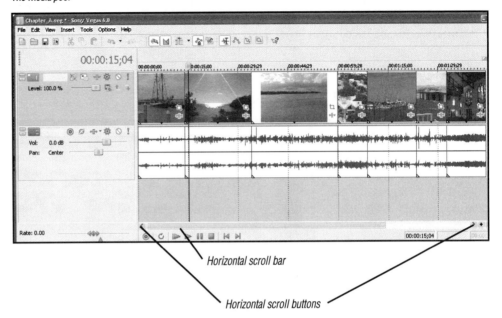

Horizontal scroll bar

Horizontal scroll buttons

Change the timeline view

1. Create a new project and add four video clips to the timeline.

2. Place your cursor over the vertical indentation at the right end of the horizontal scroll bar. When your cursor becomes a double-headed arrow, drag left to zoom in on the timeline, or drag right to zoom out.

   When you zoom in on the timeline, you see more detail. As you zoom in, Vegas refreshes the thumbnails for the video track. If you zoom in close enough, Vegas displays a thumbnail for each frame.

   QUICKTIP

   If your system sports a scroll wheel mouse, you can zoom in on the timeline by placing your cursor in the main window and turning the mouse wheel away from you. Zoom out by turning the mouse wheel toward you.

3. Click the plus sign (+) next to the right scroll button to zoom in on the timeline; click the minus sign (-) to zoom out.

   Each click of the plus sign (+) zooms in to the next highest level of magnification, whereas each click of the minus sign (-) zooms out to the next lowest level of magnification.

   QUICKTIP

   Select the Zoom tool shown in Figure 1-4 and then click and drag around the frames you want to zoom in on.

4. Click the right horizontal scroll button to scroll right. Click the left horizontal scroll button to scroll left.

   QUICKTIP

   You can also scroll the timeline by clicking the space between the horizontal scroll bar and either scroll button.

   QUICKTIP

   Click the vertical plus sign (+) to increase the height of each track; click the vertical minus sign (-) to decrease the height of each track. Drag the vertical scroll bar to scroll vertically through the tracks in your production.

LEARN THE
MENU COMMANDS

What You'll Do

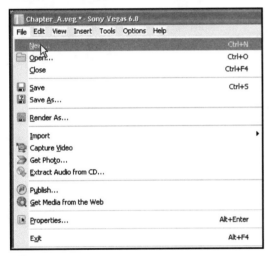

In this lesson, you learn how to access the menu commands and their counterparts from shortcut menus.

Working with Menu Commands

Vegas is a wonderfully diverse application. You can use its tools to perform many of the tasks you need to assemble video clips into a finished production. However, your first line of defense is always the menu commands. You use menu commands to open existing projects, create new projects, save projects, and so on.

You'll find all the commands neatly laid out on the menu bar at the top of the Vegas workspace. Vegas commands are divided into seven groups. In addition to using the commands to edit video, create transitions, and apply special effects, you can use menu commands to preview your projects, add video and audio tracks, and so on. Table 1-1 shows the seven menu groups you have at your disposal.

Table 1-1: Vegas Menu Command Groups

Menu Group	Description of Commands
File	Commands to create new projects, open files, save files, render projects as movies, capture video, and import media.
Edit	Commands to cut, copy, and paste events, as well as paste event attributes. This group also contains commands to split video clips, group video clips, select editing tools, apply ripple edits, and more.
View	Commands to display or hide windows in the Window Docking area, as well as other windows you might have floating in the workspace. This group also contains commands to view or hide envelopes in your productions.
Insert	Commands to insert audio and video envelopes, audio and video tracks, and audio and video buses. This group also contains commands to insert text and generated media and markers and regions.
Tools	Commands that enable you to apply effects and otherwise manipulate project media. This group also contains commands to render selections to a new track, prerender video, print video to tape, and more.
Options	Commands to apply options to the timeline tracks, such as how media events snap to the timeline, how the grid on the time ruler is spaced, which unit of measure is used for grid marks on the time ruler, and so on. This group also contains commands that determine how other media on a track is affected when you add additional media to the track.
Help	Commands to access the Vegas help document, which contains a vast array of topics designed to clarify tasks you perform in Vegas. You'll also find a list of the extensive Vegas keyboard shortcuts, in addition to links to Internet resources for Vegas.

You'll find most menu commands duplicated on shortcut menus. The upcoming lesson will give you a brief tour of the menu bar shown in Figure 1-5. In this figure, the cursor is paused over the Edit menu group, which displays the list of editing commands. You'll find instructions for menu commands when they pertain to a particular lesson or topic of discussion. The purpose of this lesson is to give you the lay of the land. You'll also discover information on the types of commands you can expect to find on shortcut menus.

FIGURE 1-5

Menu bar

Menu bar

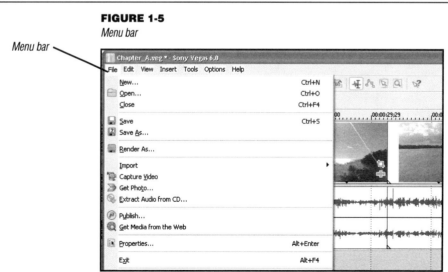

Use the Vegas menu commands

1. Create a new project. Then arrange some video clips on the timeline as outlined previously. Alternatively, you can open a previously saved project.

2. Select the Normal Edit tool. Then position your cursor over the center of the first clip.

3. Click the Edit group on the menu bar.

   A drop-down list of Edit commands appears.

4. Select the Split command.

   The video clip is split into two events. The split command is just one of the commands you'll use to edit your video productions. Notice that the new event from the clip you just split is still selected.

5. Choose Edit > Copy.

   The selected event is copied to the Clipboard.

6. Click an empty spot on the timeline. Then choose Edit > Paste.

   Vegas pastes the copied video and audio tracks to the timeline.

QUICKTIP

Choose Help > Contents and Index to display the Vegas Online Help dialog box. From within this dialog box, you can peruse a menu of available help topics or click the Search tab, where you can search for help about a specific topic.

Use the Vegas shortcut menus

1. Position your cursor over the first track name in the Track List window and right-click it.

   When you right-click a track, you display a shortcut menu that contains commands that are pertinent to the selected track.

2. Position your cursor over the second track name. Right-click to display the shortcut menu shown in Figure 1-6.

   Video and audio tracks have different shortcut menus.

3. Position your cursor over the first track timeline and right-click.

   The shortcut menu for a timeline contains commands that are pertinent to the timeline.

FIGURE 1-6
Audio track shortcut menu

EDIT WITH TOOLS

What You'll Do

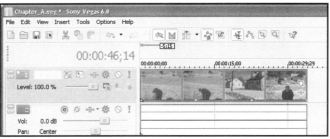

In this lesson, you learn how to use the editing tools that are available on the toolbar. You use tools to create a project, as well as select and move timeline events.

Using the Edit Tools

You'll do most of your work in Vegas on the timeline. Unlike many drawing applications where you're actually creating shapes and objects, in a nonlinear video editing application, you manipulate clips on the timeline. Each clip you add to a timeline track is known as an event. You have relatively few tools with which to work in Vegas

FIGURE 1-7
Vegas toolbar

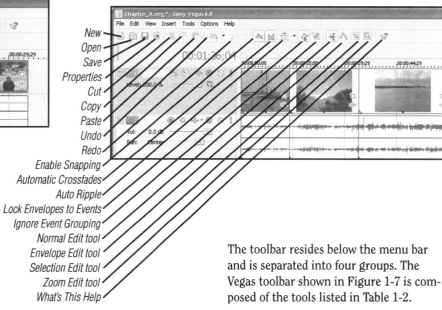

New
Open
Save
Properties
Cut
Copy
Paste
Undo
Redo
Enable Snapping
Automatic Crossfades
Auto Ripple
Lock Envelopes to Events
Ignore Event Grouping
Normal Edit tool
Envelope Edit tool
Selection Edit tool
Zoom Edit tool
What's This Help

The toolbar resides below the menu bar and is separated into four groups. The Vegas toolbar shown in Figure 1-7 is composed of the tools listed in Table 1-2.

because quite frankly, most of your work is done with menu commands and tabs within the Window Docking area.

Table 1-2: Function of Each Vegas Toolbar Tool

Tool	Function
New	Creates a new project.
Open	Opens an existing project.
Save	Saves the current project.
Properties	Opens the Project Properties dialog box. To display individual project settings, click the appropriate tab. For example, to view the project's audio settings, click the Properties button and then click the Audio tab.
Cut	Cuts selected event(s) or time range.
Copy	Copies selected event(s) or time range to system Clipboard.
Paste	Pastes Clipboard contents into the project.
Undo	Undoes the previous action. The down-arrow to the right of the Undo tool reveals a drop-down list of commands that can be undone.
Redo	Redoes the previous undone action. The down-arrow to the right of the Redo tool reveals a drop-down list of commands that can be redone.
Enable Snapping	Snaps media events to grid points on the timeline.
Automatic Crossfades	Applies a crossfade to overlapped events.
Auto Ripple	Rearranges existing events to accommodate for new events added to the timeline.
Lock Envelopes to Events	Locks envelope points to events.
Ignore Event Grouping	Disables groups.
Normal Edit tool	Selects and moves events and groups.
Envelope Event tool	Edits points in event envelopes.
Selection Edit tool	Creates a selection.
Zoom Edit Tool	Zooms in on or out of the timeline.
What's This Help	Accesses help about a specific tool or interface element.

Each tool is discussed in detail as it pertains to a specific lesson. This lesson introduces you to the toolbar and a few of the more frequently used tools.

FIGURE 1-8
Using tools to edit media clips

Use the toolbar

1. Click the New button ⬜ .

   Vegas creates a new document using the default project settings.

2. Click the Explorer tab, navigate to the folder where you store your video clips, and then drag three clips into the main window. Align the clips end to end.

3. Click the Selection Edit tool ⬚ and drag a marquee around the last two clips on the timeline.

   Vegas highlights the two clips, which indicates they have been selected.

4. Click the Normal Edit tool ⬚ and drag the selected clips to the right.

5. Click the Enable Snapping tool ⬚ to disable snapping. Then drag the selected clips to the left so that they overlap the first clip on the timeline.

   Notice that the clips did not snap to the marks on the time ruler. When you disable snapping, you can move the clips to any position on the timeline.

6. Click anywhere inside the window to deselect the clips.

7. Click the Normal Edit tool. Then drag the last clip so that it overlaps the second clip.

   Vegas creates a transition between the clips, as shown in Figure 1-8. Notice that with snapping enabled, the clip snaps to the time ruler grid marks. Crossed lines note a transition, where two clips overlap.

8. Keep this project open because you'll use it in the upcoming lesson. Alternatively, if you won't be reading the next lesson immediately, save the project.

QUICKTIP

Click the What's This Help button. Then click any button or interface element to reveal a tooltip with information about the button or interface element.

USING THE UNDO AND REDO TOOLS

When you work on a project in Vegas, every action you perform after creating a new project or opening a saved project is saved to your hard drive scratch disk as the project edit history. You can undo several actions in one fell swoop by clicking the down arrow to the right of the Undo button and selecting one or more actions from the undo list. When you undo one or more actions, they appear on the redo list, which you can access by clicking the down arrow to the right of the Redo button. When you're working on a large project, the project edit history can take up a significant amount of hard drive space. You can clear the project history and recover hard disk space by choosing Edit > Clear Edit History. When you save a project and exit Vegas, the project history is erased from your hard drive. When you reopen the project, a new project history is created that records every action performed in the current session.

SAVE A PROJECT

What You'll Do

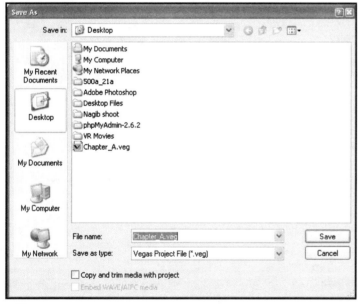

In this lesson, you learn to save a project. You can save a project with media or without.

Saving a Project

When you edit video in Vegas, your goal is to render a video file for display on a computer monitor, a Web site, or a television set. However, the editing process can often be lengthy—probably more than you'll care to undertake in one session. You can save a project at any time. When you save a project, Vegas creates a VEG file. When you save a project using the default settings, the VEG file contains all the information Vegas needs to re-create the track's timelines and all the other edits you've applied to a project, when you open the saved VEG file.

The VEG file does not save the project media; it records the path to the media along with information that the application uses to reconstruct the project, complete with all edits and transition effects you've applied and so on. If after saving the project, you move any of the media to a different folder, a warning dialog box appears the next time you open the project file telling you that the media is offline. The dialog box gives you options to locate the offline media, ignore the offline media, or cancel opening the project.

When you save a project, you can opt to save the project with media. When you choose this option, you can either save the source media with the VEG project file, or save trimmed copies of the source media with the project file. When you save a project with media, the media is stored in the same folder as the project file.

When you save a project for the first time, the Save As dialog box appears. When you use the Save command again, the project is automatically saved to the folder in which you originally saved the project. To save an existing project in a different folder or with a different name, you use the Save As command.

Save a project

1. Choose File > Save.

   The Save As dialog box opens, as shown in Figure 1-9.

2. Navigate to the folder where you want to save the project.

   > **QUICKTIP**
   >
   > You can create a new folder by clicking the New Folder button in the Save As dialog box.

3. Enter a name for the project. Then click Save.

   Your project is saved for future editing.

Save a project with media

1. Choose File > Save.

   The Save As dialog box appears.

2. Navigate to the folder in which you want to save the project.

FIGURE 1-9

Save As dialog box

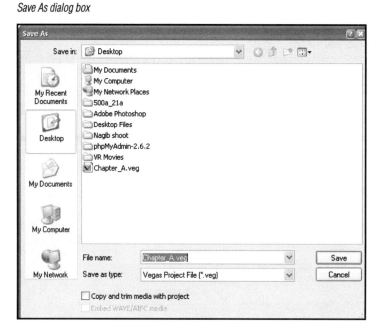

FIGURE 1-10

Copy Media Options dialog box

3. Click the Copy and Trim Media with Project check box. Then click Save.

   The Copy Media Options dialog box appears, as shown in Figure 1-10.

4. Click the Copy Source Media radio button to copy each clip used in the project in its entirety to the folder in which the project file is saved. Alternatively, accept the default option of Create Trimmed Copies of Source Media.

   Accept the default option if the clips are trimmed to your satisfaction and you don't anticipate applying additional edits to the source media or using other portions of the source media when editing the project in the future. Remember that the saved media are copies of your original source material. If you trim a 30-second clip to 15 seconds and save the trimmed media with the project, you will not be able to increase the duration of the saved media.

5. If you decide to create trimmed copies of the source media, accept the default option of adding two seconds to the head and tail of the clip, or enter a different value in the text field.

   If you add a head and tail to each clip in the project, you'll be able to fine-tune the duration of each clip when editing the project. Adding a head and tail to the clip gives you a bit of headroom with which to work.

6. Click OK.

   Your project file and copies of the source media are saved to the specified folder.

QUICKTIP

Saving a backup of a project is a good idea when you're working on a complex project that will span several sessions. After you finish work for the day, you can save a backup of a project by choosing File > Save As to save the project with a different name. If you should ever have a computer glitch that corrupts the project file, you can resort to your last saved backup version.

Lesson 5   Save a Project

VEGAS 6 REVEALED 23

CUSTOMIZE VEGAS

What You'll Do

In this lesson, you learn to customize the Vegas workspace to suit your working preferences. You learn to change the order in which windows appear in the docking window, float windows, add buttons to the toolbar, and more.

Modifying the Workspace

When you create a video project, you often use the same windows on a repetitive basis. The default Vegas workspace docks fre-

quently used windows in the Window Docking area. Each window is identified by a tab at the bottom of the Window Docking area. If you prefer, you can float a window in the workspace, which is handy when you're working with the same window for an extended period of time. For example, when you're modifying events by adding Effects, it's beneficial to float the Video Preview window so that you can view the effects of your edits.

When you float a window, you can also resize it. For example, you can resize the Video Preview window to get a better look at the video as you preview it. You can easily resize any window that you float in the workspace by dragging a handle. For that matter, you can also change the height of

the Window Docking area. You can also float windows within the Window Docking area. This is handy when you need to view multiple windows within the Window Docking area. If you float a window within the Window Docking area, you can change its width. You can save window layouts by pressing Ctrl+ Alt+D and then a number key across the top of the keyboard. This assigns this layout to that number. To recall a layout, press Alt+D and the number. However, when you exit the application, Vegas records the positions in which you left the workspace windows. When you launch Vegas again, the windows will be as you last left them.

Modifying the Toolbar

Another option at your disposal is changing the layout of the toolbar. You can change the order in which buttons appear on the toolbar, delete buttons you infrequently use, and add buttons for commands you use often.

FIGURE 1-11

Modifying the Window Docking area

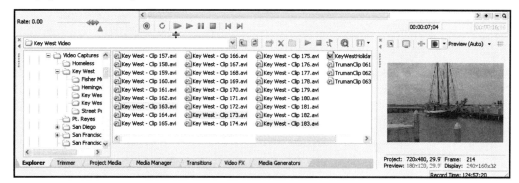

1. Move your cursor toward the top of the Window Docking area. When your cursor becomes two parallel horizontal lines with up- and down-pointing arrows, click and drag up to increase height, or click and drag down to decrease height, as shown in Figure 1-11.

2. Click the handle (six dots aligned vertically) on the left side of the window and drag it to the right to float it within the Window Docking area.

    After you float a window within the Window Docking area, a separator bar appears between the windows.

3. Move your cursor toward the separator bar on the right side of a window that's docked within the Window Docking area. When your cursor becomes two parallel vertical lines with right- and left-pointing arrows, click and drag right to increase width, or click and drag left to decrease width.

4. Click the Close button to close the currently displayed window.

5. Click the left-pointing arrow below the Close button to expand the a docked window to fill the Window Docking area. Click the right-pointing arrow to collapse a window docked within the Window Docking area to its normal width.

Float a docked window

1. In the docking window, click the tab of the window you want to float.

2. Click the handle (six dots aligned vertically) on the left side of the window and drag it to the desired position in the workspace.

3. Move your cursor toward the lower-right corner of the floated window. When your cursor becomes a diagonal line with two arrows, click and drag to resize the window.

4. Move your cursor toward the left or right border of the floated window. When your cursor becomes a horizontal line with two arrows, click and drag right or left to change the window width.

5. Move your cursor toward the upper or lower border of the window. When your cursor becomes a vertical line with two arrows, click and drag up or down to change the height of the window.

6. Click the title bar of the floated window. Then drag it to a different location in the workspace.

Figure 1-12 shows the Video Preview Monitor floating in the workspace.

FIGURE 1-12
Floating a window

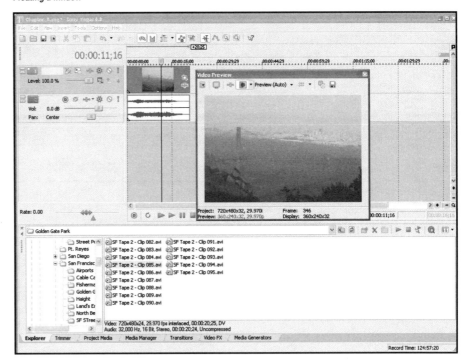

FIGURE 1-13

Customizing the toolbar

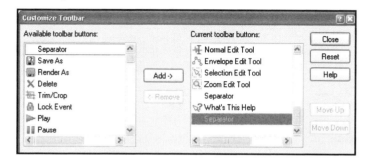

1. Choose Options > Customize Toolbar.

The Customize Toolbar dialog box appears, as shown in Figure 1-13. The left window of the dialog box contains a list of all available buttons, whereas the right side of the dialog box contains a list of the buttons currently displayed on the toolbar.

2. Select a button on the left side of the window. Then click Add.

The Add button adds an available button to the toolbar.

QUICKTIP

Add a separator to divide one group of tools from another.

3. Select a button in the right window. Then click Remove.

The Remove button removes the selected button from the toolbar.

4. On the right side of the window, click the Move Up or Move Down button to change the order in which the button appears on the toolbar.

5. Click Close to apply your changes to the toolbar.

QUICKTIP

To restore the toolbar to its default settings, open the Customize Toolbar dialog box; then click Reset.

SET VEGAS PREFERENCES

What You'll Do

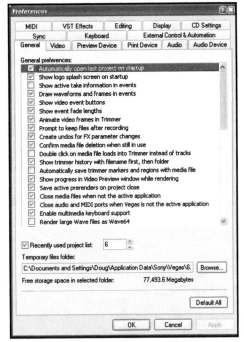

In this lesson, you get an introduction to Vegas preferences. You learn about the tabs that make up the Vegas Preferences dialog box and set a preference.

Setting Your Preferences

Software users have different ways of working with and using applications, which is the reason that most applications give you the option of setting preferences. When you set preferences, you modify the way Vegas performs to suit your working style. Vegas is a robust application, and as such, it has many preferences with which you can work. The Vegas Preferences dialog box is divided into the following tabs:

- **General.** In this tab, you set preferences for launching Vegas, auto saving, opening media files, determining the number of files displayed on the recently saved list, and so on.

- **Video.** In this tab, you set the amount of RAM that Vegas uses to create a Dynamic Ram Preview, set the preferred video capture application, set video preview options, track fade colors, and so on.

- **Preview Device.** In this tab, you can configure an external monitor on which to preview your video.

- **Print Device.** In this tab, you can configure the device to which you print projects to tape.

- **Video Devices.** In this tab, you set preferences for external video devices such as external monitors that are attached to FireWire IEEE-1394 capture devices and some MJPEG capture cards.

- **Audio.** In this tab, you set options for waveform display, the preferred external audio editor, and the metronome.

- **Audio Device.** In this tab, you set preferences for the default audio driver used by Vegas 5.1 audio devices attached to your system and the default audio recording device.

- **Sync.** In this tab, you set MIDI timecode defaults for MIDI devices that are attached to your system.

- **Keyboard.** In this tab, you can edit existing keyboard shortcuts, and create new ones.

- **External Control and Automation.** In this tab, you can choose and configure external devices that are connected to your machine.

- **MIDI.** In this tab, you configure MIDI devices that are connected to your computer to work with Vegas software.
- **VST Effects.** In this tab, you specify the location of any VST plug-ins you have installed on your machine.
- **Editing.** In this tab, you set preferences for event looping, JKL keyboard shuttle speed, audio quick fade, default display duration for timeline images, and envelope fade defaults.

- **Display.** In this tab, you can modify the display colors for tracks and envelopes. You can also change the saturation.
- **CD Settings.** In this tab, you set preferences for the default CD-ROM burner used by Vegas, the default burn speed, and the CD-ROM audio extraction defaults.

Individual preferences will be covered when they pertain to a topic of discussion, whereas other preferences are self-explanatory. The best course of action to take concerning preferences is to work with Vegas with the default preference settings. After you have a few video projects under your belt, the settings in each tab will make more sense to you. At this time, you can set preferences to streamline your workflow.

Hide the docking window

1. Choose Options > Preferences.

   The Preferences dialog box shown in Figure 1-14 appears.

2. If it's not already selected, click the General tab.

   You click this tab to display the available preferences for a category.

3. Drag the scroll bar until you see an option labeled Automatically Hide the Docking Window.

4. Click the check box to select the preference option.

   Clicking a check box selects the option. Preference options currently in effect are signified by a filled check box next to the preference name. Click a filled check box to deselect the option.

5. Click OK to close the Preferences dialog box.

6. Click anywhere inside the workspace.

   The docking window is hidden.

7. Move your cursor to the bottom of the work-space.

   The docking window is revealed. This is just one example of using Preferences to modify the manner in which Vegas reacts to user input.

FIGURE 1-14

Vegas Preferences dialog box

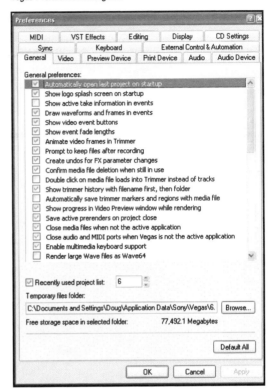

Getting Online Help

1. Launch Vegas.

2. Choose Help > Contents and Index.

3. Click the Search tab, shown in Figure 1-15.

4. Enter Timeline in the Type In the Words to Search For field.

5. Click List Topics to display the list of topics shown in Figure 1-16.

6. Choose a topic to display.

7. Click Display.

8. Double-click a different topic.

FIGURE 1-15
Help Search tab

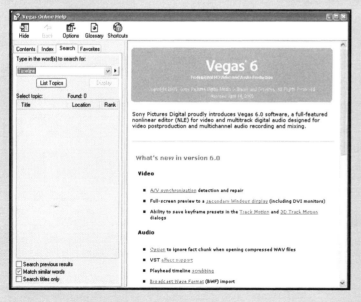

FIGURE 1-16
Timeline Help topics

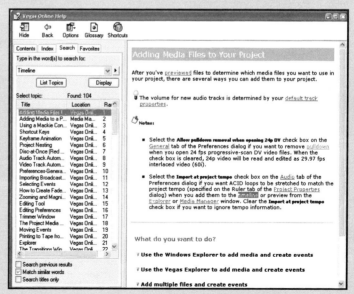

SKILLS REVIEW

Creating a New Document, Importing Media, and Saving a Project

1. Launch Vegas.

2. Click the New button on the toolbar.

3. Click the Explorer tab in the Window Docking area shown in Figure 1-17.

4. Navigate to the folder where you store your video clips.

5. Select a video clip, and then Ctrl-click two other video clips.

6. Drag the clips into the main window and align them to the start of the time ruler to create three events, as shown in Figure 1-18.

7. Choose Project > Save.

8. Name the file Skills_1. Then click Save.

FIGURE 1-17
Explorer tab

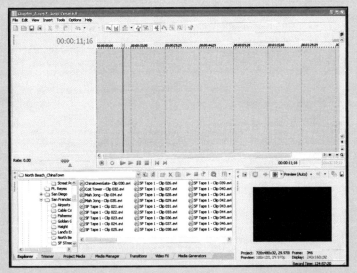

FIGURE 1-18
Adding clips to a project

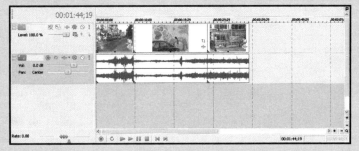

Opening and Editing an Existing File

1. Choose File > Open.

2. Select the file Skills_1. Click Open.

3. Select the second event and drag it to the end of the third event.

4. Use the Selection Edit tool to select the last two events, as shown in Figure 1-19.

5. Use the Normal Selection tool to align the selected events to the end of the first event, as shown in Figure 1-20.

6. Leave the file open and proceed to the next skills review.

Using the Shortcut Menu

1. Right-click the second event. If your video event has embedded audio, Shift-click the audio track for the event.

2. Choose Copy from the shortcut menu, shown in Figure 1-21.

3. Place your cursor at the end of the third event. Then click the mouse button.

4. Right-click and choose Paste from the shortcut menu.

5. Save the project.

FIGURE 1-19

Selecting events with the Selection Edit tool

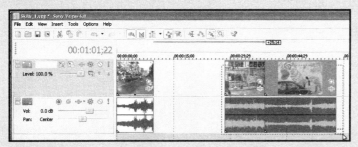

FIGURE 1-20

Moving selected events with the Normal Selection tool

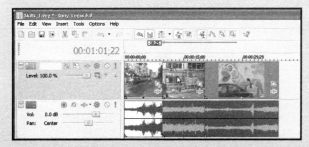

FIGURE 1-21

Shortcut menu

PROJECT BUILDER 1

Your production manager has just returned from a field trip. She's captured some wonderful video of a historic park that she wants to include in the project you've just created. At this point, nothing is set in stone. Your current goal is to assemble your assets for future editing.

1. Save three new video clips to the Chapter_1 folder.

2. Launch Vegas and open the Chapter_1.veg file.

3. Locate the three new video clips using the Explorer in the Window Docking area.

4. Import the files directly into the Project Media window. Your Project Media window should now have six clips and look similar to Figure 1-22.

5. Save the project for future editing.

FIGURE 1-22

Sample Project Builder 1

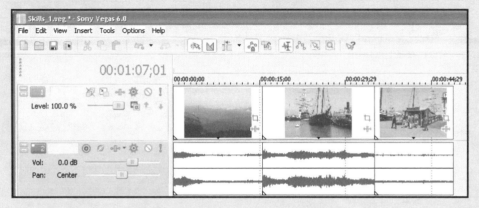

A travel agency has hired your company to create promotional videos. You've just received an assignment from your manager to create a project that will feature scenes from your town. At this point, you have only three video clips with which to work. Eventually, the project will be a 30-second promo commercial. You'll create a new project, import the clips into the Media Pool, and then save the project for future use.

1. Obtain three video clips of your town. The clips should be between 10 and 20 seconds in duration.

2. Create a new folder on your hard drive. Name the folder Chapter_ 1.

3. Copy the video files to the Chapter 1 folder.

4. Launch Vegas.

5. Create a new project. Save it as Chapter_1.

6. Use the Import Media command to import the media files into the project. Your project at this point should resemble Figure 1-23.

7. Align the clips to the start of the timeline. Your project should resemble Figure 1-24.

8. Save the project.

FIGURE 1-23
Project Builder 2, Sample 1

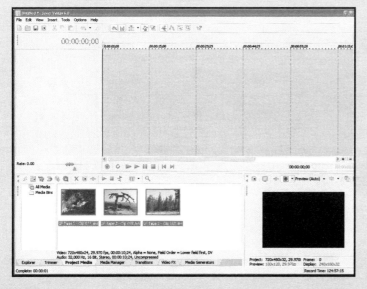

FIGURE 1-24
Project Builder 2, Sample 2

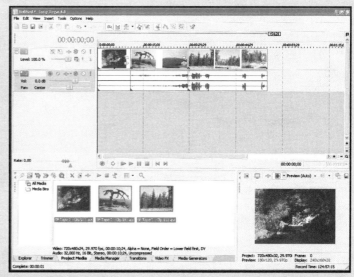

If you work for an organization that has a multimedia department, you'll be working with other video editors and you might share projects. Therefore, it's imperative that you be able to grasp what is happening when you are asked to work on a project that has already been started. Figure 1-24 shows a project that has been started, yet needs additional editing before it can be rendered as a finished video.

1. Log onto the Internet and navigate to http://www.course.com.

2. Navigate to the Web page for this book, click the Online Companion link, and then click the link for Chapter 1.

3. Right-click DesignProj1.zip, choose Save Target As (Internet Explorer) or Save Link Target As (Netscape Navigator), and then download the file to your Chapter_1 folder.

4. Unzip the file and then double-click the DesignProj1.veg file.

5. Create a new document in your word processing application and save the file as DesignProj1.

6. Review the project file and answer the following questions:

   - How many video events are on the timeline?
   - How many audio events are on the timeline?
   - How many clips are in the Project Media window?

- What is the frame size for the project?
- What is the video frame rate for the project?
- What is the audio sampling rate for the project?

FIGURE 1-25

Design project

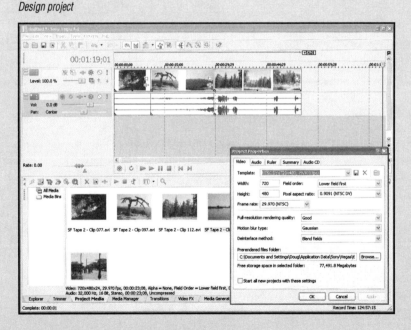

CHAPTER SUMMARY

This chapter introduced you to Vegas 6 and the exciting features of the application. You began your discovery of Vegas with an exploration of the workspace. The timeline is where you build your projects by adding clips, which are known as events. Menu commands are used to create new projects, edit projects, view windows, and more. You also have a toolbar at your disposal for selecting and editing timeline events. When you finish editing a project prior to rendering it, you can save the project for future editing.

What You Have Learned

In this chapter, you:
- Explored the Vegas workspace.
- Learned how to navigate the timeline.
- Learned about the various menu commands you use to create and edit your projects.
- Learned about the tools you use to edit your projects.
- Learned to save a project for future editing.
- Learned to customize the Vegas workspace.
- Learned to set Vegas preferences to suit your work habits and methods.

Key Terms from This Chapter

- **Acid Pro.** A Sony application that enables you to create music by assembling sampled music loops on a timeline that is similar to that used by Vegas.
- **Audio Busses.** Devices that you use to control the audio output in your projects. You can add up to 26 audio busses to a project, which in theory works like a sound mixing board.
- **Crossfade.** A video transition for events that are overlapped where one event fades into the next. Vegas gradually decreases the opacity of the first event while increasing the opacity of the second event.
- **Event FX.** A filter that is applied to an event.
- **Events.** Media you add to the Vegas timeline. You can change the duration of events and then enhance them with Event FX.
- **Master Mixer.** A device used to adjust the combined level of all audio tracks and busses in your project.
- **Media Manager.** A new feature in Vegas 6 that enables you to manage the media you use in your projects. You can add tags to media. Tags can be used when searching the Media Manager.
- **Plug-in Chain.** Multiple FX applied to an event.
- **Sony Sound Forge.** A Sony application used to edit sound clips. Sony Sound Forge works interactively with Sony Vegas, enabling you to use Sound Forge to edit audio events.
- **Video Bus.** A track that enables you to add and animate event FX to the entire production. You animate effects applied to a track through the use of keyframes. You can also add envelopes to the video bus track to modify the entire production device.
- **Video Preview Window.** Displays a project's video output at the current curosr position during editing and playback.
- **Window Docking Area.** The bottom of the Vegas workspace, which is used to dock windows. You can drag windows from the Window Docking area and float them in the workspace.

chapter

2

CREATING A
New Project

1. Specify project settings.

2. Import media.

3. Use the Project Media window.

4. Capture video.

5. Extract audio and capture images.

6. Add media to a project.

7. Preview a project.

chapter 2 CREATING A
New Project

When you create a project in Vegas, the rendered video can be anything from a 30-second promo or commercial to a movie-length documentary. The project you create might involve hundreds of individual clips, takes, audio clips, **voice-over recordings**, transitions, and video effects. When you're working on a complex project, organization becomes a key issue.

When you create a project, all the media that is used in the project is organized in a device known as the Project Media window. The Project Media window is found in the Window Docking area. From within the Project Media window, you can select media and add it where needed on the timeline. You can have multiple instances of any clip or image in your project. You can apply different effects to instances of a clip, trim the clip, speed up or slow down the clip, and so on. When you modify a clip in a Vegas project, you're not altering the original media in any way. The fact that your source media is not altered gives you carte blanche to use your creative ideas to achieve unique and interesting effects. If your idea doesn't pan out, you can change

it to suit your product, and your source material will be unaffected.

When you create a new project, you specify the settings for the project. If you're capturing video from a digital camcorder, you'll be working with **DV (Digital Video)-compliant media**, and the default settings are just what you need. If, however, you are working with other media that has a different **frame rate** and size, you can change project settings to match the media you are using. When you specify project settings, you can also specify audio settings and how the time ruler is divided. You can add summary information such as the project title, copyright information, and any comments that are pertinent to the project.

Tools You'll Use

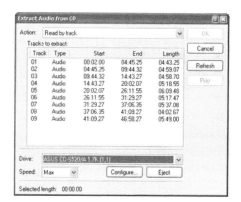

SPECIFY PROJECT
SETTINGS

What You'll Do

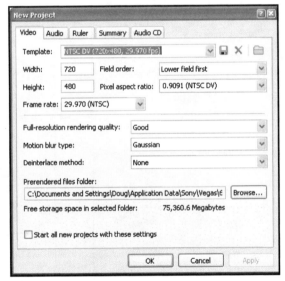

Mixing Formats and Media

Vegas is a diverse application that supports a wide range of formats and
media types. When you create a project
in Vegas, you generally work with
media of a specified frame rate and
size. When you specify properties for a
project, you determine how Vegas handles the media in your project, as well
as the output of the project. Other settings are merely informational details
about your project, such as the title of
the project.

Specifying Project Settings

When you start a new project, the first
thing that typically appears is the
Project Settings dialog box. The
Project Settings dialog box is what
you use to specify project settings.
It's divided into the following tabs:

- **Video.** In this tab, you specify the settings that determine how project video
  is handled. You can choose from a
  wide variety of preset templates or create a custom template.

- **Audio.** In this tab, you specify the settings that determine how project
  audio clips are handled. You specify
  the audio sampling rate, whether the
  project audio is stereo or 5.1 Surround
  Sound, and specify other settings,
  such as the audio bit depth, resample
  quality, and so on.

- **Ruler.** In this tab, you determine
  how the time ruler is divided for the
  project.

- **Summary.** In this tab, you enter information that is pertinent to the project.

- **Audio CD.** You use this tab when
  you're burning an audio project to
  CD-ROM.

FIGURE 2-1

Project video settings

1. Choose File > New or press Ctrl+N.

   The New Project dialog box appears and the Video tab is selected, as shown in Figure 2-1.

   ### NOTE

   If you choose the New command and currently have a project open, you will be prompted to save the project.

2. Click the Template down arrow; then choose a preset from the drop-down list.

   The Template drop-down list contains a list of preset templates. You can modify preset templates and save them as custom templates. Choose the preset that matches the intended destination of your project. For example, if you are rendering video for a DVD that will be played on a DVD player in North America, choose NTSC DV (720x480, 29.970 fps).

3. Enter values in the Width and Height fields to set the frame size of the rendered movie.

   All presets will enter appropriate values for the Width and Height fields. If, however, the intended destination of your video is a device such as a computer monitor, you can enter different values. If you enter different values, make sure they match the aspect ratio of the original preset, otherwise the video will be distorted. For example, if the preset Width is 640 and the preset Height is 480, this is a 4 to 3 aspect ratio; the height of the video is 75 percent of the width. Keeping the same aspect ratio, you can resize the video to 480x320, 320x240, or 160x120.

4. Click the Field Order down arrow; then choose an option from the drop-down list.

Choose Lower Field First if your output is for DV video. If the output video is jittery and not smooth, or if specified by your output hardware, choose Upper Field First. Choose None (Progressive Scan) if your rendered video will be viewed on a computer monitor.

5. Click the Pixel Aspect Ratio down arrow; then choose an option from the drop-down list.

Choose Square [1.000] for a video that will be viewed on a computer monitor. Video that will be viewed on a television has a rectangular aspect ratio. Choose the proper pixel size for the television broadcast standard with which your project will be viewed. All options clearly delineate the broadcast standard and whether the preset is widescreen video.

6. Click the Frame down arrow; then choose an option from the drop-down list.

This option determines the number of frames per second at which your rendered video will be played back. A higher frame rate results in smoother video. If you're creating a project that will be played back on a television, choose the frame rate that matches the broadcast standard of the intended playback device.

7. Click the Full-Resolution Rendering Quality down arrow; then choose an option from the drop-down list.

This option determines the quality at which your project will be rendered. The default option of Good works well in most cases. However, if your video contains a lot of detail, you might want to consider using the Best setting. Note that this setting can dramatically increase rendering time. Choose Draft or Preview to create a test render for the project.

8. Click the Motion Blur down arrow; then choose an option from the drop-down list.

This option determines how video effects and transitions that involve motion are handled. Motion blur makes computer-generated animation appear more natural and realistic. For most effects and transitions, the default Gaussian option works well.

9. Click the Deinterlace Method down arrow; then choose an option from the drop-down list.

This setting determines how Vegas deinterlaces fields when rendering effects. If you choose None, Vegas will not deinterlace the video. If you choose Blend Fields, Vegas blends information from both fields. The Blend Fields option works well for video that contains a lot of detail and little motion. Choose Interpolate Fields if your project video contains a lot of motion but little detail.

10. Accept the default Prerendered Files Folder, or click the Browse button; then choose a different directory.

FIGURE 2-2

Specifying audio settings

11. Click OK to apply the settings to the project or choose another tab to modify additional settings.

About Broadcast Standards

When you create video that will be copied to VHS tape or DVD, you must choose the correct broadcast standard for the area in which your video will be viewed. If your project will be played back on television sets sold in America and Japan, use the NTSC broadcast standard. If your project will be played back on television sets sold in Europe and the rest of the world, use the PAL standard. NTSC video frame size is either 704×480 pixels or 720 pixels×480 pixels with a frame rate of either 23.97 fps (frames per second) or 29.97 fps. PAL video frame size is either 704×576 pixels or 720×576 pixels with a frame rate of 25 fps.

Specify audio settings

1. Create a new project and specify video settings as outlined in the previous steps.

2. Click the Audio tab.

The New Project dialog box is reconfigured, as shown in Figure 2-2.

3. Click the Master Bus Mode down arrow; then choose an option from the drop-down list.

   Choose Stereo for two-channel stereo sound, or 5.1 Surround Sound if your project will be viewed on devices that support 5.1 Surround Sound. When you choose 5.1 Surround Sound, each audio track will contain a 5.1 Surround Sound mixer that enables you to specify how the sound is distributed between speakers. In addition, a 5.1 Surround Sound project has a mixer for each channel in the Mixer window.

4. Click the Number of Stereo Busses spinner buttons to specify the number of stereo busses. Alternatively, you can enter a value no greater than 26 in the text field.

   You can have a maximum of 27 stereo busses in a project (26 news busses and the Master bus). The number of busses you specify are added to the Mixer window.

5. Click the Sample Rate down arrow; then choose an option from the drop-down list.

   Choose one of the default settings, or enter a different value. You can specify a rate between 2,000 and 192,000 kHz. A higher sampling rate results in better-quality sound at the expense of a larger file size. For broadcast-quality audio, choose a rate of 48,000 kHz.

6. Click the Bit Depth down arrow; then choose an option from the drop-down list.

   A higher value results in better-quality sound at the expense of a larger file size.

7. Click the Resample Quality down arrow; then choose an option from the drop-down list.

Choose Preview, Good, or Best. Good works well in most instances. If your project has a music soundtrack, you might want to consider using the Best setting.

8. Click the Enable Low-Pass Filter on LFE check box. Note that this option is for 5.1 Surround Sound only and is dimmed out if you choose Stereo for the Master Bus Mode.

   This option applies a low-pass filter to each track in the 5.1 Surround Sound that is applied to the LFE (Low Frequency Effects) channel.

9. Click the Cutoff Frequency for Low-Pass Filter down arrow; then choose an option from the drop-down list. This option is only available for 5.1 Surround Sound.

   This option specifies the frequency above which the LFE channel will ignore sound.

10. Click the Low-Pass Filter Quality down arrow; then choose an option from the drop-down list.

    This option determines the sharpness of the rolloff curve for the low-pass filter. Choose Best for the sharpest curve.

11. Accept the default option for Recorded Files Folder, or click the Browse button and specify a different folder.

   QUICKTIP

   The available disc space for the Recorded Files folder is displayed below the field.

12. Click OK to apply the settings, or click another tab to specify other project settings.

FIGURE 2-3

Setting Ruler options

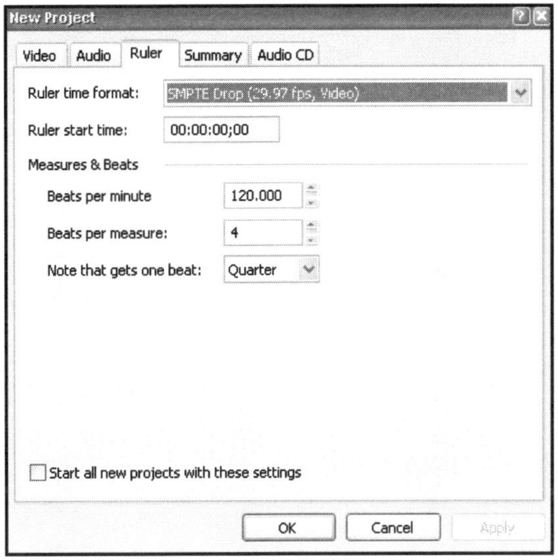

1. Choose File > New and set the video and audio options as outlined previously.

2. Click the Ruler tab.

   The Ruler tab appears, as shown in Figure 2-3.

3. Click the Ruler Time Format down arrow; then choose an option from the drop-down list.

   You can display the time ruler tick marks as individual frames of a television broadcast frame rate, samples, time, seconds, or time and frames.

4. Accept the default ruler start time, or enter a different value in the Ruler Start Time text field.

   The default ruler start time is 0 seconds, which is formatted according to the time format you chose in step 1. If needed, you can enter a different start time to synchronize the audio **timecode** with the original time-code of a trimmed video clip.

5. In the Beats per Minute section, accept the default value, or enter a different value for the project tempo. Alternatively, you can click the spinner buttons to specify a value.

   Accept the default (120.000), or enter a different value.

6. In the Beats per Measure field, accept the default value, or enter a different value. Alternatively, you can click the spinners buttons to specify a value.

   Accept the default value (4), or enter a different value.

7. Click the Note That Gets One Beat down arrow; then choose an option from the drop-down list.

8. Click OK to apply the settings, or click a different tab to set other project settings.

Add project summary information

1. Choose File > New and set the video, audio, and ruler options as outlined previously.

2. Click the Summary tab.

The Summary tab appears, as shown in Figure 2-4.

3. Enter the desired text in the Title field.

> **QUICKTIP**
>
> The information you enter is displayed in certain media players. For example, if you render the project in the WMV format, the Title and Artist information are displayed when the video is played in the Windows Media Player.

4. Enter the name of the project creator or featured artist in the Artist field.

5. Enter the name of the editors who mixed and created the project in the Engineer field.

6. Enter any copyright information in the Copyright field.

> **QUICKTIP**
>
> Create your copyright information in a word processing application that supports symbols. Create copyright text such as © 2005 Doug Sahlin, All Rights Reserved. Select the text, and then press Ctrl+C. In Vegas, place

FIGURE 2-4

Adding summary information

FIGURE 2-5

Setting Audio CD options

your cursor in the Copyright field and press Ctrl+V to paste the copyright information.

7. Enter any desired text pertaining to the project in the Comments field.

Set Audio CD options

1. Choose File > New and set the video, audio, ruler, and summary options as outlined previously.

2. Click the Audio CD tab to reveal the dialog box shown in Figure 2-5.

3. Enter a 13-digit number for the UPC or MCN code in the Universal Product Code/Media Catalog Number field.

    You can use this option to write the UPC or MCN code to disc if your CD ROM burner supports this feature.

4. Accept the default value of 1 for First Track Number on Disk or enter a different value.

    This option sets the number for the first track on the disc.

5. Click OK to apply the settings, or click a different tab to modify other project settings.

QUICKTIP

In the Video tab, click the Start New Projects with These Settings check box to apply the current project settings to future projects you create.

What You'll Do

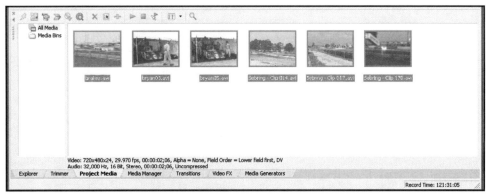

 In this lesson, you import media from the Explorer into the Project Media window.

Using the Explorer

When you use the Explorer to navigate to a folder that contains media, you see a list of names and extensions of each file in the folder. You can then select a file and drag it into the main window, or drag it directly into the Project Media window. If the file-name doesn't give you an apt description of what the file is all about, you can preview the file before adding it to your project.

Importing Media into the Project Media Window

In previous lessons, you learned how to import media into a project by using a menu command. There is, however, a much easier way to import media into your project from anywhere in your system.

The Explorer, which resides in the Window Docking area, is just like the Windows Explorer: You use it to navigate from one folder to another.

FIGURE 2-6

The Explorer tab

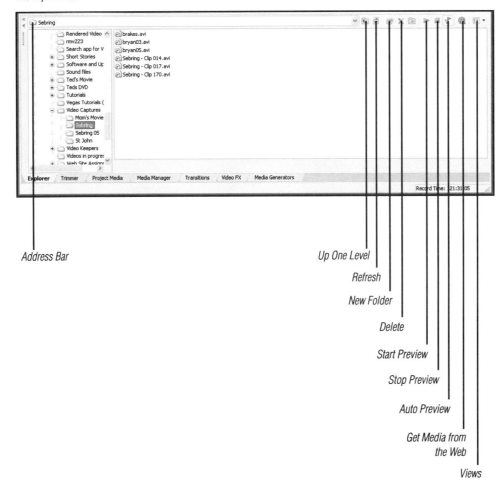

Address Bar

Up One Level

Refresh

New Folder

Delete

Start Preview

Stop Preview

Auto Preview

Get Media from
the Web

Views

1. Create a new project as outlined previously.

2. Click the Explorer tab in the Window Docking area.

3. Navigate to the folder where you store your video files. This process is identical to navigating the Windows Explorer directory tree, as shown in Figure 2-6.

    Directory folders that contain subfolders are designated with a plus sign (+). Click the plus sign (+) to expand that folder and display the subfolders. Expanded folders are designated with a minus (-) sign, indicating the folder can be collapsed to its root folder. Click the minus sign (-) to collapse the folder.

4. Select a video, audio, or image file and click the Start Preview button to preview the file.

    QUICKTIP

    Click the Auto Preview button. As soon as you select a file, it automatically begins playing.

    If you select an image or video file, the selected file is displayed in the Video Preview window. If you select an audio file, the sound plays. If you select a video file, the video plays at the file's frame rate. If you select an image file, the image is displayed for five seconds.

    QUICKTIP

    To rename a file, right-click it and choose Rename from the shortcut menu.

5. Click the Stop Preview button to stop the preview.

From within the Explorer, you can also add folders, delete files, and change the manner in which files are displayed in the Explorer. To reveal newly added folders or the new name of a renamed file, click the Refresh button.

Organizing Media with the Media Manager

A wonderful addition to Vegas 6 is the Media Manager. With the Media Manager, you can organize the media on your computer, rate media, and create media libraries. The Media Manager is located in the Window Docking area and contains thumbnails of all media you've imported into Vegas. The Media Manager works similarly to the Project Media Window in that you can preview clips and add them to a project. However, you can do much more with the Media Manager. You can search for media on your system and add tags to classify your media. If you have a large media collection, this is the ideal tool with which to organize it. The Media Manager has a built-in help menu that will guide you through every task.

Add files to the Project Media window

1. Click the Explorer tab.
2. Navigate to the desired folder as outlined in the previous lesson.

   You can preview each file as outlined in the previous lesson, or you can select multiple files for import into the project. You can select a range of files by selecting a desired file and then Shift-clicking the last file in the

range. You can select noncontiguous files by clicking the first file and then Ctrl-clicking the other files you want to add to the selection.

3. Select four video files from the folder. Drag them over the Project Media tab.

   The Project Media window opens.

4. Continue to press the mouse button as you move your cursor into the Project Media window.

   The cursor becomes a document icon with a plus sign, indicating that you can add the selected files to the Project Media window.

5. Release the mouse button.

   The video clips are added to the Project Media window, as shown in Figure 2-7. Each video clip is designated by a thumbnail image of the clip's first frame.

6. Choose File > Save.
7. Name the project file **mediaWindow** and click OK.

FIGURE 2-7
Importing media directly into the Project Media window

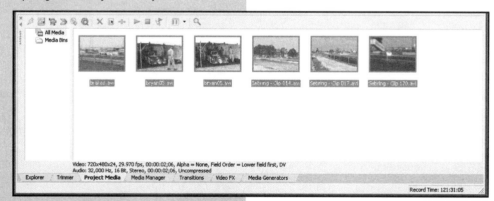

USE THE PROJECT
MEDIA WINDOW

What You'll Do

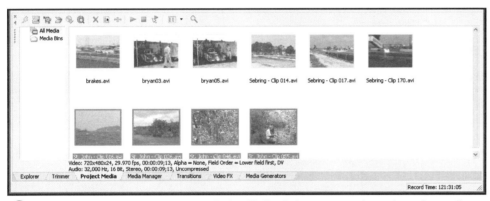

 In this lesson, you learn how to use the Project Media window to store and organize project media.

Working with the Project Media Window

When you're working on a complex project, organization is integral. Vegas takes care of a lot of the organization for you by adding clips that you import to the Project Media window. As you learned in earlier lessons, you can add instances of a video clip—or

for that matter, any asset in the Project Media window—to a project by dragging it from the Project Media window to the desired position on a track timeline. However, if you only use the Project Media window to drag clips into your project, you're missing the power of this multifaceted workhorse.

Capturing and Organizing Media

From within the Project Media window, you can import media, capture video from your digital camcorder, capture audio from your CD-ROM drive, capture images from your scanner, delete unused assets you've imported into the project, and more. You can also preview media assets from within the Project Media window and change the way assets are displayed in the Project Media window.

If you're working on a complex project with a hodgepodge of assets, you might find it beneficial to organize the Project Media window by adding folders, which are known as media bins in Vegas. When you organize project media in bins, you can create separate bins for your video clips, audio clips, images, and other assets. Sifting through a bin is much easier than trying to scroll through hundreds of mixed media files. You can also use the powerful Search tool to locate assets in any bin in the Project Media window.

Work with the Project Media window

1. Open the mediaWindow.veg file that you saved from the previous lesson.

2. Click the Project Media window tab.

   The Project Media window opens and all media that have been imported into the project are displayed. By default, a thumbnail of each media object is displayed until you select a different view. A thumbnail consists of the first frame of a video file, a thumbnail of a still image, or a media icon for a sound file. The file name is displayed beneath the thumbnail.

3. Select two video clips from the Project Media window; then drag them into the main window.

   The clips are added as timeline events. If the video contains embedded audio, separate video and audio tracks are created.

4. Click the Remove All Unused Media from Project icon.

   Vegas removes the two unused clips from the Project Media window.

   ### QUICKTIP

   You can remove selected files from the Project Media window by clicking the Remove Selected Items icon. If one or more of the selected items are being used in the project, Vegas displays a warning dialog box to that effect, prompting you to remove all instances of the items from the project.

5. Click the Import Media icon .

Vegas opens the Import dialog box, which enables you to navigate to a folder and import the desired file into the project. You can also import multiple files with this dialog box.

6. Import several noncontiguous media files into the project.

   Vegas adds the files to the Project Media window, as shown in Figure 2-8.

7. Select a file in the Project Media window; then click the Media Properties icon.

   The Properties dialog box appears and displays the selected object's properties. The properties displayed depend on the type of file you have selected.

FIGURE 2-8
The Project Media window

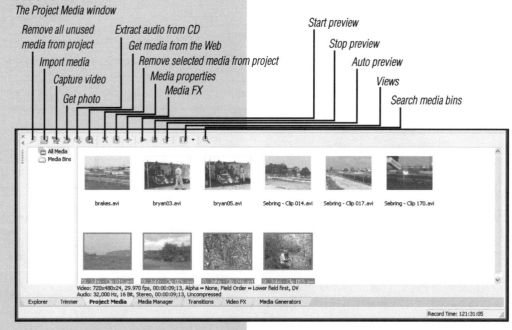

Remove all unused media from project
Extract audio from CD
Get media from the Web
Import media
Remove selected media from project
Capture video
Media properties
Get photo
Media FX
Start preview
Stop preview
Auto preview
Views
Search media bins

Video: 720x480x24, 29.970 fps, 00:00:09;13, Alpha = None, Field Order = Lower field first, DV
Audio: 32,000 Hz, 16 Bit, Stereo, 00:00:09;13, Uncompressed

brakes.avi   bryan03.avi   bryan05.avi   Sebring - Clip 014.avi   Sebring - Clip 017.avi   Sebring - Clip 170.avi

Explorer   Trimmer   **Project Media**   Media Manager   Transitions   Video FX   Media Generators

Record Time: 121:31:05

FIGURE 2-9

Displaying files with the Detail view option

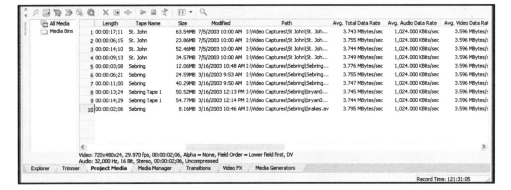

8. Close the Properties dialog box, then click the Views down arrow; then choose List from the drop-down list.

   Vegas displays a list of all files in the media bin.

9. Click the Views down arrow; then choose Detailed from the drop-down list.

   Vegas displays details about each file, as shown in Figure 2-9.

Organize media with media bins

1. Create a new project as outlined previously.

2. Click the Project Media window tab.

3. Right-click the Media Bin icon.

   When you know a project will have more media clips than you can easily manage, it's a good idea to create additional media bins before importing project media files.

4. Choose Create New Bin from the shorcut menu.

   Vegas creates a new media bin with the default name of New Media Bin.

5. Before deselecting the bin, type **Audio**.

   You can give a bin a unique name by entering the name right after you create the new bin.

6. Repeat steps 3 through 5 to create a new bin named **Video**.

   QUICKTIP

   You can rename any bin you've created by right-clicking the bin and then choosing Rename from the shortcut menu.

7. Click the Audio bin to open it.

8. Click the Import Media icon and import some audio files.

   When you open a media bin and import files, the media files are organized in that bin. Remember that a listing in the Project Media window is just the path to the directory where the media is stored on your hard drive; the media is not physically moved.

9. Click the Video Bin icon and import some video files.

   After you open a media bin, you can import files directly into it. After you import video files, your media bin should resemble Figure 2-10.

Using the Project Media Window Detailed View

When you display the Project Media window in detailed view, you can change the order of columns by clicking and dragging columns to a different position. You can hide a column by clicking and dragging it beyond the border of the Project Media window. You can also determine which columns are displayed by right-clicking anywhere in the Project Media window, choosing View from the shortcut menu, and then clicking the column name to show/hide the column. You can sort Project Media window files by column by clicking the column. For example, to sort files by name, click the Name column. A downward-pointing arrow indicates that the column has been sorted in ascending order, and an upward-pointing arrow indicates that the column has been sorted in descending order.

FIGURE 2-10

Organizing media into bins

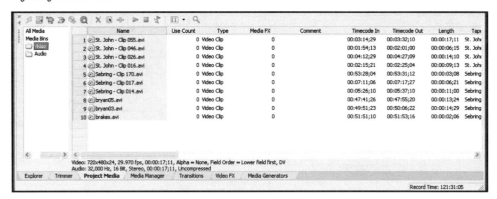

CAPTURE VIDEO

What You'll Do

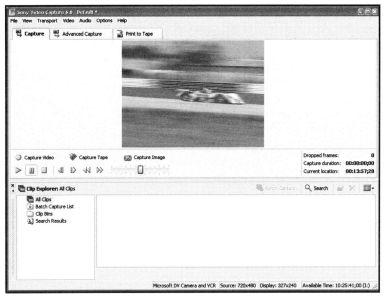

In this lesson, you capture video from your digital camcorder by using Sony Video Capture. To capture video with Vegas, you must connect your camera to an IEEE 1394/OHCI (Open Host Controller Interface)-compliant video card.

Using Sony Video Capture

If you're a videographer, you can capture video shot with your digital camcorder directly into Vegas and use it to create a finished production. You can use Sony Video Capture after connecting your digital camcorder to an IEEE 1394 port on an OHCI-compliant video capture card. When you capture video in Vegas, you end up with an AVI file that has been compressed using the powerful Sony DV (Digital Video) compression codec. The Sony DV codec assures you of high-quality video using the least amount of disk space possible. If you start with high-quality footage from a digital camcorder, the Sony DV codec allows you to render a broadcast-quality video from Vegas. You can also capture HDV (High Definition Video) using Vegas Capture.

Setting Video Capture Preferences

Every application you use has preferences, and Sony Video Capture is no exception. There are default Sony Video Capture preferences, but you can modify the preferences to suit your tastes. One default option you should consider changing is the default location for storing captured clips (the My Documents folder). If you have an auxiliary hard drive with plenty of room, you should store your clips there.

Capturing Video

Even when you're using the Sony DV codec, captured video takes up a tremendous amount of hard drive space. For example, to capture a minute of video, you'll use approximately 200MB of disk space. If you do a lot of video capture, it's recommended that you devote a folder of a large auxiliary hard drive to video capture. You should also refrain from capturing video on the same hard drive on which you've installed your operating system. You should keep the capture hard drive in good order by defragmenting the drive and deleting any video files that are no longer in use.

When you're capturing video, it's a good idea to use the Vegas Capture application to avoid problems with incompatible codecs from other capture programs. It's also a good idea to disable any screen savers and other nonessential TSR applications.

When you capture video, it is added to the Project Media window. You can capture video to an existing project, or begin a new project and then capture video. After you connect your digital camcorder to an IEEE 1394 port on an OHCI-compliant video capture card, you can use either a menu command or a button in the Project Media window to capture your video. By default, captured video is separated into scenes. A scene begins when the videographer begins recording a clip, and it ends when the videographer presses the Record button again to stop recording.

FIGURE 2-11

The Sony Video Capture Preferences dialog box

1. Choose File > Capture Video. Choose between the external capture application (for DV) or the internal caputure utility (for HDV and Decklink).

   The Sony Video Capture application launches.

2. Choose Options > Preferences.

   The Preferences dialog box appears, as shown in Figure 2-11.

3. Click the Disk Management tab.

   Within this tab, you'll find a list of all capture folders that are currently in use on your system. The default capture folder is the My Documents folder. You can accept the default folder and add other capture folders, or you can replace the default capture folder with a folder on an auxiliary hard disk drive, which is recommended.

   CAUTION

   It's best not to specify an external USB or FireWire hard drive for video capture because the data transfer speed is not fast enough and will cause Sony Video Capture to drop frames to keep up with the DV tape.

4. Right-click the default folder; then choose Browse from the shortcut menu.

   The Browse dialog box appears. If you haven't previously set up a capture folder on your system, you can do so by navigating to the hard disk you want to use for video capture and then clicking the Make New Folder button.

5. Navigate to the desired folder; then click OK.

Sony Video Capture replaces the default My Documents folder on the Capture Folders list with the specified folder, as shown in Figure 2-12. If desired, you can have more than one capture folder by clicking the Add Folder button at the top of the Disk Management tab. This opens the Browse dialog box, which enables you to browse to and add an additional folder to the list.

QUICKTIP

After creating an additional capture folder, click its check box to enable the folder for video capture.

NOTE

When you have more than one capture folder, make sure you disable the folders you do not want to use for video capture; otherwise an error may occur. Disabled capture folders are not checked. To disable an active folder, click its check box.

6. Click the Maximum Size per DV Clip check box if you want to limit the maximum size of captured clips.

When you enable this option, you can specify a different maximum clip size by manually entering a different value in the text field.

7. Accept the default option for Overflow When Disk Space Below, or enter a different value in the text field.

When disk space falls below this value, Sony Video Capture stores captured video clips to a different drive. The default value is calculated at 3 percent of the capture hard drive's capacity. This headroom prevents a disk from being filled with video, which could

FIGURE 2-12

Specifying Capture folders

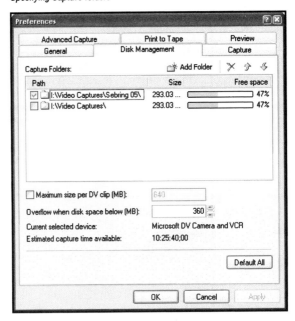

potentially render the disk useless and unrecoverable in the event of a system crash. This also gives the operating system sufficient disk space with which to work when you defragment the drive.

8. Click OK to apply the changes, or click a different Preferences tab to modify additional settings.

QUICKTIP

At the bottom of the Disk Management section of the Preferences dialog box, you'll find text that indicates the currently selected capture device and the estimated capture time available on the specified capture hard disk drive.

Capture video from a digital camcorder

1. Connect your digital camcorder to an IEEE 1394 port on an OCHI(Open Host Compliant Interface)-compliant video capture card.

   Refer to your digital camcorder and video capture card instruction manuals for information on how to connect your camcorder to the capture card or **FireWire** port.

2. Turn your camcorder on and switch to playback mode.

   Most digital camcorders have a VCR or VTR button that switches the camera to playback mode. Refer to your digital camcorder instruction manual for information on how to play back DV tapes. You do not need to rewind the tape because Sony Video Capture has a video transport bar that you can use to control the playback of the DV tape. After you switch the camera to VTC or VTR mode, Windows makes a sound signifying that the operating system has recognized the camcorder as a video device.

3. Click the Capture Video button inside the Project Media window.

   The Sony Video Capture dialog box appears, as shown in Figure 2-13.

QUICKTIP

You can also access the Sony Video Capture dialog box by choosing File > Capture Video.

FIGURE 2-13
The Sony Video Capture application

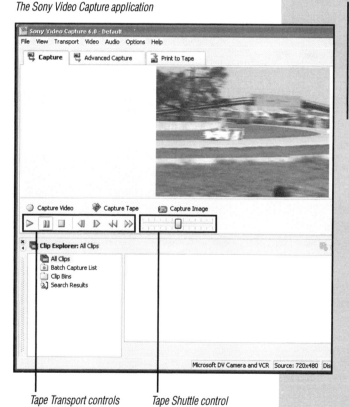

Tape Transport controls   *Tape Shuttle control*

4. Click the Capture Video button 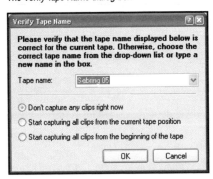 to capture the entire tape.

The Verify Tape Name dialog box appears, as shown in Figure 2-14. From within this dialog box, you name the tape you are capturing. You can also specify whether to capture all clips from the beginning of the tape, capture all clips from the current tape position, or not capture any clips right now.

5. Click OK.

What occurs next depends on the option you selected in step 4. If you chose the option to capture clips from the current tape position, Sony Video Capture sends a signal to your digital camcorder, the tape begins playing, and the tape is captured by Vegas as clips. A clip is when the video camera operator starts recording video footage by pressing the Record button and then presses the Record button again to stop. If you chose to capture the entire tape, Sony Video Capture sends a signal to your digital camcorder to rewind the tape to the beginning and play back the tape. If you chose not to capture clips right now, you can use the Tape Transport controls to play, fast forward, rewind, pause, and stop the tape. When you reach the desired point, click the Capture Video button to begin recording a clip from the tape. Press Stop to stop recording. You can then play the tape and when you reach additional footage you want to record, click the Capture Video button again.

QUICKTIP

You can use the Shuttle control to preview the tape. Drag the control to the right to fast

FIGURE 2-14

The Verify Tape Name dialog box

Verify Tape Name

Please verify that the tape name displayed below is correct for the current tape. Otherwise, choose the correct tape name from the drop-down list or type a new name in the box.

Tape name: Sebring 06

○ Don't capture any clips right now

○ Start capturing all clips from the current tape position

○ Start capturing all clips from the beginning of the tape

OK   Cancel

FIGURE 2-15

The Capture Complete dialog box

forward and to the left to rewind. Dragging the control toward either extreme causes the tape to fast forward, or rewind quicker.

Click the Capture Image button to capture the current frame of the DV tape as a JPEG image.

6. Click the Stop button or press Esc to finish capturing the tape.

The Capture Complete dialog box appears, as shown in Figure 2-15. This dialog box displays a summary of the session statistics and gives you the option of adding the captured clips to the Project Media window, along with other options such as showing the clips, renaming the clips, or deleting the clips.

7. Click Done to exit the Capture Complete dialog box.

Sony Video Capture saves the clips to the specified folder. This process might take some time, depending on the quantity and length of the clips you've captured.

8. Accept the default file name for the capture, or enter a different name. Then click Save.

Sony Video Capture saves the session file.

Batch capture with Advanced Capture options

1. Connect your digital camcorder to your computer, as outlined in the previous steps.

2. Click the Advanced Capture tab.

The Advanced Capture section of the Sony Video Capture dialog box appears. From within this section, you can manually set the

In and Out points of each segment of the tape you want to capture, which is saved as a clip. You can specify multiple clips and then begin a batch capture.

3. Enter a name for the clip in the Clip Name field.

   This designates the name for an individual clip you are capturing from a DV tape.

4. Enter a name for the tape in the Tape Name field.

   This designates the tape name that is used in the session capture information and is also a part of each clip's name.

5. Enter any applicable comments in the Comment field.

   This step is optional. Any text you enter in this field is displayed in the clip's Video Capture Comment column when you view the Project Media window in Detailed format. This information is useful because you can use the Project Media window Search tool to search for clips based on the text entered in each clip's Comment field.

6. Click the Rating down arrow; then choose an option to rate the clip from the drop-down list.

   This is optional and can be used to rate the quality of the video. However, this option is useful as you can sort clips in the Project Media window based on rating.

7. Use the Shuttle control or the Transport Control buttons to preview the tape.

8. When you find the start of a clip you want to capture, click the Mark In button to set the timecode for the start of a clip. Alternatively,

you can enter a value in the Timecode In field.

9. Use the Shuttle control or the Transport Control buttons to advance the tape to the last frame of the clip you want to capture.

10. Click the Mark Out button to set the timecode for the end of a clip you want to capture. Alternatively, you can enter a value in the Timecode Out field.

    The Timecode Out specifies the last frame of the clip to be captured.

    QUICKTIP

    Click the Left Bracket key ([) to set the In point of a clip you want to capture, and the Right Bracket key (]) to set the Out point of a clip you want to capture.

11. Click the Log In/Out button to add the clip to the Clip Explorer section of the Video Capture dialog box.

12. Specify additional clips from the tape as needed.

    Figure 2-16 shows the Advanced Capture dialog box after several clips have been logged for batch capture.

FIGURE 2-16

Using Advanced Capture options

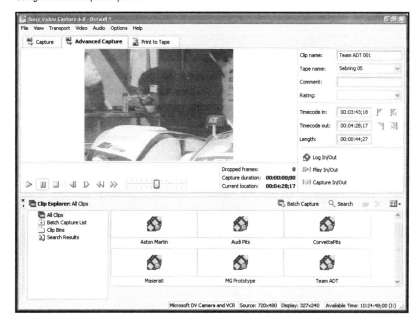

NOTE

You can specify clips from multiple tapes.

13. If desired, click the Play In/Out button to preview the clips you've specified.

14. Click the Batch Capture button.

The Batch Capture dialog box appears. All clips that you've logged are selected for capture. Click a clip's check box to deselect it and remove it from the batch capture.

15. Click OK to begin batch capture.

Sony Video Capture sends a signal to your digital camcorder to advance to the timecode of the first clip and begin playing the clip. Sony Video Capture captures the clip and then sends signals to the digital camcorder to advance to the next clip, which is then captured, and so on.

EXTRACT AUDIO AND
CAPTURE IMAGES

What You'll Do

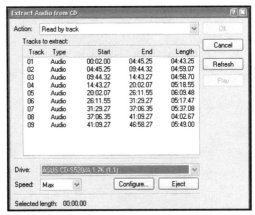

In this lesson, you capture audio from a CD-ROM disc and capture an image from your scanner.

Mixing Media

When you create a project in Vegas, you're not limited to a single audio and video track. You can have an unlimited number of audio and video tracks, which is where the power of Vegas shines. You add interest to the finished production by adding additional video and audio tracks. With audio tracks, you mix them and add busses and effects to create the desired soundtrack for your production.

You can also mix video with still images to achieve interesting results. You can add still images to a track and then composite them with video. Another use for still images is as backdrops for titles and ending credits. However, before you can add images or audio from CD-ROMs to your production, you must capture them.

Extracting Audio Tracks

You can capture audio tracks from CD-ROM discs and add them to the Project Media window. After you capture an audio soundtrack, you can create a new track and add it to your production. Adding a soundtrack to a video production heightens viewer interest. When Vegas captures an audio track from a CD-ROM, it rips a digital copy of the track to your hard drive. The file is in the Wave (*.wav) format.

Capturing Still Images

If you have a scanner attached to your system, Vegas recognizes it as a capture device. You can capture an image from your scanner and add it to the Project Media window. When you add images to a timeline, they are displayed for five seconds by default.

FIGURE 2-17

Extracting audio tracks from a CD-ROM

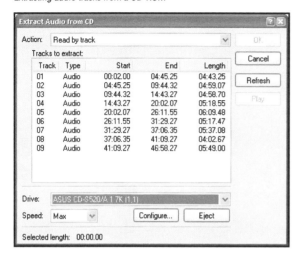

1. Insert the CD-ROM that contains the audio you want to add to the project.

2. Click the Project Media window tab.

3. Click the Extract Audio from CD button . (It looks like a CD.)

   QUICKTIP

   You can also extract audio from an audio CD by choosing File > Extract Audio from CD.

   Vegas searches your system for CD-ROM devices. After Vegas locates a supported device, the Extract Audio from CD dialog box appears and lists the tracks from the Audio CD, as shown in Figure 2-17.

   NOTE

   If you have more than one CD-ROM drive on your system, you can select a different drive by clicking the Drive down arrow and selecting the desired device from the drop-down list.

4. Click a track; then click Play to preview it.

   Vegas plays the selected track and the Play button becomes the Stop button. You can click the Stop button to stop playing the track and then preview another track.

   CAUTION

   It is illegal to copy audio tracks to which you do not own the rights. If you're creating a project for distribution, make sure you are extracting audio from a royalty-free music disc or that you can option a license or rights to use the audio track you intend to extract.

5. After you select the desired track, click OK.

The Save As dialog box appears, prompting you for a file name and folder in which you want to save the extracted audio file.

6. Navigate to the desired folder, enter a file name, and then click Save.

The Extracting Audio dialog box appears. A progress bar scrolls from left to right indicating the status of the operation and how much time is remaining. After the audio file is saved to disk, the title is added to the Project Media window.

Capture an image from your scanner

1. Insert the image in your flatbed scanner.

2. Click the Project Media window tab.

3. Click the Get Photo button , which looks like a flatbed scanner with its top open.

The Select Scanner/Camera dialog box appears, as shown in Figure 2-18. If you have more than one scanner or camera attached to your system, they are listed on the Device drop-down list. Accept the currently selected device, or select a different device.

4. Click OK.

FIGURE 2-18

Selecting the scanning device

FIGURE 2-19

Scanning the image

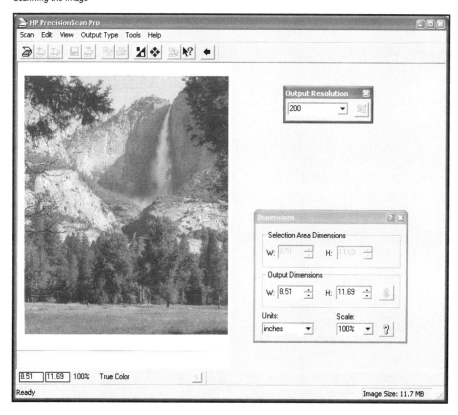

6. Follow the scanning application's prompts to capture the scanned image to the desired folder on your system.

After the scanning application completes its handiwork, the Scanned Images dialog box appears. Click Done to save the scanned image to your hard drive. Alternatively, you can click Rename to give the image a more meaningful name. After you've saved the image, Vegas adds the file name of the scanned image to the Project Media window.

ADD MEDIA
TO A PROJECT

What You'll Do

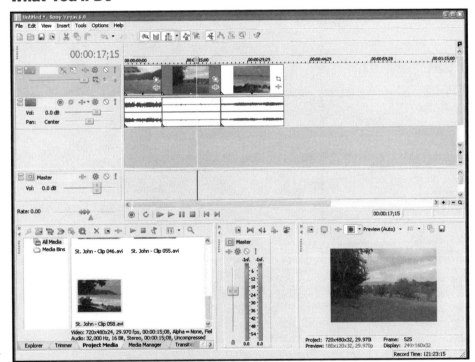

In this lesson, you learn the different methods for adding media to the timeline. You learn to add mixed media to the timeline and multiple clips.

Adding a Clip to the Timeline

After you import media into a project or capture media, you're ready to assemble your production on the timeline. When you add media to a project, you create a track. When you add video clips with embedded audio to a project, Vegas creates a separate video track and audio track, which enables you to fine-tune each track to suit your project.

When you add a clip to the timeline, you create an event. You can manipulate and edit each event as a single entity. For example, if you place two video clips next to each other, and one clip is noticeably darker, you can rectify the problem by applying a filter (known in Vegas as an Event FX) to the event, without affecting the other clips on the timeline. When you edit individual events the original media is not changed in any way. If desired, you can remove one of the tracks associated with the event without having to ungroup them.

You can add a clip to a track by selecting it from the Project Media or Explorer window, and dragging it to the desired position on the timeline. You can also quickly add a clip by double-clicking it in the Explorer window, which positions the clip at the current position of the cursor on the timeline.

Adding Multiple Clips

If desired, you can add multiple clips to the timeline. Common logic might lead you to believe that the clips will be stacked end to end on the timeline. Although this is an option, you can also assign each clip to its own track or add the clips as takes. Each

option gives you tremendous versatility. When you assign clips to individual tracks, you can composite them for special effects. When you add clips as takes, you can preview each take to see which clip is ideally suited to your project. Working with takes is covered in Chapter 4, " Using Advanced Video Editing Techniques."

Add a media clip to the project

1. Create a new project and add four clips to the Project Media window, as outlined previously.

2. Drag a video clip with embedded audio from the Project Media window into the workspace.

   As you move your cursor into the workspace, a rectangular bounding box depicts the current position of the clip, as shown in Figure 2-20.

3. Align the bounding box to the beginning of the timeline; then release the mouse button.

   After you release the mouse button, Vegas creates an audio track and video track for the clip, as shown in Figure 2-21.

4. Click the video clip, Shift-click the Audio track, and then press Delete.

   When you move video clips with embedded audio along the timeline, the event tracks act as a group. However, when you want to delete an event, you must select both audio and video.

5. Leave the project open and proceed to the next lesson.

Double-click a clip to add it to the timeline

1. Position your cursor at the beginning of the timeline.

2. Double-click the first clip's thumbnail in the Project Media window.

FIGURE 2-20
Aligning a media clip to the timeline

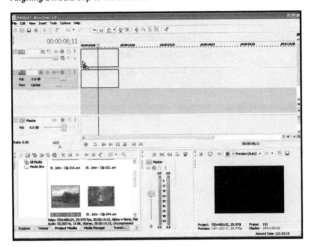

FIGURE 2-21
Adding a clip with audio and video tracks

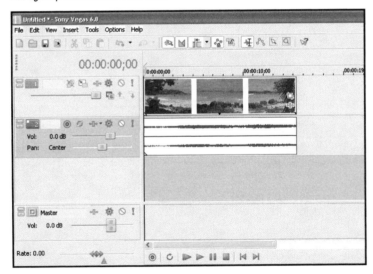

FIGURE 2-22

Double-click to add clips

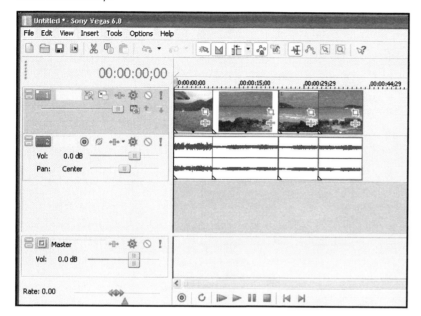

Vegas adds the clip at the current cursor position and moves the playhead to the end of the event.

> **CAUTION**
>
> If you work in detailed mode and double-click the clip's name, the clip will not be added to the project. In detailed mode, double-clicking the name opens a text box, which enables you to rename the clip.

3. Double-click the second clip's thumbnail in the Project Media window.

   Vegas aligns the head of the second clip with the tail of the first and moves the cursor to the tail of the second clip.

4. Double-click the third and fourth clip's thumbnail to add them to the timeline.

   Your timeline should resemble Figure 2-22. Note that you can only add one clip at a time when double-clicking.

Add multiple clips as tracks

1. Create a new project and add three clips to the Project Media window, as outlined previously.

2. Select the first clip and then Shift-click the remaining clips to add them to the selection.

3. Right-click and drag the clips into the workspace.

4. Align the clips with the beginning of the timeline and release the mouse button.

The shortcut menu shown in Figure 2-23 appears. If you choose Add Across Time, the clips are arranged end to end in the order you selected them in the Project Media window. If you choose Add Across Tracks, Vegas adds the necessary tracks to accommodate the selected clips at the cursor insertion point. If you choose Add as Takes, Vegas stacks the clips at the cursor insertion point, with the first clip displayed on the timeline. You can play different takes to find the one best suited to your project. If the clip contains audio and video, you have the option to add only video, or audio across time, across tracks, or as takes. For more information on working with takes, refer to Chapter 4.

5. Choose Add Across Tracks.

Your project should resemble Figure 2-24.

FIGURE 2-23
Add Multiple Clips shortcut menu

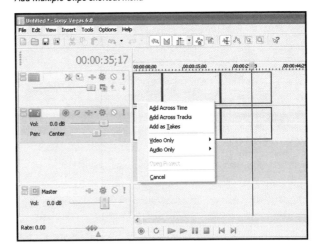

FIGURE 2-24
Adding multiple clips across tracks

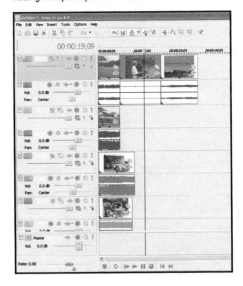

PREVIEW A PROJECT

What You'll Do

 In this lesson, you learn to navigate the timeline with keyboard shortcuts and the Scrub control. You also learn to preview your project in the Video Preview window.

Scrubbing the Timeline

When you have a relatively short project, with few events, it's easy to navigate to a specific point on the timeline by viewing the video track thumbnails and then clicking the timeline. However, when you have a project that comprises hundreds of events and is several minutes or perhaps an hour or longer in length, finding a specific frame is difficult. Fortunately, you don't have to use the scroll bar or scroll buttons to find your way.

You can quickly navigate forward or backward from any point in the timeline with the **Scrub control**. You can control the speed at which you scroll the timeline. When you get close to the desired frame, you can slow the scrub speed and then release the control when you've reached the desired frame.

If you prefer keyboard controls, you can scrub the timeline by using the J, K, and L keys. You can control the speed at which the frames advance (also known as shuttle speed) by changing preferences.

Previewing the Project

As you build a project, the timeline tracks provide a visual representation of the clips you've added to the project. You can also play the movie in the Video Preview window. This option is useful after you've just applied video effects and you want to preview the results before working with additional clips, or when you just want to see how the project is coming along. When you preview the video, you can control the quality of the preview, change the size of the preview, and so on.

You can use the VCR-like controls at the bottom of the main window to play, pause, stop, fast forward, or rewind the production. You can also control playback using the keyboard. The quality of the playback varies depending on the power of your processor and the number of video effects you've applied to the timeline events. If you preview a project with no effects applied, the playback is smooth.

Scrub the timeline

1. Create a new project and arrange several clips on the timeline.

2. If the Video Preview window is not currently visible, choose View > Video Preview.

3. Click the Scrub control shown in Figure 2-25; then drag to the right.

   As you drag the Scrub control to the right, the Rate value becomes a positive number and the video plays back. A Rate value of 1.0 plays the video at normal speed. As you drag the Scrub control farther to the right, the rate increases and the project plays back at a faster rate.

   > **QUICKTIP**
   >
   > You can drag the playhead directly above the Time Ruler to scrub the timeline. Press Ctrl+Alt while dragging the playhead to scrub the video without hearing the audio.

4. Release the Scrub control to stop playback.

5. Drag the Scrub control to the left.

   As you drag the Scrub control to the left of center, the Rate value becomes a negative number, indicating that the video is playing back in reverse. Drag the control farther to the left to increase the rate of speed.

   > **QUICKTIP**
   >
   > Press Alt, click the Time Ruler, and then drag to begin scrubbing the timeline at that point.

6. Release the Scrub control to stop playing the project in reverse.

7. Press the L key.

FIGURE 2-25
Using the Scrub control

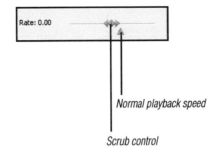

Normal playback speed

Scrub control

FIGURE 2-26

Using the Transport Bar controls

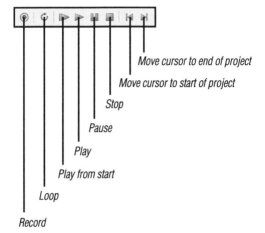

Move cursor to end of project

Move cursor to start of project

Stop

Pause

Play

Play from start

Loop

Record

Press the L key for forward playback. Each time you press the L key, the playback rate increases until the maximum forward playback rate of 20 is achieved.

QUICKTIP

Press Alt-right arrow to advance forward a frame at a time; press Alt-left arrow to move backward a frame at a time.

8. Press the K key to halt playback.

9. Press the J key.

Pressing the J key causes the project to play back in reverse. Each time you press the J key, the playback rate increases until the maximum reverse playback rate of –4 is achieved. If you press and hold the J or K key, maximum playback is achieved.

QUICKTIP

To change the playback rate when you're scrubbing the timeline with the J, K, or L keys, choose Options > Preferences; then click the Editing tab. Click the JKL/Shuttle down arrow. Then choose Slow (maximum playback rate from –2.0 to 2.0), Medium (the default playback rate from –4.0 to 4.0), or Fast (playback rate from –20 to 20). Note that this has no effect on the speed with which the Shuttle control plays back your project.

10. Leave the project open because you'll be using it in the next lesson.

Preview a project

1. Click the Play from Start button that's shown in Figure 2-26.

The Play from Start button begins playback

from the beginning of the project. If you want to begin playback on the currently selected frame, click the Play button, or press Enter or the spacebar.

QUICKTIP

To change the playback rate, click the Normal Playback Speed triangle below the Scrub control. Drag it to the right to increase playback speed, or drag it to the left to decrease playback speed. Alternatively, you can right-click the Normal Playback Speed triangle and then choose a rate from the shortcut menu. Double-click the icon to return playback speed to normal.

2. Click the Pause button.

Playback pauses on the current frame. Alternatively, you can press Enter to pause playback on the current frame. If you click the Stop button, playback stops and your cursor is positioned at the frame where you first pressed the Play button. Pressing the spacebar also stops playback, but returns the project to the initial frame from which you began reviewing the project.

3. Click the Play button.

Playback resumes. Alternatively, you can press the spacebar to resume playback. You can also press Enter to resume playback.

QUICKTIP

To position your cursor at the first frame in the project, click the Move Cursor to Start of Project button; to position your cursor on the last frame, click the Move Cursor to End of Project button. Alternatively, you can press Ctrl+Home to position the cursor at the start of the project, or Ctrl+End to move your cursor to the end of the project.

SKILLS REVIEW

Creating a New Project for a Multimedia Application

1. Launch Vegas.

2. Choose File > New.

3. Click the Template down arrow, and then choose Multimedia.

4. Enter a value of 30 in the Frame Rate field, as shown in Figure 2-27.

5. Click the Audio tab.

6. Change Sample Rate to 22,050 kHz as shown in Figure 2-28.

7. Click OK and keep the project open for the next skills review.

FIGURE 2-27
Select a template

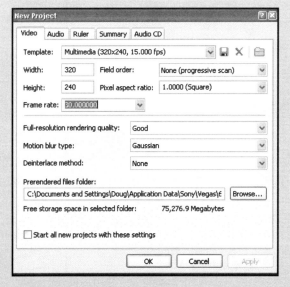

FIGURE 2-28
Select an audio sample rate

SKILLS REVIEW

Adding Multiple Files to the Project Media Window

1. Click the Explorer tab and navigate to a folder where you've stored video files.

2. Select four noncontiguous files and add them to the Project Media window as shown in Figure 2-29.

3. Select three of the files and add them as tracks as shown in Figure 2-30.

4. Select the fourth file and align it to the tail of the event in the first track.

5. Preview the project.

6. Keep the project open for the next skills review.

FIGURE 2-29
Add clips to the Project Media window

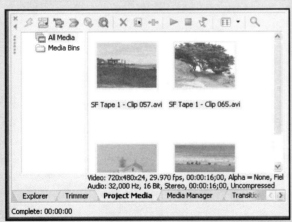

FIGURE 2-30
Add events to the project

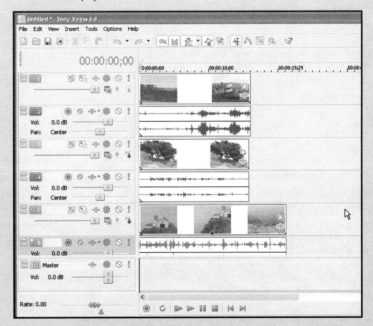

SKILLS REVIEW

Scrubbing the Timeline

1. Use the Scrub control to move forward along the timeline as shown in Figure 2-31.
2. Use the Scrub control to play back the timeline in reverse as shown in Figure 2-32.

3. Use the keyboard to move forward along the timeline.
4. Use the keyboard to halt playback.
5. Use the keyboard to play back the timeline in reverse.
6. Keep the project open for the next skills review.

Managing Project Media

1. Delete the media from the second and third tracks from the timeline. Alternatively, if the media you imported has audio, delete the media from the third, fourth, fifth and sixth tracks.
2. Delete any unused media from the Project Media window.
3. Rename one of the remaining clips in the Project Media window.
4. Create a new media bin.
5. Rename the media bin Images.
6. Import some images into the new media bin, as shown in Figure 2-33.

FIGURE 2-31
Scrub forward along the timeline

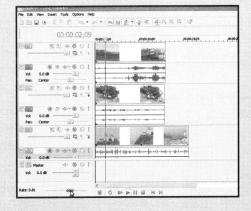

FIGURE 2-32
Scrub the timeline in reverse

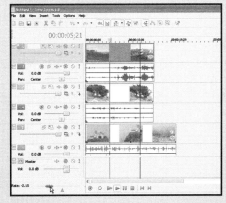

FIGURE 2-33
Import images into a media bin

PROJECT BUILDER 1

Your production supervisor has given you the assignment of shooting video for an upcoming promotion for a real estate company. You're shooting video of an open house in an upscale part of town. After shooting the video, you'll capture the video to your computer using Sony Video Capture.

1. Connect your digital camcorder to your IEEE 1394 port on an OHCI-compliant Capture card.

2. Launch Vegas.

3. Create a new project.

4. Save the project as Project_1.

5. Switch your camcorder to VCR or VTR mode.

6. Click the Capture Video button in the Project Media window or choose File > Capture Video.

7. Capture the desired portion of the tape as clips and save the captured video to a new media bin named **Chapter_2**. Your Project Media window should resemble Figure 2-34.

FIGURE 2-34

Sample Project Builder 1

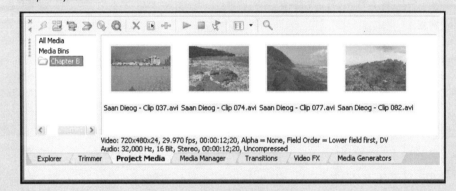

PROJECT BUILDER 2

Your production supervisor looked over your shoulder as you captured the video from the open house shoot to your PC.

He thinks the footage looked terrific, and he wants you to assemble a 20-second teaser for the client. You've been instructed to create a multimedia file that can be transferred to CD-ROM.

1. Open the Project_1.veg file.

2. Click the Project Properties button.

3. Choose the Multimedia template and accept the default settings.

4. Preview the clips you captured. Remember that you can click the Auto Preview button in the Project Media window to begin playing a clip as soon as you select it as shown in Figure 2-35.

5. Add enough events to the project to create a 20-second video. Your time-line should resemble Figure 2-36.

6. Preview the project. See Figure 2-37.

FIGURE 2-35
Previewing a clip

FIGURE 2-36
Project Builder 2 Sample 1

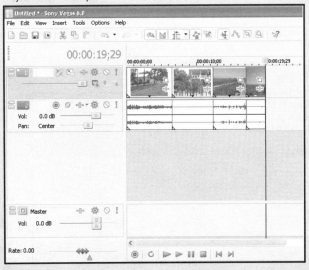

FIGURE 2-37
Project Builder 2 Sample 2

DESIGN PROJECT

Your client's advertising department presents you with several video clips and several images that you'll be using to create a series of 30-second advertisements. The client has informed you that this is just the beginning, and there will be additional video clips, images, sound files, and voice-overs. You decide it's in your best interests to create a new project and organize the media the client has already presented you in bins. You'll use the base project as a template for all future projects with the client because all the material will be organized in a logical manner for easy access.

1. Create a folder on your hard drive and name it **Design Project 2**.

2. Create three subfolders and name them **Video**, **Audio**, and **Images**.

3. Copy some video, audio, and image files into the folders you've just created.

4. Launch Vegas and create a new project.

5. Save the project as **Client_B**.

6. In the media bin, create three bins and label them Audio, Video, and Images.

7. Import the **Audio**, **Video**, and **Image** files from the Design Project 2 folder into the project, making sure the proper media is segregated in the proper media bin. The easiest way to

do this is to use the Explorer to navigate to the folder, select the files, and then drag them into the appropriate media bin.

8. Arrange one image and three video files on the timeline, as shown in Figure 2-38. Your Project Media window should have bins, as shown in Figure 2-39.

FIGURE 2-38
Project sample timeline

FIGURE 2-39
Project sample Project Media window

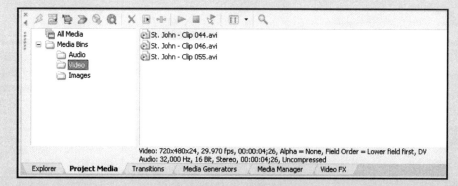

CHAPTER SUMMARY

This chapter covers importing media into your project. Media can be imported into a project using menu commands, or by dragging files from the Explorer into the Project Media window. After you've populated the Project Media window with clips, you can add them directly to the desired track. When adding multiple clips to a project, you can add them to a track, add them across tracks, or add them as takes.

What You Have Learned

In this chapter, you:
- Learned to specify project settings.
- Learned to import media using menu commands and the Explorer.
- Captured video from your camcorder.
- Used the Project Media window to extract audio from CDs and capture images from your scanner.
- Learned to add multiple media clips to tracks.
- Learned to add multiple media clips across tracks.
- Learned to add multiple media clips as takes.
- Learned to navigate the timeline with the Shuttle control.

Key Terms from This Chapter

- **Audio bit depth.** The number of bits used to represent a single sample. Higher bit depths ensure cleaner audio. 8-bit samples use less memory and disk space, but are inherently noisier.
- **Audio sampling rate.** The number of samples per second used to store a sound. Higher sampling rates ensure better fidelity at the expense of a larger file size.
- **DV (Digital Video)-compliant media.** Media such as miniDV and microDV tapes that are used to digitally record video.
- **The Explorer.** A device in the Window Docking area that is used to navigate to system folders. The Vegas Explorer is similar to the Windows Explorer.
- **FireWire.** An external device for transmitting data from devices to a computer. FireWire supports data transfer rates of 400 Mbps (1394a) or 800 Mbps (1394b).
- **Frame rate.** The number of frames played per second.
- **HDV.** An acronym for High Definition Video. HDV video format has a 16:9 (widescreen) aspect ratio MPEG-2 compliant transport stream that is

captured on digital videotape. Supported frame rates are 60i (frames-per-second interlaced), 30p (progressive), 50i, and 25p.
- **Scrub control.** A slider used to rapidly navigate (scrub) through a project. You can scrub forward or backward.
- **Sony DV codec.** The codec used by Vegas when compressing video during capture, and when decompressing video for playback within Sony Vegas.
- **Sony Video Capture.** An application installed with Vegas that is used to capture video from camcorders and other video playback devices such as video decks, that you connect to a computer via an IEEE 1394 port of an OHCI-compliant video capture card.
- **Timecode.** A method of measuring time in a video project. Timecode is measured as hh:mm:ss:ff where hh is hours, mm is minutes, ss is seconds, and ff is frames. For example, 01:20:05:10 is 1 hour, 20 minutes, 5 seconds, and 10 frames into the project.
- **Voice-over recordings.** Audio recordings that can be used to narrate videos.

3

WORKING WITH
Media Events

1. Understand track events.

2. Modify event duration.

3. Compress and expand events.

4. Understand ripple editing.

5. Add Event Effects.

6. Create event groups.

7. Cut, copy, and paste events.

chapter 3 WORKING WITH
Media Events

When you add a clip from the Project Media window to your project, you are creating an event. An event is defined as a single audio, video, or image clip. You can alter the duration of an event, apply effects to an event, and group events. The beauty of editing individual events is that the original clip is not affected. In fact, you can have a carbon copy of a clip at a different point in your production (a different event) and apply different effects. For example, you can align two video clips end to end and choose a command from the shortcut menu that causes the second event to play in reverse.

When you add an event to a project, you can trim the event to remove unwanted footage. You can split an event on any frame. After splitting an event, you have two events. You can delete one of the events, or split one of the new events further down the timeline and then delete the middle of the event. Splitting an event is a quick and easy way to remove unwanted footage from anywhere in an event.

You can copy, cut, and paste events. The ability to paste an event you've already

trimmed is a tremendous benefit that speeds up your workflow. You can also speed up or slow down an event by compressing or stretching it. When you compress an event, you're squeezing the original footage into a smaller period of time. When you stretch an event, you expand the event to fit a longer duration on the timeline.

After you add an event to your project, you can add one or more Event FX to the event. You have two categories of Event FX: audio and video. Video Event FX are similar to filters you find in an image-editing application. For example, if you have clips that are too dark, you can use the Sony Brightness and Contrast Event FX to breathe some life back into the footage. If you have several events that need the same effects, you can add the Event FX to one clip and adjust the parameters to suit your project. You can then paste the event attributes to other events that need the same effects.

When you create a project with hundreds of events, it can be a chore to manage the project. Selecting and moving several events to a different position on the timeline is time consuming. Fortunately, you can create a group of events. After you create a group of events, they behave as a single entity. Select one event in the group, and you can move the entire group to a different position or track. You cannot however apply effects to a group in one fell swoop. You can only apply an effect to an individual event.

You can, however, paste event attributes to several events before combining them as an event group.

Tools You'll Use

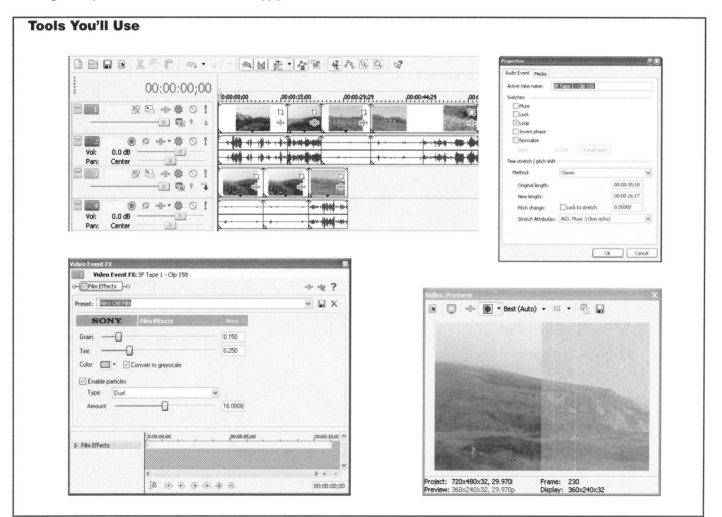

UNDERSTAND
TRACK EVENTS

What You'll Do

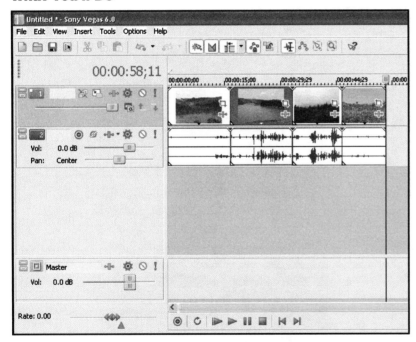

 In this lesson, you gain an understanding of the relationship between track events and the original clip.

Understanding Media Files and Events

An event is the lowest common denominator in a Vegas project. An event can be an audio clip, video clip, or static image that you add to a track timeline. When you add media to a project, the path to the file is stored in the Project Media window. When you add a clip from the Project Media window to your project, you are creating an instance of the clip, which is known as an event. An event can be the media clip in its entirety, or a portion of the original clip.

An event contains all of the information of the original media clip. You can trim an event to a shorter duration than the original without affecting the original clip as stored on your hard drive. **Non-destructive editing** in Vegas is a tremendous plus. In Vegas, you have the following types of events:

- **Generated Media.** Generated Media video events are items you create in Vegas such as solid color backdrops, gradient backdrops, text overlays, title clips, and credit rolls.

- **Audio.** Audio events are sound files that can be part of a video clip such as an MPEG or AVI file, or they can be audio clips such as MP3 or WAV files. You can modify audio events by changing characteristics such as speed, volume, and balance between speakers. Audio events appear on a separate track and cannot be mixed with video event tracks. You can mix audio events to control the soundtrack of the rendered video file.

- **Video.** Video events can be full motion video, or still images. Video events appear on their own tracks and cannot be mixed with audio events. You can alter video characteristics such as speed, duration, size, and so on. When you have multiple video tracks, you can control the way each track is composited with the others to determine the look of the rendered video file.

1. Create a new project and add a video clip to the Project Media window.

2. Double-click the clip to add it to the project.

3. Double-click the clip again to add a second event to the project.

4. Your timeline should resemble Figure 3-1.

5. Move your cursor towards the head of the second clip.

6. When your cursor becomes a dual-headed arrow with a rectangle, click and drag to the right.

The rectangle part of the icon that appears when you hold your cursor over the head or tail of an event points to the event that will be altered when you click and drag. When you drag the head or tail of a clip, you change the duration of the event. Dragging the head of the clip to the right effectively shortens the event. You can also drag the tail of the event to the left to shorten an event, which removes footage from the tail of the clip. You can also extend an event by dragging the head of the clip to the left or the tail of the clip to the right, which in essence replays the footage. When looping is on, a notch appears in an event whose duration has been extended, the notch signifying the point at which the frames will be replayed.

FIGURE 3-1

Create multiple instances of a clip

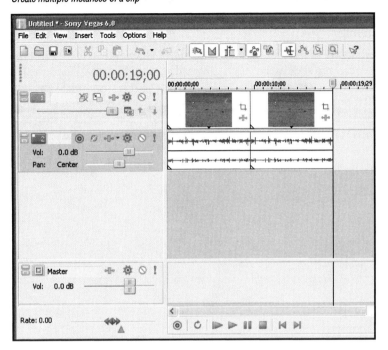

FIGURE 3-2

Modify an event

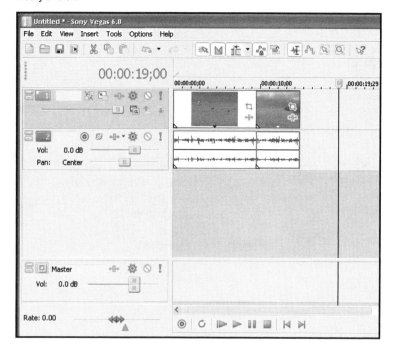

7. Release the mouse button.

Your timeline should resemble Figure 3-2. For the purpose of this illustration, the screen capture software is zoomed to the second clip so that the icon is visible.

8. Press Ctrl+Home to navigate to the beginning of the timeline.

9. Press the spacebar to preview the project.

When the first event plays, notice that it is identical to your original clip, in spite of the fact that you changed the duration of the second event. When the second clip plays, it begins at a different frame than the original.

MODIFY EVENT
DURATION

What You'll Do

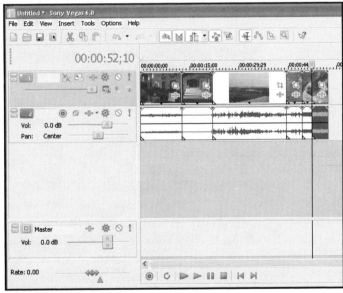

 In this lesson, you change the duration of an event and split an event.

Trimming an Event's In and Out Points

In the previous lesson, you changed the duration of an event by changing the point at which the event begins, which is known in video editing as trimming the **In** point. You can also modify the duration of an event by trimming the **Out** point.

When you trim the In and Out points of an event, you watch the Video Preview window to see which frame you are choosing for the In or Out point. In the last lesson, you dragged the head of the clip to a random position which then became the In point. This is fine when you're editing video in which the frames are similar. However, when you need to trim the clip to a specific frame, this method leaves a bit to be desired. In this lesson, you navigate to the precise frame and then trim the clip.

Splitting an Event

Another manner in which you can trim an event is by splitting it. When you **split an event**, you end up with two events. You can delete one of the events, or split the second event and then delete the middle event. Splitting an event is useful when you need to remove a large amount of unwanted footage, or need to trim unwanted footage from the middle of a clip. You split a clip while previewing it with the Video Preview window. You play the event and then stop it at the precise frame where you want the event to be split.

FIGURE 3-3

Setting the In point of an event

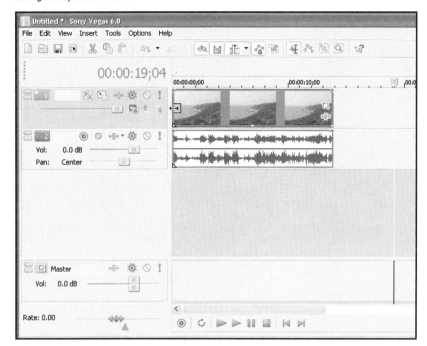

1. Create a new project and add a video clip with embedded audio to the Project Media window.

2. Double-click the clip to create an event.

   Vegas snaps the clip to the beginning of the timeline. Remember, you can also create an event by dragging a media clip into the workspace. When you drag a clip into the workspace, you can drop it anywhere on the timeline.

3. If the Video Preview window is not currently displayed, choose View > Video Preview.

4. Press the spacebar to begin previewing the project.

5. Press Enter to pause the event on the frame that you want to become the new In point.

   A flashing vertical line indicates the frame where you've paused the video. Remember if you need to fine-tune the position of the cursor, you can navigate to the next or previous frame by using the right and left arrow keys.

6. Move your cursor towards the head of the event until it becomes a dual-headed arrow with a right-pointing rectangle, as shown in Figure 3-3.

7. Click and drag toward the flashing line.

8. Release the mouse button when the cursor snaps to the flashing line.

   Vegas trims the event to the desired In point and the event snaps to the beginning of the timeline. When you trim the In point of an event in the middle of a timeline, Vegas snaps the head of the trimmed event to the tail of the neighboring event, unless you've disabled Auto Ripple.

9. Press Ctrl+Home to move the cursor to the start of the project, and then press the spacebar to preview the project.

   Alternatively, you can click the Go to Start button ◁ and then click the Play button ▷.

10. Press Enter when you've reached the desired frame for the new Out point.

11. Move your cursor towards the tail of the event until it becomes a dual-headed arrow with a rectangle that points left, as shown in Figure 3-4.

12. Click and drag towards the flashing line.

13. Release the mouse button when the cursor snaps to the flashing line.

   Vegas trims the event to the desired Out point. When you trim the Out point of an event that occurs in the middle of a timeline, Vegas snaps the head of the next event on the timeline to the tail of the trimmed event, unless you have Auto Ripple disabled. All remaining events are moved to fill in the space vacated by the frames you've trimmed.

   QUICK TIP

   You can also trim an event beyond the end point, by moving your cursor toward the tail of an event. When your cursor becomes a double-head arrow with a right-pointing rectangle, drag right. As you drag, a notch appears at the end of the original event indicating that the event repeats from the first frame. If you drag the head of a clip to the left, a notch appears at the beginning of the

FIGURE 3-4

Setting the Out point of an event

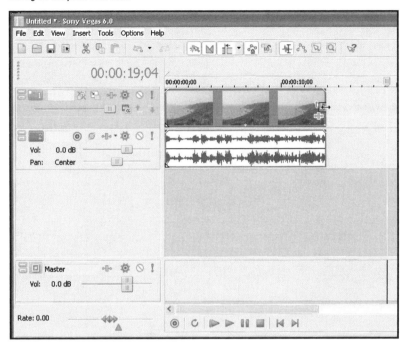

FIGURE 3-5

Trimming adjacent events

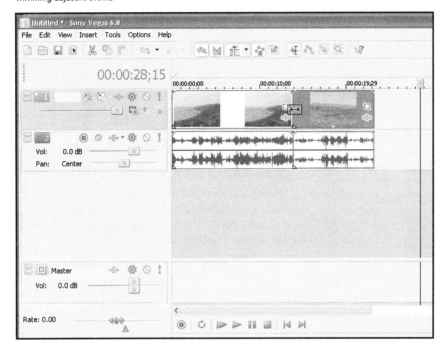

clip. The modified event will begin playing at a frame in the clip, which is determined by how far you dragged, and will continue playing to the end of the clip, and playing again from the start when the playhead approaches the notch.

Trim adjacent events

1. Begin a new project and add two video clips with embedded audio to the Project Media window.

2. Select the two clips and drag them into the main window, aligning the clips to the beginning of the timeline.

3. Move your cursor to the border between the events and then press Ctrl+Alt.

   Your cursor should resemble the one in Figure 3-5.

4. While pressing Ctrl+Alt, click and drag.

   Drag right to extend the first clip and trim the second, or drag left to extend the second clip and trim the first.

Split a clip

1. Create a new project and add a video clip with embedded audio to the Project Media window.

2. Double-click the clip to create a new event.

3. If the Video Preview window is not currently displayed, choose View > Video Preview.

4. Press the spacebar to begin previewing the project.

5. Press Enter to pause the event on the frame where you want to split the event.

6. Press S.

The event is split at the desired frame and the video and audio track for the latter half of the split event is selected. At this point, you can press Delete to remove the selected event. To remove unwanted footage from the middle of an event, you'll split the selected clip and then select and delete the middle portion, as you'll do next.

7. Press the spacebar to begin previewing the video again.

8. Press Enter when the frame on which you want to split the event is reached.

9. Press S.

Your original event is now split into three events and should resemble Figure 3-6. Alternatively you can choose Edit > Split to split an event at the current frame.

10. Click the middle video event, Shift-click the middle audio event, and then press Delete.

11. Vegas removes the unwanted footage and snaps the head of the last event to the tail of the first, unless you've disabled Auto Ripple.

FIGURE 3-6

Splitting an event

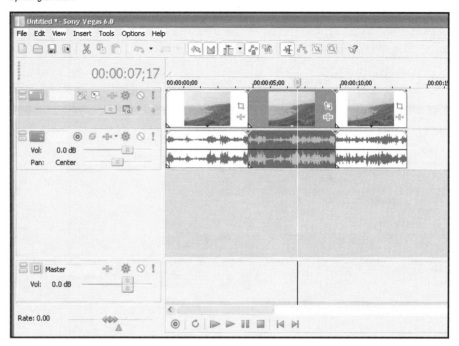

COMPRESS AND
EXPAND EVENTS

What You'll Do

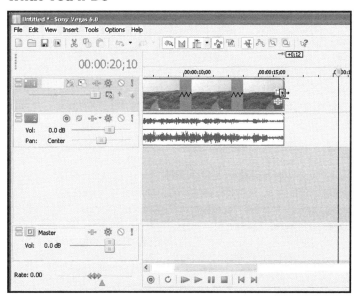

▶ In this lesson, you stretch and compress a video to make it a longer or shorter event.

Stretching an Event

When you want an event to play for a longer duration, without looping the event, you can stretch the event. When you stretch an event, you're extending the amount of time that the event plays, which in essence, slows the motion. You can slow an event down by applying a velocity envelope to it, but the event still occupies the same number of frames on the timeline. When you stretch an event, Vegas creates extra frames so that the stretched video matches the project frame rate. By default, Vegas uses **Smart Resampling.** You can modify this by changing a video event's properties and choosing Force Resample, or Disable Resample. In most instances, Smart Resampling is just the ticket.

Compressing an Event

When you want an event to play faster, you can apply a velocity envelope and set the speed at up to 300 percent of the original speed of the clip. You can also compress the event to speed up the motion. When you compress an event, you shorten it.

A stretched or compressed event is designated by a zig-zag line in the middle of the event. You can speed up or slow down several events by grouping them, as outlined in the upcoming lesson on grouping, and then stretching or compressing the group.

Changing the Pitch of a Compressed/Stretched Event

When you compress or stretch an event with embedded audio, the audio track is compressed or stretched as well. By default, when you compress or stretch an event, the length of the audio event and the pitch is changed. You can, however, modify this by changing the properties of the audio event.

Stretch an event

1. Create a new project and add a video clip with embedded audio to the Project Media window.

2. Double-click the clip to create a new event.

3. Move your cursor towards the tail of the event while holding down the Ctrl key.

4. When your cursor becomes a dual-headed arrow with a rectangle and squiggly line, as shown in Figure 3-7, click and drag right.

   You can also move your cursor towards the head of an event while holding down the Ctrl key. In this case, the rectangle points in the opposite direction. Drag to the left to stretch the event.

5. Release the mouse button when you've stretched the event to the desired duration.

6. Keep the project open, because you'll be using it in the next objective.

   You can only stretch an event until the playback rate reaches .25, in other words, a quarter of its original speed. When you stretch an event to its maximum, it is four times its normal duration. A stretched event has a stretched squiggly line in the middle, as shown in Figure 3-8.

FIGURE 3-7

Stretching an event

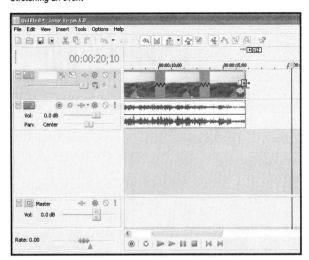

FIGURE 3-8

A stretched event on the timeline

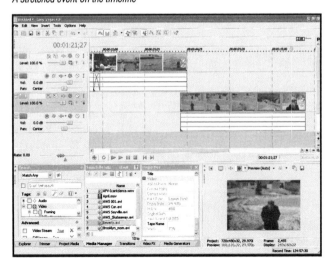

FIGURE 3-9

A compressed event

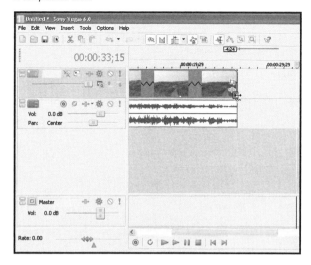

FIGURE 3-10

Changing the pitch of a compressed event

Compress an event

1. Choose Edit > Undo Stretch Event.

2. Move your cursor towards the tail of the event while holding down the Ctrl key.

3. When your cursor becomes a dual-headed arrow with a rectangle and a squiggly line, as shown previously in Figure 3-7, click and drag left.

4. Release the mouse button to finish compressing the event.

   Your timeline should resemble Figure 3-9.

5. Keep the project open for the next objective.

   The maximum you can compress an event is to a playback rate of 4.0, which is four times as fast as the original speed of the clip. The duration of an event compressed to the max is one-quarter the original event duration.

Change the pitch of a compressed event

1. Right-click the audio event for the event you just compressed and choose Properties from the shortcut menu.

   When you view the properties for a compressed or stretched event, the original length and new length of the event are listed, as shown in Figure 3-10.

2. Accept the default Classic method, or click the Method drop-down arrow to choose an option for the audio event.

   The default option changes the length of the audio track to correspond with the length of the video track while preserving the audio

Lesson 3   Compress and Expand Events

pitch. Your other choices are None and Classic. If you choose None, the audio event reverts to its original duration. If you choose Classic, you can manually adjust the duration of the audio event by typing a value in the New Length text box shown in Figure 3-10. You can also shift the pitch of the event by typing a value in the Pitch Change text box.

NOTE

If you are changing the pitch on an audio event that has been edited in Sony Sound Forge or Sony Acid, and the event has been ACIDized, a third option of Acid appears on the drop-down menu. This option enables you to stretch the audio by specifying a new tempo.

3. Accept the new event length, or type the desired value in the New Length field.

Changing the event length will cause the audio event to be longer or shorter than the stretched/compressed video event.

4. Accept the default Pitch Change value of 0.00000, or type the desired pitch shift (in **semitones**) in the Pitch Change field.

This option changes the pitch of the event. A value of 12 semitones raises the pitch one octave.

5. Click the Lock To Stretch check box to have the pitch determined by the new length of the audio event.

For example, if the length of an event is doubled, and you choose the Lock To Stretch option, the pitch of the event is raised by one octave. If you do not use the Lock To Stretch option, you can choose an option from the Stretch Attributes drop-down list to determine the sound of the stretched audio event.

6. Accept the default Stretch Attributes options, or click the Stretch Attributes down arrow and choose an option from the drop-down list.

This option determines how the stretched/compressed audio event is divided and crossfaded. The optimum choice depends on your source material. Experiment with the different options to determine which one is right for the audio event whose properties you are modifying.

7. Click OK to apply the changes.

UNDERSTAND
RIPPLE EDITING

What You'll Do

In this lesson, you learn how to use automatic ripple editing to keep your timeline intact after editing one or more events on the timeline. You also learn to ripple tracks after editing an event.

Using Auto Ripple

When you move, delete, or trim an event in the middle of a track, Vegas reshuffles the other events in order to keep the timeline track intact. This prevents you from leaving any gaps in your production, which would show up as black frames when the video is played. When Auto Ripple is enabled, Vegas automatically applies a ripple edit when you edit events on a timeline. For example, if you select an event in the middle of a track and drag it right, the events downstream from the selected event move to the right as well. If you disable Auto Ripple and move an event, it overlaps the event you move it over, which in essence creates a crossfade. However, you can easily create a crossfade by dragging an event to the left and overlapping the adjacent event. With Auto Ripple enabled, the downstream clips will follow and your timeline will remain intact. When Auto Ripple is enabled, the contents of the timeline will be rippled when you:

- Trim an event
- Slip trim or slide an event
- Compress or stretch an event
- Cut an event
- Paste an event
- Delete an event
- Move an event

Understanding Ripple Edit Types

Auto Ripple is a powerful tool, especially when you create complex projects with hundreds of events and lengthy timelines. The default Auto Ripple mode will rearrange the downstream clips on the affected tracks. However, when you start adding regions and markers to your project, you'll need those to be rippled when you edit track events. If you have multiple tracks in your project, those may also need to be rippled when you edit events on other tracks. You can choose any of the following ripple edit methods:

- Affected Tracks. Choose this method and the tracks you edited are rippled. This option also ripples the points on any envelopes you've applied to the effected tracks.

- Affected Tracks, Bus Tracks, Markers, and Regions. Choose this option and the tracks you edited are rippled, as well as any associated bus tracks. Any markers, regions, CD markers, or command markers you've applied to the project are rippled as well.

- All Tracks, Markers, and Regions. Choose this option and the tracks you've edited are rippled, along with the other tracks in your project. This option also ripples any markers, regions, CD markers, or command markers you've applied to the project.

Applying Rippling after Editing

If desired, you can disable automatic rippling and manually ripple tracks after you've performed an edit to one or more events in your project. If you choose this option, Vegas displays a marker above the timeline after you apply one of the previously discussed edits to one or more events on the timeline. The marker shows you the direction in which the ripple will be applied. You can then use a menu command or keyboard shortcut to ripple affected tracks; affected tracks, bus tracks, markers, and regions; or all tracks, markers, and regions.

FIGURE 3-11

Creating a multi-track project

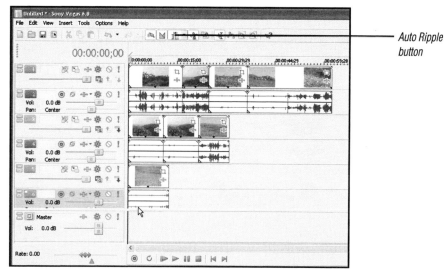

Auto Ripple button

FIGURE 3-12

Editing an event

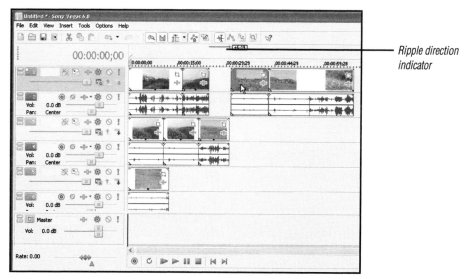

Ripple direction indicator

1. Create a new project.

2. Use the Explorer to navigate to a folder in which you store video clips.

3. Select three clips, right-click, and then drag the clips into the project.

4. Align the clips to the start of the timeline and choose Add Across Tracks.

5. Select three more clips and align them to the tail of the last clip on the first video track, and add two more clips to the end of the second video track.

   Your timeline should resemble Figure 3-11.

6. Click the Auto Ripple button's down arrow and choose Affected Tracks from the drop-down list. Make sure the Auto Ripple button is clicked as well.

7. Drag the second event on the first video track to the right.

   As you drag the event, a blue marker appears above the timeline, indicating the direction in which events will be rippled, as shown in Figure 3-12.

8. Release the mouse button.

   Vegas ripples the events on the first video track, and first audio track if the video clip has embedded audio. The other tracks are unaffected.

9. Choose Edit > Undo Move Events. Alternatively, you can press Ctrl+Z.

10. Click the triangle to the right of the Ripple Edit button and choose All Tracks, Markers, and Regions from the drop-down list.

11. Drag the second event on the second video track to the right and release the mouse button.

The events on the first video track and audio track (if the video file has embedded audio) are rippled, as well as the events on the second video and audio track.

12. Keep the project open, as you'll be using it in the upcoming objective.

Apply post-edit rippling

1. Choose Edit > Undo Move Events.

2. Click the Auto Ripple button to disable automatic rippling.

3. Drag the second video event in the first video track to the right and release the mouse button.

The second video event overlaps the third, as shown in Figure 3-13. Notice the blue line with the right-pointing arrow at the top of the timeline. This indicates the direction in which the timeline will ripple if you decide to apply a post-edit ripple. If you're working on a complex project, you may want to create a crossfade, and then fill in the gap with another clip. Otherwise, you can apply a post-edit ripple and the last event on the video timeline will ripple to make room for your previous edit.

4. Choose Edit > Post-Edit Ripple > Affected Tracks.

> **QUICK TIP**
>
> Press F to apply a post-edit ripple to affected tracks.

FIGURE 3-13
Post-edit rippling

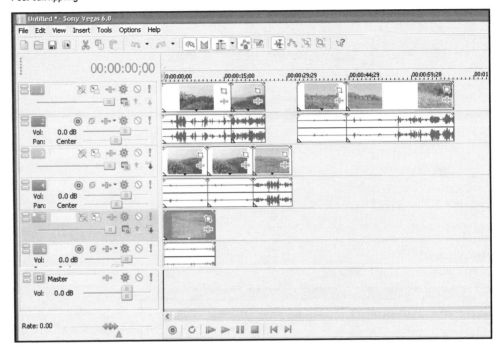

FIGURE 3-14

Applying a post-edit ripple to all tracks, markers, and regions

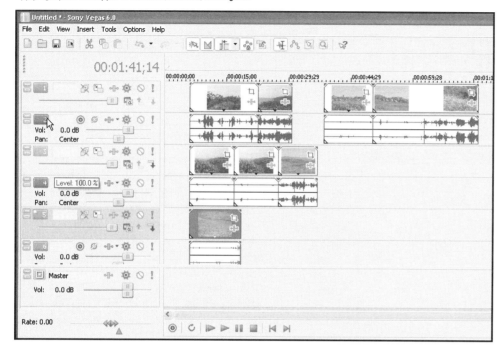

The third event is rippled to the right to make room for the event you just moved.

5. Drag the video event on the third video track to the right and release the mouse button.

A ripple direction marker appears on the top of the timeline, but no events are rippled.

6. Choose Edit > Post-Edit Ripple > All Tracks, Markers, and Regions.

> **QUICK TIP**
>
> Press Ctrl+Shift+F to apply a post-edit ripple to all tracks, markers, and regions in a project.

Events on all tracks are rippled to the right and align to the head of the event you just moved, as shown in Figure 3-14. One use for a post-edit ripple of all tracks is to make room for a clip you want to insert at the beginning of the project, or for that matter, at any point in the project. After inserting the new clip into one of the tracks, you can align an event to the tail of the event you just inserted, and then apply a post-edit ripple to all tracks to align the rest of the events to the newly inserted event.

ADD EVENT
EFFECTS

What You'll Do

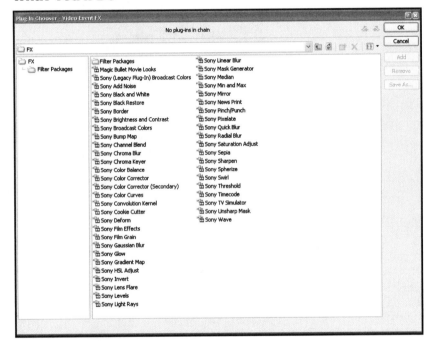

In this lesson, you are introduced to effects. You use effects to alter events in your projects.

Understanding Effects

Another very powerful feature of Vegas is the ability to apply an effect to individual events in your project. You have two types of effects. Video Event FX can be applied to events on video tracks, and audio Non-Real-Time Event FX can be applied to events on audio tracks. Effects are very much like filters you use in an image-editing program. And they are used for similar things. For example, if the color balance of a clip is out of whack, you can use the Sony Color Balance, or Sony Color Corrector effect to correct the deficiency.

Adding Effects to Events

When you create an event by adding a video clip to a track, a small icon appears at the lower-right corner of the event's thumbnail on the timeline. You add a Non-Real-Time Event FX to an audio track by choosing it from the shortcut menu. Either method gives you access to the Plug-in chooser dialog box. The contents of the dialog box vary depending on whether you're working with an audio event or a video event. Either way, the dialog box is a treasure trove of useful effects that you can use to add pizzazz to your project, or correct a deficiency in the original clip.

Creating a Plug-In Chain

If one effect is good, are two or more better? Of course the answer to this question depends on your artistic vision and the needs of the individual clip with which you're working. But you can apply as many effects to a track event as needed. When you add more than one effect to a track event, you're creating a plug-in chain. However, the Carte Blanche use of multiple effects on several, or several hundred, track events will significantly increase the amount of time needed to render your project. If you're working with an older system that barely meets the Vegas minimum system requirements, your machine may be tied up for several hours when rendering a lengthy production to which you have added plug-in chains to multiple events.

Previewing an Effect

Some effects are quite subtle. For example, when you apply color correction to an event, it can be hard to see how the added effect changes the overall quality of the clip. You can, however, configure the Video Preview window to display a before and after. You can preview the effect in the left or right half of the window, or drag a marquee around the area of the window that remains unchanged by the effect.

Add an event effect

1. Create a new project and add a video clip to the timeline.

2. Click the Event FX button on the video track of the event you just created, as shown in Figure 3-15.

   The Video FX Event dialog box and the Plug-In Chooser-Video Event FX dialog box shown in Figure 3-16 appear.

3. Select Sony Film Effects and then click Add in the upper-right corner.

   The effect is added to the event.

4. Click OK to exit the Plug-In Chooser-Video Event FX dialog box.

   After adding one of more effects to an event, you edit event parameters in the Video FX dialog box.

5. Click the Preset down arrow and choose Very Old Film from the drop-down list.

FIGURE 3-15

The Event FX button

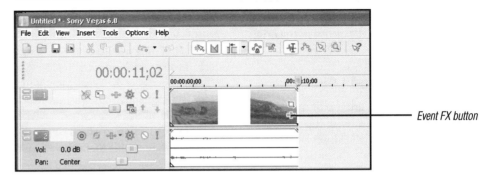

Event FX button

FIGURE 3-16

The Plug-In Chooser -Video Event FX dialog box

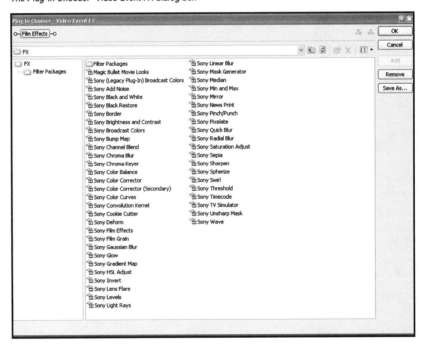

FIGURE 3-17
The Video Event FX dialog box

Plug-in Chain

Remove Selected
Plug-in

Save Preset

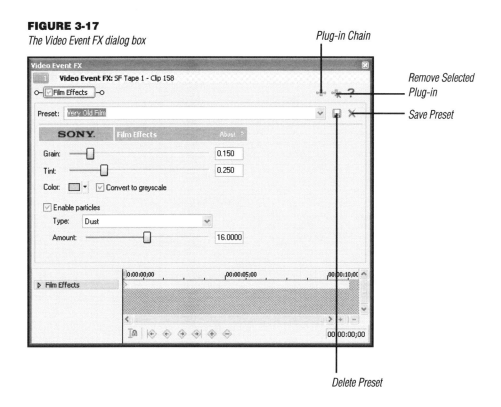

Delete Preset

The dialog box for the Sony Film Effects plug-in is shown in Figure 3-17. When you add an effect to an event, you can modify the parameters to suit your artistic taste, or choose a preset. You can preview the effect each parameter change has on the event by opening the Video Preview window. As you change each parameter, the window updates in real time. You can start with one of the presets and tweak the parameters. If you create a variant of an effect you'll want to use in the future, you can save it by clicking the Save Preset button. After naming and saving the modified preset, it will appear on the Preset drop-down list the next time you open the dialog box for the selected effect.

6. After setting the plug-in parameters, click the Close button.

   The effect is applied to the event and the event's Event FX button is now a bright green color.

7. Leave the project open, as you'll be using it in the next objective.

Create a Plug-In Chain

1. Click the Event FX button on the event you created in the last objective.

   The Video Event FX dialog box opens. You can now edit any effect you've applied to the event, or as you're about to do, add an additional effect.

2. Click the Plug-In Chain button shown in Figure 3-17.

The Plug-In Chooser-Video Event FX dialog box shown in Figure 3-16 appears.

QUICK TIP

You can open the Plug-In Manager dialog box by pressing Ctrl+Alt+1. After the dialog box opens, click the Audio or Video folder. If you click the Video Folder, choose FX. Then select the desired effect and drag it to the desired audio or video event to open the Video Event FX dialog box, where you can set the parameters for the effect. You can also click Transitions to apply a preset transition to a crossfade.

3. Select the Sony Film Grain effect and then click Add.

At this point you could add additional effects if needed. When you have multiple effects in a plug-in chain, you can change the order in which they are applied by clicking an event and dragging it right or left. You can also remove an effect from the plug-in chain by selecting it and then clicking Remove.

4. Click OK to exit the Plug-In Chooser-Video Event FX dialog box.

You can now edit the added effect in the Video Event FX dialog box, which should look like Figure 3-18. You can also change the order in which events execute by selecting an event and then dragging it left or right. If you're not sure how to set parameters for a selected effect, click the Plug-in Help button to open a dialog box that explains how to use the selected effect.

FIGURE 3-18
Creating a plug-in chain

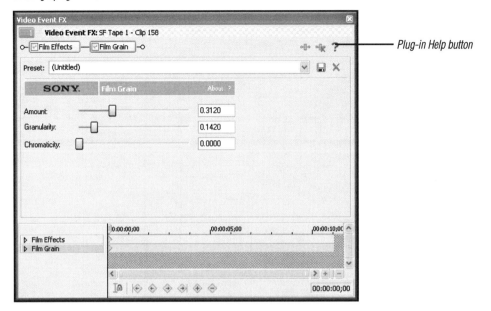

Plug-in Help button

FIGURE 3-19
Previewing an effect

Split Screen View button

Video Preview

Best (Auto) ▾

Project: 720x480x32, 29.970i
Preview: 360x240x32, 29.970p

Frame: 230
Display: 360x240x32

5. Click the Preset down arrow and choose Subtle from the drop-down list.

   After creating a plug-in chain for an event, your logical course of action is to preview the event before doing any additional work on your project. If the effects don't achieve the desired result, you can edit them by opening the Video Event FX dialog box as outlined previously.

6. Leave the project open, as you'll be using it in the next objective.

Preview event effects

1. If it's not already open, choose View > Video Preview.

2. If desired, float the window in the workspace and resize the window.

   When working with intricate effects, it's often desirable to view a larger version of the video.

3. Click the Split Screen View down arrow and choose a viewing option.

   Choose Select Left Half to view the original video in the left half of the window, or choose Select Right Half to view the original video in the right half of the window. Alternatively, you can choose Select All, and then drag a marquee inside the Video Preview window to have that portion of the window display the original video.

4. Press the spacebar to preview the video.

   Figure 3-19 shows the Video Preview window with the left half showing the original video. This figure shows an event with the effects you worked with in the previous two objectives.

CREATE EVENT
GROUPS

What You'll Do

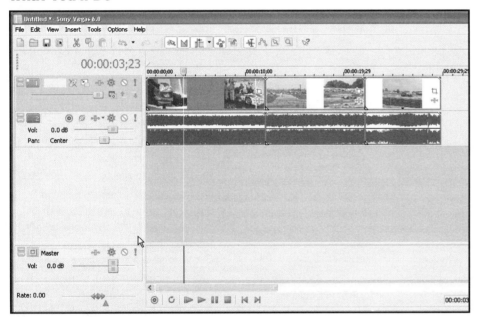

In this lesson, you create an event group. You also learn how to momentarily ignore the group to edit an individual event within the group.

Creating a Group

When you have several events on a timeline that you want to combine as a single entity, you can create an event group. When you create an event group, you can move all of the events within the group as a single unit. You cannot, however, apply an effect to an entire group. You must apply effects to each individual clip before creating the group.

Working with a Group

After you create a group, you can select it by clicking any event in the group and then dragging the group to the desired position on the timeline. If you have Auto Ripple enabled, the other events or event groups on the timeline ripple when you move the event downstream on the timeline. You can also use post-edit rippling with an event group. If, however, you need to edit an individual clip in a group, you can do so by using a menu command or toolbar button to ignore event grouping. After editing the clip, you can once again restore event grouping.

Create an event group

1. Create a new project and arrange six clips end to end on the timeline.

   If desired, you can select all six clips at once and drag them into the main window. Remember that you can select a range of clips by clicking the first clip you want to select and then Shift-clicking the last clip. You can select non-contiguous clips by clicking the first clip, and then Ctrl-clicking additional clips to add them to the group.

2. Select the second, third, and fourth event.

   If the events have both audio and video, make sure you select both tracks for each event.

3. Choose Edit > Group > Create New.

   The selected events are now a group and will act as a single entity. Note that you can also create a group of non-contiguous events.

4. Select any event in the group and drag to the right.

   If you have automatic rippling enabled, the downstream clips move to accommodate the position of the group, as shown in Figure 3-20.

5. Click the Ignore Event Grouping button 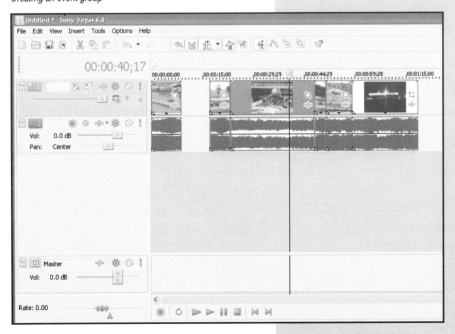 .

   When you click this button, you can move events within the group independently of the other event.

6. Select the second event in the group and overlap it with the first to create a crossfade.

   The clip moves independently. If you have automatic rippling enabled, the third clip tags along for the ride.

7. Select the third event in the group and overlap it with the second to create a crossfade.

   Again the event moves independently of the group. Click the Ignore Event Grouping button anytime you need to edit individual events in a group.

8. Click the Ignore Event Grouping button to restore event grouping.

9. Click any event in the group and then move the group to a different location on the timeline.

FIGURE 3-20

Creating an event group

CUT, COPY, AND
PASTE EVENTS

What You'll Do

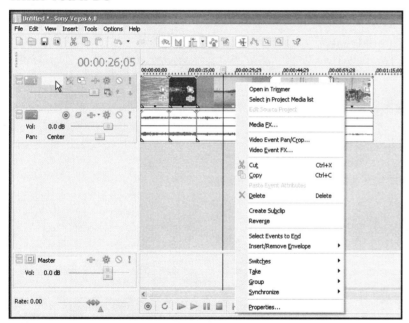

 In this lesson, you copy, cut, paste, and delete events from the timeline. You also learn how to paste attributes from one event to another.

Cutting, Copying, and Deleting Events

When you select a clip from the Project Media window and add it to a timeline track, you create an event. You can add additional instances of any clip in a Project Media window to a track. When you do so, you create a copy of the original media clip, which is an independent event on the track timeline. As you've learned previously, you can edit a timeline event and the original clip is unaffected. When you edit an event that you want to use in other places on the timeline, you can copy the event and then paste it into another track, or paste it farther downstream on the timeline.

You can also cut a clip to remove it from a track. When you cut a clip with automatic rippling enabled, adjacent clips downstream from the cut clip ripple to fill in the void. A cut or copied event replaces the current contents of the Clipboard.

When an event is no longer needed on a track, you can delete it. When you delete an event, it is not copied to the Clipboard, and therefore is unavailable for pasting. When you delete an event from the timeline, the original clip is unaffected and is still listed in the Project Media window.

Pasting Events

You can paste events on different tracks and then change the compositing mode to create special effects. When you paste a copied or cut event, you can paste a single copy anywhere on the timeline, paste multiple copies on the timeline, or insert the copied or cut event between two events on the timeline. If you've applied effects to an event, you can paste the event attributes to a single event, or several events. Pasting attributes is a powerful feature. For example, when you color-correct a single event that is part of several events that were shot in the same lighting, you can apply the same color correction to the other events by pasting attributes.

Copy, cut, and paste events

1. Create a new project and import a video clip into the project using either the Import Media command or the Explorer.

2. Drag the clip from the Project Media window into the main window, aligning the clip with the start of the timeline.

3. Select the clip, right-click, and then choose Copy from the event shortcut menu shown in Figure 3-21.

   The event is copied to the Clipboard. You can also copy multiple events. Alternatively, you can Choose Edit > Copy, or press Ctrl+C to copy selected events.

   > **QUICK TIP**
   >
   > To cut an event from the timeline, choose Edit > Cut or press Ctrl+X. You can paste a cut event to another track or to a different position in the timeline.

4. Position your cursor to the right of the clip you just copied and then choose Edit > Paste.

   The copied event is pasted to the timeline. Alternatively, you can press Ctrl+V to paste a copied event to the timeline.

5. Import a different media clip into the project and align it to the tail of the last clip in the timeline.

6. With the third clip still selected, choose Edit > Copy.

7. Position your cursor between the first and second clip and then choose Edit > Paste Insert.

FIGURE 3-21
The event shortcut menu

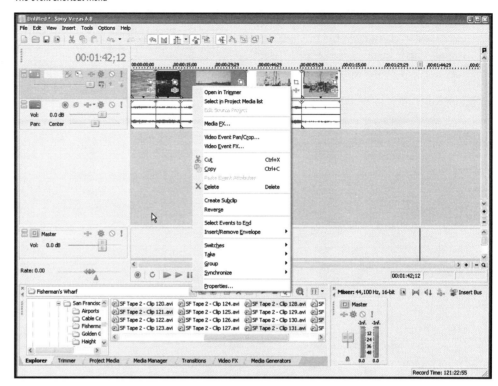

FIGURE 3-22

Inserting a copied event between existing events

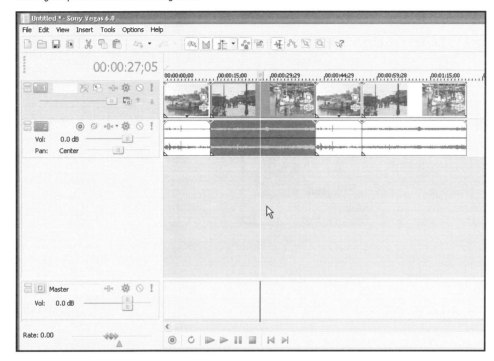

FIGURE 3-23

The Paste Repeat dialog box

Vegas inserts the clip where your cursor is positioned and the downstream clips move to accommodate the duration of the inserted event, as shown in Figure 3-22.

8. Position your cursor at the tail of the last clip on the timeline.

9. Choose Edit > Paste Repeat. Alternatively, you can press Ctrl+B.

   The Paste Repeat dialog box shown in Figure 3-23 appears.

10. Enter a value in the Number of Times to Paste field.

   This value determines how many copies of the clip are pasted at the cursor insertion point. Alternatively, you can click the spinner buttons to specify a value.

11. In the Paste Spacing section, accept the default End to End option, or click the Even Spacing button.

   If you choose the End to End option, the copies are aligned head to tail. If you choose the Even Spacing option, the Paste Every text field becomes available. The default spacing value is one second, but you can enter any value. Note that if you enter a value that is less than the event duration, the pasted events overlap.

12. Click OK.

   Vegas pastes the desired number of copies spaced as you specified.

Paste event attributes

1. Create a new project and import five video clips into the Project Media window.

2. Select the clips in the Project Media window and drag them into the main window, aligning the clips to the start of the timeline.

   QUICK TIP

   While working in the Project Media window, you can change focus to track view (the timeline) by pressing Alt+0 (zero).

3. Click the Event FX button on the first video event.

   The Video Event FX and Plug In Chooser-Video Event FX dialog boxes appear.

4. Select the Sony Lens Flare plug-in and then click the Add button.

   The effect is added to the event's plug-in chain.

5. Click OK to exit the Plug In Chooser-Video Event FX dialog box.

6. Accept the default parameters for the effect and then click the Close button to exit the Video Event FX dialog box.

   The effect is applied to the event and the Event FX button is highlighted in green. Figure 3-24 shows the Video Preview window after the effect is applied to the event.

7. Select the video event you just applied the effect to and then choose Edit > Copy.

8. The video event and its attributes are copied to the Clipboard.

9. Select the second event, and then Shift-click the last event.

FIGURE 3-24
Applying the Lens Flare effect

FIGURE 3-25

Pasting event attributes

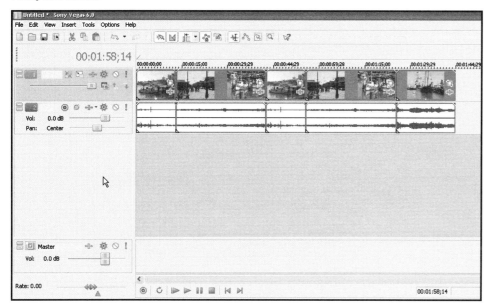

The range of events is selected. Alternatively, you can select the Selection Edit tool and drag a marquee around the events you want to select.

10. Choose Edit > Paste Event Attributes.

Vegas pastes the lens flare plug-in to the selected events. Notice that the Event FX button for each selected event is now green, as shown in Figure 3-25. Preview the project and you'll see the lens flare on each event.

QUICK TIP

To apply an effect to every event in a track, apply the effect to the first track and then choose Edit Copy. Select the second event, right-click, and choose Select Events To End from the shortcut menu. Choose Edit > Paste Event Attributes to paste the attributes copied from the first event to the selected events.

SKILLS REVIEW

Trimming a Clip

1. Create a new project and import a video clip into the Project Media window.

2. Double-click the clip to create an event, as shown in Figure 3-26.

3. Trim some footage from the event In point.

4. Monitor your work in the Video Preview window and release the mouse button to set the trim point at the desired frame.

5. Trim some footage from the event Out point, as shown in Figure 3-27.

FIGURE 3-26
Create an event

FIGURE 3-27
Trim a clip

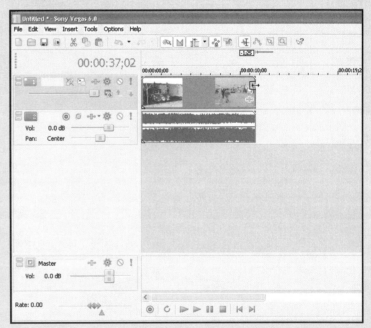

Splitting an Event

1. Create a new project and import a video clip into the Project Media window.

2. Double-click the clip to create an event.

3. Press the spacebar to begin previewing the project.

4. Press Enter to pause the clip at the desired frame.

5. Press S to split the event, as shown in Figure 3-28.

6. Delete the downstream section of the event.

Stretching an Event

1. Create a new project and import a video clip with embedded audio into the Project Media window.

2. Double-click the clip to create an event.

3. Press Ctrl and move your cursor towards the tail of the event.

4. When your cursor becomes a squiggly line with a dual-headed arrow, as shown in Figure 3-29, click and drag to the right.

FIGURE 3-28
Split a clip

FIGURE 3-29
Stretch an event

5. Release the mouse button when the event cannot be stretched any farther.

6. Right-click the event audio track and choose Properties from the shortcut menu.

7. Click the Lock To Stretch check box, as shown in Figure 3-30, and then click OK to apply the change.

8. Move your cursor toward the head of the clip and press the spacebar to preview the event.

Applying a Post-Edit Ripple

1. Create a new project and import four video clips into the Project Media window.

2. Drag the first three clips into the main window, aligning them with the beginning of the timeline.

3. Click the Auto Ripple button to disable automatic rippling.

4. Select the second clip, and move it downstream on the timeline, leaving enough room to insert another clip, as shown in Figure 3-31.

FIGURE 3-30
Changing the time stretch method

FIGURE 3-31
Editing the timeline

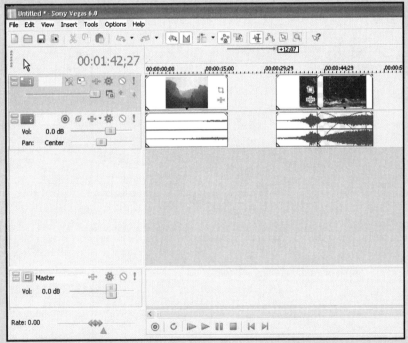

5. Choose Edit > Post-Edit Ripple > Affected Tracks. Alternatively, you can press F.

6. Drag the fourth clip from the Project Media window and insert it into the space that was created after you moved the second event. Align the clip you're inserting with the tail of the first event, as shown in Figure 3-32.

7. Align the third event with the tail of the second.

8. Choose Edit > Post-Edit Ripple > Affected Tracks. Alternatively, you can press F.

Creating an Event Group

1. Create a new project and import five video clips into the Project Media window.

2. Make sure automatic rippling is enabled.

3. Drag the clips into the main window, aligning them to the beginning of the timeline, as shown in Figure 3-33.

FIGURE 3-32
Aligning events

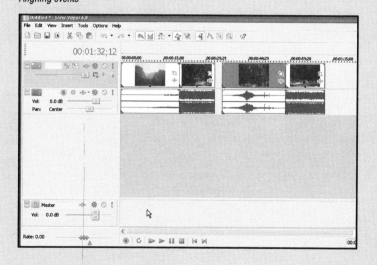

FIGURE 3-33
Adding clips to the timeline

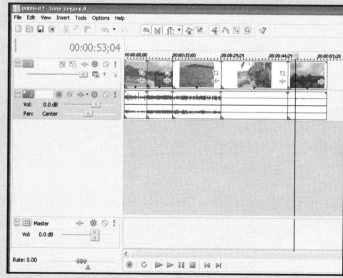

4. Select the second, third, and fourth events and press G. If the events have embedded audio, make sure you select the video and audio tracks for each event.

5. Move the event group you just created downstream on the timeline, leaving enough room to insert another clip.

6. Select the last clip and press Ctrl+C.

7. Position your cursor at the tail of the second clip and press Ctrl+V.

8. Align the event group to the tail of the clip you just pasted, as shown in Figure 3-34.

Paste Inserting a Clip

1. Create a new project and import four video clips into the Project Media window.

2. Drag the clips into the main window, aligning them to the beginning of the timeline, as shown in Figure 3-35.

FIGURE 3-34
Aligning an event group

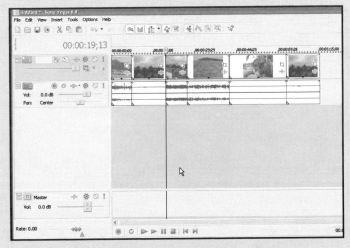

FIGURE 3-35
Adding events to a project

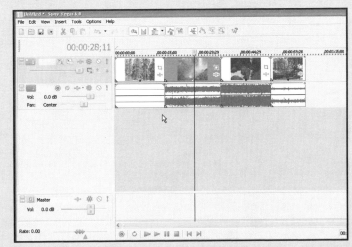

3. Select the fourth event and Choose Edit > Cut. Alternatively, you can press Ctrl+X. If your video clip has embedded audio, be sure to select both the audio and video event.

4. Position your cursor between the second and third event.

5. Choose Edit > Paste Insert to insert the event, as shown in Figure 3-36.

FIGURE 3-36

Paste inserting an event

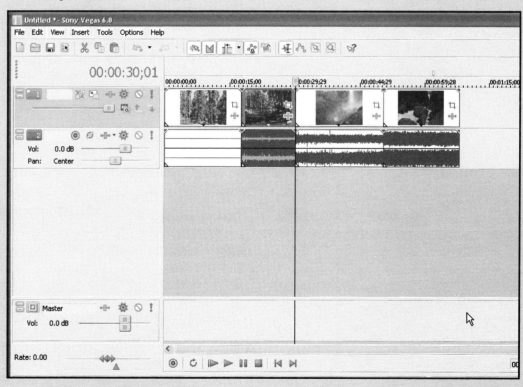

PROJECT BUILDER 1

You work for a multimedia company that specializes in creating multimedia CD-ROM presentations and DVD promotions. Your production supervisor has given you a CD-ROM with 10 video clips shot by one of your firm's clients, a travel agency. Your supervisor's parting comment was, "This is hodge-podge. There are some gems buried in this mess. Mine them and create a 60-second video." After previewing the footage, you determine there is a lot of unnecessary footage at the head and tail of several of the clips.

1. Create a new project using appropriate settings for multimedia video.

2. Save the project as **Proj_1**.

3. Import 10 clips into the Project Media window.

4. Select the clips and drag them into the main window.

   Your timeline should resemble Figure 3-37.

5. Press the spacebar to begin previewing the project.

6. Press Enter to pause the preview on a frame that will become the new In point for the first event.

7. Trim the In point to the current playhead position.

8. Press the spacebar to continue previewing the project.

9. Press Enter to pause the movie on a frame that will become the new Out point for the first event.

10. Trim the Out point to the current playhead position.

11. Continue previewing the project, trimming the In and Out points of each clip to weed out unnecessary footage of each event in your production. Your timeline should resemble Figure 3-38. Note that the current time indicator shows that the edited project is just over a minute in duration.

FIGURE 3-37

Sample project builder 1 before trimming clips

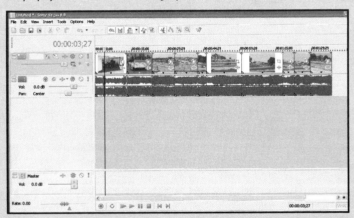

FIGURE 3-38

Sample project builder 1 after trimming clips

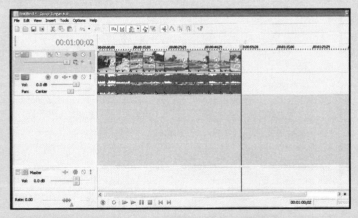

While previewing material for the travel agency project, your production supervisor notices a clip that contains out-of-focus footage in the middle of the clip. He contacts his video editing guru (which would be you) and asks if there's any way to salvage the clip. You know this can be done easily in Vegas, but you pause a few seconds to make it appear as though the problem might be unsolvable. Several seconds later, you smile and say, "No sweat. Come back in an hour." As your supervisor leaves, you wonder what you'll do for the 55 minutes that remain after you remove the out-of-focus footage.

1. Create a new project.
2. Save the project as Proj_2.
3. Import a clip into the Project Media window.
4. Drag the clip into the main window, aligning it with the beginning of the timeline.
5. Press the spacebar to begin previewing the project.
6. Press the Enter key when you encounter the first frame that you want to remove. Remember you can always use the right and left arrow keys to nudge forward or backward a frame at a time.
7. Choose Edit > Split. Alternatively, you can press S.
8. Press the spacebar to continue previewing the project.
9. Press Enter to pause the project on the last frame you want to remove.
10. Choose Edit > Split. Alternatively, you can press S.

    Your clip is now split into three events.
11. Select the middle event. If the event contains video and audio, make sure you select both tracks.
12. Press Delete. Figure 3-39 shows a project event that needs to have footage removed from the middle. Figure 3-40 shows the project event after the event was first split into three events and then the middle event with the unwanted footage was deleted.

FIGURE 3-39

Sample design project with event that needs footage removed

FIGURE 3-40

Sample design project with edited event

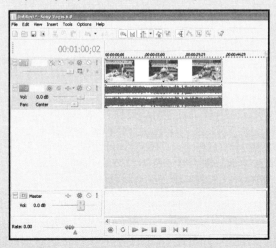

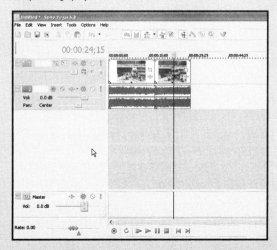

DESIGN PROJECT

You work for a television station preparing video clips for news reports. An amateur videographer captured footage of a crime. The footage is presented to your company on a miniDV tape. After capturing the footage and reviewing it, you notice that the footage is dark. Your production supervisor asks you to attempt to salvage the video, because this footage is the only known recording of the crime.

1. Create a new project.

2. Import five video clips that were recorded at the same time into the Project Media window.

3. Select the clips and drag them into the main window.

4. Apply the Brightness/Contrast plug-in to the first video event. Adjust the parameters to suit your footage.

5. Select the first event and press Ctrl+C.

6. Select the second video event, right-click, and choose Select To End from the shortcut menu.

7. Choose Edit > Paste Attributes. Each event's Video FX button should be highlighted in green, as shown in Figure 3-41.

FIGURE 3-41

Design project sample

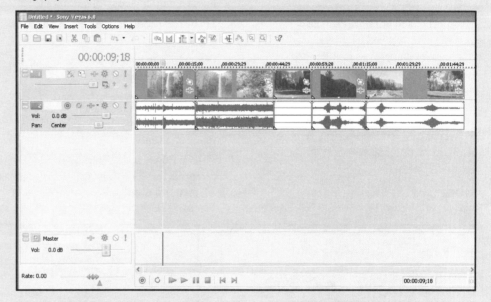

CHAPTER SUMMARY

This chapter covers the relationship between events and the original media. Event duration can be modified by manually dragging the head or tail of the event. Events can also be modified by compressing or expanding them. When an event is compressed or expanded, the contents of the event are unchanged, but a compressed event plays faster, and an expanded event plays slower. When events are added to the timeline, other events are rippled to make room for the new event if you have Auto Ripple enabled. You can also manually ripple the timeline after adding an event.

What You Have Learned

In this chapter, you:

- Discovered how events are related to the original media.

- Learned how to modify event duration by changing the In and Out points.

- Compressed an event to make it play faster without changing the content.

- Stretched an event to make it play slower without changing the content.

- Learned how to change the audio properties of a compressed or stretched event.

- Learned how to use the Auto Ripple feature.

- Learned to manually ripple affected tracks after adding events to a project.

- Modified events through the use of Event FX.

- Created event groups.

- Learned how to copy, cut, and paste events.

- Learned how to paste event attributes from events you have copied.

Key Terms from This Chapter

- **Event group.** A group of events that acts as a single entity on the timeline. You can reposition an event group, but you cannot apply Event FX to an event group.

- **In point.** The point at which an event begins playing, as compared to the original media. By specifying a different In point, you can prevent unwanted footage at the beginning of a media clip from playing, without altering the original media.

- **Non-destructive editing.** The capability to edit events without modifying the original media.

- **Non-Real-Time Event FX.** Plug-ins that are applied to audio events, and cannot be previewed in real time. When you apply a Non-Real-Time

Event FX to an audio event, Vegas makes a copy of the event with the plug-in applied and adds it as a take.

- **Out point.** The point at which an event stops playing, as compared to the original media. By specifying a different Out point, you can prevent unwanted footage at the end of a media clip from playing, without altering the original media.

- **Ripple editing.** Changing the position of events on the timeline that are downstream from events you add to a timeline. In essence, ripple editing makes room for the newly inserted events.

- **Semitones.** An interval equal to a half tone in the standard diatonic scale.

- **Smart Resampling.** Vegas uses Smart Resampling to synchronize a stretched or compressed event with the project frame rate.

- **Splitting an event.** Using a menu command to split an event into two events.

- **Stretching an event.** Increasing the duration of an event without changing or repeating the contents.

4

USING ADVANCED VIDEO
Editing Techniques

1. Slip and slide events.

2. Work with takes.

3. Work with multiple tracks.

4. Understand composite modes.

5. Work with event and track envelopes.

6. Use the Trimmer.

chapter 4 USING ADVANCED VIDEO
Editing Techniques

When you create a project and compile events on a single timeline, you can create a compelling production. However, when you add multiple tracks to the equation, you take your production to the next level. When you have multiple video tracks, you can vary the level (opacity) and composite blend mode of each track to achieve compelling visual effects by displaying video tracks over still images or vice versa. If you've worked with layers in an image-editing application such as Adobe Photoshop, you'll be familiar with composite blend modes. When you add tracks to a project, the tracks at the top of the list eclipse the tracks beneath it.

In addition to selecting a composite blend mode and specifying the level (opacity) for a video track, you can set the volume and pan for an audio track. You'll learn to work with audio tracks in Chapter 6, "Working with Sound." The upcoming lessons in this chapter show you how to add tracks, use the video track controls, and specify composite blend modes.

When you want to speed up or slow down a video event, you can stretch or compress it to fit a specified duration along the timeline, as discussed in Chapter 3, "Working with Media Events." You can achieve a similar result by applying a Velocity envelope to a clip. When you apply a Velocity envelope to a clip, you don't change the duration of the event; you increase the speed of a clip up to 300 percent of its original speed, or slow down an event. You can also use the Velocity envelope to play a clip in reverse.

When you create a project with multiple events, you can trim events on the timeline as you learned in Chapter 3. However, if you're a stickler for details, and the event's got to be precisely trimmed, you may find it more beneficial to use the Trimmer. The Trimmer makes it possible for you to select a clip from the Explorer or Project Media window, trim it with frame-by-frame accuracy, and then insert the trimmed clip into a track.

You can create a **subclip**, which is a trimmed portion of a media clip you import into a project. You can create a subclip using an existing timeline event, a handy feature, because the subclip is trimmed to the exact In and Out points of the original event. You can also create a subclip from within the Trimmer.

Tools You'll Use

SLIP AND SLIDE
EVENTS

What You'll Do

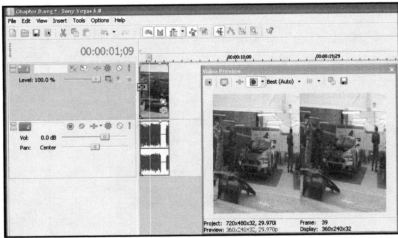

In this lesson, you learn how to slip and slide events.

Trimming, Slipping, and Sliding an Event

After you meticulously trim an event to length, you may discover that the In and Out points are not as desired. You can reset the event's In and Out points without altering the length of the event. This is known as slipping an event. When you slip an event, you shift the frames that comprise the event to the left or right. In other words, after slipping the event, the event is the same duration, but contains a different sequence of frames from the original media clip. When you slip an event, the event maintains its position on the timeline.

Slipping an Event

Picture an event as a small window that displays the portion of the media clip you are using on the timeline. For example, the original media clip is 30 frames long and the event plays frames 10 through 20. You can slip the event so that it plays frames 5 through 15, or frames 15 through 25, and so on, of the original media.

Mastering Slip-Trimming

You can also trim an event and specify the desired In and Out points in one fell swoop. This time-saving procedure is known as slip-trimming an event.

Sliding an Event

When you're modifying the contents of an event, you can simultaneously alter the frames that are displayed in the event, and change its position on the timeline. This is known as sliding an event. When you slide an event, the duration of the event is unaltered, but the content and the event's position on the timeline changes.

FIGURE 4-1

Slipping an event

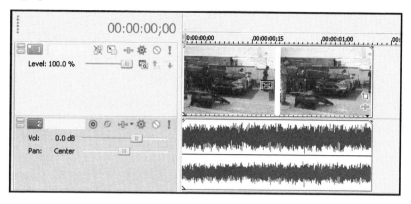

FIGURE 4-2

Previewing a slip edit

1. Create a new project and import a video clip into the project. Use a video clip that is several seconds long.

2. Drag the media clip into the main window to create an event.

3. Trim the In and Out points of the clip until the clip is approximately four seconds in duration.

4. If the Video Preview window is not visible, choose View > Video Preview.

   When you slip or slide an event, the Video Preview window is divided into two panes.

5. Press Alt and move your cursor over the clip.

   Your cursor becomes a rectangle with an arrow on each end, as shown in Figure 4-1.

6. Drag your cursor to the left or right.

   When you begin dragging inside the event, the Video Preview window is split into two panes. The left pane displays the In point and the right frame displays the Out point, as shown in Figure 4-2. As you drag inside the event, the frames update in real time showing you the current In and Out points.

7. Release the mouse button when you see the desired In and Out points in the Video Preview window.

Slip-trim an event

1. Create a new project and import a video clip into the project. Use a video clip that is 10 seconds or longer in duration.

2. Drag the media clip into the main window to create an event.

3. If the Video Preview window is not currently displayed in the workspace, choose View > Video Preview.

4. Press Alt and move your cursor towards the tail of the event.

5. When your cursor becomes a dual-headed arrow with a left-pointing rectangle, as shown in Figure 4-3, click and drag left.

   QUICK TIP

   You can also slip-trim the head of an event. When you move your cursor towards the head of an event while slip-trimming, the rectangle shown in Figure 4-3 is reversed.

   As you drag, the Video Preview window is split in two panes. When you trim the head of a clip, the right pane is static and the left pane changes to reflect the current In point. If you trim the head of a clip, the image in the left pane is static and the image in the right pane changes to reflect the current Out point.

6. Release the mouse button when the clip is Video Preview window displays the desired In point, as shown in Figure 4-4.

   If you're slip-trimming the head of an event, release the mouse button when the Video Preview window displays the desired Out point.

FIGURE 4-3
Slip-trimming the tail of an event

FIGURE 4-4
Slip-trimming an event

FIGURE 4-5

Sliding an event

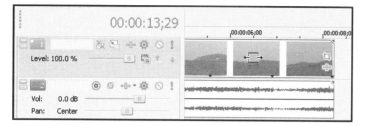

Slide an event

1. Create a new project and import a video clip into the project. Use a video clip that is several seconds long.

2. Drag the media clip into the main window to create an event.

3. Trim the In and Out points of the clip as desired.

4. If the Video Preview window is not currently displayed, choose View > Video Preview.

5. Press Ctrl+Alt and move your cursor towards the center of clip.

   Your cursor changes into a rectangle with an arrow at each end, as shown in Figure 4-5.

6. Drag and release the mouse button when the desired In or Out point appears in the Video Preview window.

LESSON 2

WORK WITH TAKES

What You'll Do

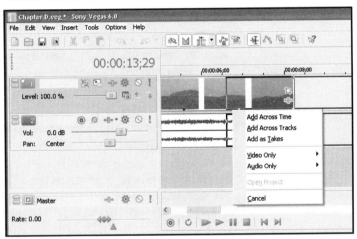

In this lesson, you learn how to add several media clips to the timeline as takes. You preview each take, select the desired take, and delete the unneeded media clips.

Adding Media Clips as Takes

In the previous chapter, you learned to add multiple media clips to a timeline as takes. In this lesson, you learn to preview individual takes to see how they mesh with the rest of the production. The ability to work with takes gives you tremendous flexibility. If the takes are of the same scene, you can choose the one with the footage best suited for your production. If the takes are different media clips, you can preview each one to determine which is the best for your production.

Previewing Takes

When you add clips of differing lengths as takes, the duration of the track event matches the longest media clip. Other clips are looped to fill the duration of the event. After you add clips as takes, you can preview each take using menu commands, commands from a shortcut menu, or keyboard shortcuts.

FIGURE 4-6

The multiple clips shortcut menu

Add Across Time
Add Across Tracks
Add as Takes

Video Only ▶
Audio Only ▶

Open Project

Cancel

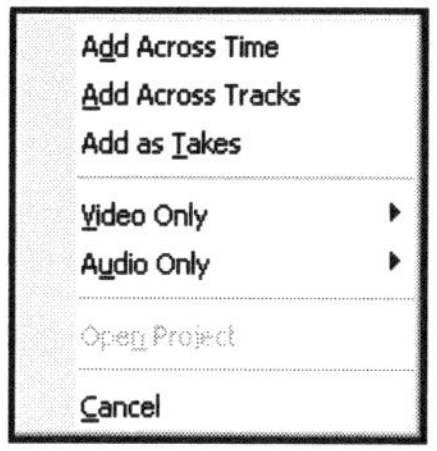

FIGURE 4-7

Takes appear as a single event on the timeline

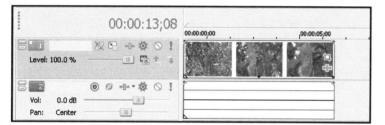

1. Create a new project and import five video clips into the Project Media window.

2. Select the clips, right-click, and drag the clips into the main window, aligning them to the beginning of the timeline.

3. Release the mouse button.

   The multiple clips shortcut menu is shown in Figure 4-6.

4. Choose Add As Takes.

   Vegas creates an event for the selected clips. When you add clips as takes, the thumbnail for the first frame of last clip you select appears on the timeline, as shown in Figure 4-7.

5. Keep the project open, as you'll be using it in the next lesson.

   QUICK TIP

   When you add clips as takes that have audio and video, you can add the audio only, or the video only as takes by choosing the applicable command from the shortcut menu.

1. If the Video Preview window is not currently displayed, choose View > Video Preview.

2. Press the spacebar to preview the current take.

   The current take plays in the Video Preview window.

3. When you're finished previewing the take, press the spacebar to return the cursor to the beginning of the project. Alternatively, you can press Ctrl+Home.

4. Right-click the current take, and move your cursor over Take on the shortcut menu.

The Take flyout menu appears, as shown in Figure 4-8.

> **QUICK TIP**
>
> Select Rename Active from the Take shortcut menu to display a text box over the current take thumbnail and then enter a new name in the text box.

5. Choose Next Take to display a thumbnail of the first frame of the next take.

When you choose different takes, you can preview them as outlined previously. When you've added takes between events in a large production, place your cursor in the event prior to the event with your takes. This will enable you to preview each take in conjunction with the previous event of your production. Alternatively, you can create a region and loop the preview. Creating regions is discussed in detail in Chapter 6.

> **QUICK TIP**
>
> Press T to display the next take or Shift+T to display the previous take. You can also use this shortcut to change takes while previewing a project.

FIGURE 4-8

The Take shortcut menu

?>

FIGURE 4-9

The Take Chooser dialog box

Stop

Play

FIGURE 4-10

The Delete Takes dialog box

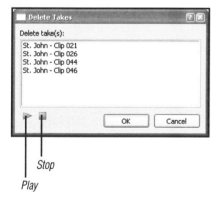

Stop

Play

6. Right-click the current take and then choose Take > Choose Active from the shortcut menu.

   The Take Chooser dialog box shown in Figure 4-9 appears. Select a clip and then click the Play button to preview the clip in the Video Preview window. Click Stop to stop previewing the clip.

7. After previewing the clips, select the desired clip. Then click OK.

   The thumbnail of the first frame of the selected take is displayed in the Event window on the timeline.

8. Right-click the current take and then choose Take > Delete from the shortcut menu.

   The Delete Takes dialog box appears, as shown in Figure 4-10. Select a clip and then click the Play button to preview the clip in the Video Preview window. Click Stop to stop previewing the clip.

9. Choose the clip to delete and click OK.

   Vegas deletes the selected clip. You can select multiple clips by selecting one clip and then Shift-clicking additional clips you want to delete.

QUICK TIP

Right-click the current take and choose Take > Delete Active to delete the current take.

QUICK TIP

A list of all takes is displayed on the Take fly-out menu, which is accessed from the shortcut menu when you right-click an event with takes.

WORK WITH
MULTIPLE TRACKS

What You'll Do

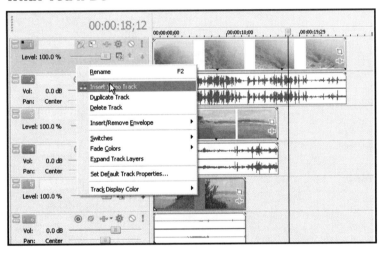

 In this lesson, you learn the different methods for adding tracks to a project. You learn to add tracks, duplicate tracks, and delete tracks.

Adding Clips Across Tracks

In previous lessons, you've learned how to create projects with multiple tracks. When you have multiple tracks in a project, you can mix the tracks, determine the opacity of tracks, determine how tracks are blended together, and so on. If you begin a project with a single audio and video track, you can add tracks at any time. You can add blank tracks, duplicate existing tracks, or drag clips from the Project Media window below the lowest track in the project to create a new track (or tracks if the clip is audio and video) and event in one fell swoop. You can also select multiple clips to create a new track and multiple events at the same time.

Compositing Tracks

When you work with multiple tracks, you can create special video effects by compositing tracks and using different blend modes. With multiple audio tracks, you can control the volume of each track and blend the overall mix using the Master Mixer. Working with audio in Vegas is covered in detail in Chapter 6.

FIGURE 4-11

Creating a multi-track project

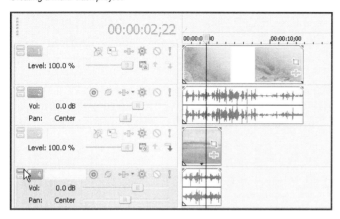

FIGURE 4-12

Inserting a blank video track

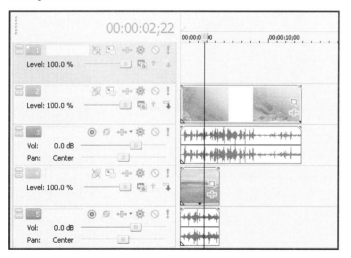

1. Create a new project.

2. Import four video clips with embedded audio into the Project Media window.

3. Select two of the clips, right-click, and drag the clips into the main window.

4. Align the clips with the beginning of the timeline and release the mouse button.

   A shortcut menu with options for inserting multiple clips appears.

5. Choose Add Across Tracks from the shortcut menu.

   Vegas creates two video and two audio tracks, as shown in Figure 4-11.

   NOTE

   If you choose the Add Across Tracks option while adding clips to a project that already contains video tracks, Vegas adds the required number of tracks for the new clips, and does not alter existing tracks in the project.

6. Right-click the first video track listing in the track list and choose Insert Video Track from the shortcut menu shown in Figure 4-12. Note that you cannot add a video track when you select an event.

   Vegas adds a blank video track to the project. When you insert a new track, it appears directly above the currently selected track.

7. Select the third clip in the Project Media window and drag it into the video track you just created.

Vegas adds the clip to the video track and creates an accompanying audio track. Remember when you add clips to a track, Vegas does not align them to any events currently in the track, nor does it align the clip to the beginning of the timeline when you add a media clip to a blank timeline. If you have auto-rippling enabled, Vegas will move any downstream events to accommodate the newly inserted clip. If you have auto-rippling enabled for all tracks, Vegas shuffles downstream events on all tracks to accommodate for the newly inserted clip.

8. Select the fourth clip in the Project Media window, drag it into the main window, and drop it beneath the last track in the project.

Vegas creates a video and audio track for the clip you just inserted, as shown in Figure 4-13, and automatically creates space below the added track, which enables you to add additional tracks as needed.

> **NOTE**
>
> You must have a blank space in the main window before you can create new tracks in this manner. If you do not have available space, Vegas adds the clip to the closest available tracks in the main window. If the main window does not have room to accommodate new tracks, drag the vertical scroll bar until a blank space appears below the last track in the project.

FIGURE 4-13

Multi-track project

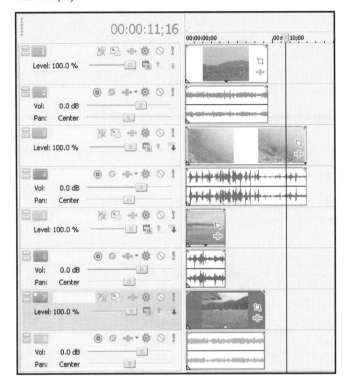

FIGURE 4-14

A multi-track event with overlapping events

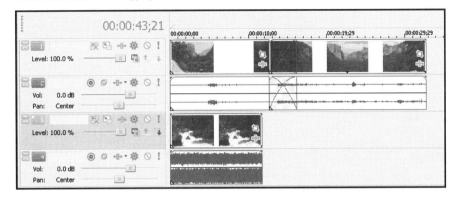

FIGURE 4-15

Video track controls

Minimize Track Height

Track number

Track FX

Automation settings

Mute

Solo

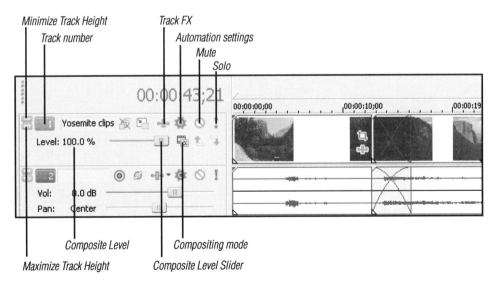

Composite Level

Compositing mode

Maximize Track Height

Composite Level Slider

1. Create a new project and import three video files with embedded audio to the Project Media window.

2. Select two clips and create a track for each clip as outlined previously.

3. Drag the third video clip to the first track and overlap it with the first event on the first video track, as shown in Figure 4-14.

4. Double-click the first video track's Track Name box.

5. Enter a name for the track.

   When you create a track, by default it has no track name. However, when you name a track, it makes it easier to ascertain the track's purpose when editing a complex multi-track project. If you enter a long name for a track, it may be truncated in the track list. You can rectify this by moving your cursor over the border between the track list and the track timelines. When your cursor becomes two parallel vertical lines with opposite pointing arrows, click and drag to expand the size of the track list. Figure 4-15 shows a named video track as it appears in the Track List, and the video track controls.

   QUICK TIP

   You can also manage tracks by changing their colors. To change a track's color, right-click the Track Number, choose Track Display Color, and then click the desired color swatch.

6. Click the Video Track FX button.

The Plug In Chooser Video Track FX dialog box opens. This dialog box works the same as the Plug In Chooser Video Event FX dialog box discussed previously in Chapter 3, enabling you to apply a plug-in to an entire track. You can adjust the plug-in parameters to suit your production. After closing the Plug In Chooser Video Track FX dialog box, close the Video Track Event FX dialog box. You can add as many plug-ins to a track as desired.

7. If the Video Preview window is not displayed, choose View Video Preview.

8. Move your cursor to the start of the timeline and press the spacebar to begin previewing the project.

9. Click the Mute button in the first video track.

When you click the Mute button, the track does not play.

QUICK TIP

Click a track in the track list to make it the active track. The active track is highlighted in the track list.

10. Click the Solo button in the first video track.

When you click a track's Solo button, all other project tracks are muted.

11. Click and drag the Level slider to the left.

When you drag the slider to the left, the track level (opacity) is reduced and more of the underlying tracks are used in the composition. Alternatively, you can double-click the current value to reveal a text box and enter a value between 0 (track is not visible) and 100 (track is fully opaque).

QUICK TIP

You can also change the level of the active track by pressing the right (to increase track opacity) or left (to decrease track opacity) arrow key.

NOTE

If the level is not displayed on the track, you will not be able to alter the track opacity with the arrow keys. To display the track level, position your cursor on the divider between the track list and the main window. When your cursor becomes two vertical lines with arrows, click and drag right until the track level is displayed.

12. Right-click the first video track, and choose Expand Track Layers from the shortcut menu.

Vegas splits the track into three layers. The A and B layers alternate, displaying neighboring events on the track. The A layer displays the first, third, fifth event and so on; the B layer displays the second, fourth, sixth events and so on, whereas the middle track displays the transition between adjacent events. Splitting a track into layers is a convenient way to edit a multi-track, multi-event project.

13. Click the Maximize Track button.

Vegas maximizes the video track to fill the main window. Maximizing a track is useful when you need to get a better look at an event. It's also beneficial when editing points on a track envelope. After you maximize a track, the Maximize Track button becomes the Restore Track Height button.

14. Click the Restore Track Height button.

Vegas restores the track to its previous height, making it possible to select and edit other tracks in your project.

15. Click the Minimize Track button.

Vegas shrinks the track to a minimal height and the Minimize Track button becomes the Restore Track Height button. Minimizing a track makes it possible to view more tracks in the main window.

16. Click the first audio track.

17. Move your cursor to the start of the timeline and press the spacebar to begin previewing the project.

When you create a project with multiple audio tracks, Vegas mixes the tracks, which becomes the audio track when the project is rendered. Audio will be discussed in detail in Chapter 6. The upcoming steps introduce you to the audio track controls.

18. Drag the Volume control slider left and right.

The audio track controls are similar to the video track controls. Audio tracks have a Volume control instead of a Level control, and a Pan control. As you drag the Volume slider shown in Figure 4-16, the track volume increases and decreases.

QUICK TIP

Double-click the current dB (**decibel**) value to display a text box and then a value between –12 and 12. You can also press the left arrow key to decrease the volume, or the right arrow key to increase the volume. As you press the key, a tooltip appears showing you the current dB value. Release the key when the desired value is displayed.

19. Drag the Pan slider left and right.

As you drag the Pan slider, the track's audio balance between speakers changes. As you drag towards the right or left, a value appears followed by an L or an R, which indicates the percentage of the audio that is being sent toward that speaker.

FIGURE 4-16

Audio track controls

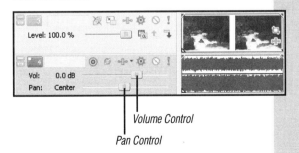

Volume Control

Pan Control

UNDERSTAND
COMPOSITE MODES

What You'll Do

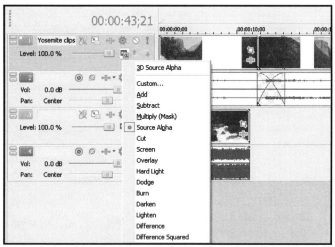

In this lesson, you learn to use the track composite control to select the desired composite method. You also gain an understanding of what you can expect to achieve when using a specific composite method.

Working with Multiple Tracks

When you add several video tracks to a project, the uppermost track eclipses all lower tracks. When you vary the track level, you reveal more of the underlying tracks. The track level control is similar to an opacity control you find in image-editing applications. When you combine the track level with a composite mode, you determine how much of each track shows up and how the tracks are combined for the final video. You can use composite tracks for special visual effects such as montages, or you can composite tracks to correct for video clips that are deficient in some way. For example, if you have a couple of events in a track that are dark, you can create a new video track, copy the dark events, and then paste them to the new video track. Use the Screen composite method and vary the level of the top track to achieve the desired result. This effectively lightens the clips.

Understanding the Composite Modes

Compositing tracks is also a wonderful way to create visual interest. For example, if you are creating a video of an athletic event such as a triathlon, you can create several tracks and align different clips of participants in the running phase of the triathlon. Apply Video FX to individual tracks and then vary the level and composite mode of each track to achieve the desired result. Depending on the effects you use, the end result is a montage in motion that can be very ethereal in nature. Table 4-1 shows the different composite modes from which you can choose and explains what each mode does.

Table 4-1: The Composite Modes

Composite Mode	Description
Custom	Opens the Plug-In Chooser—Track Composite Mode dialog box enabling you to choose one of the track composite mode plug-ins: Sony Bump Map, Sony Displacement Map, or Sony Height Map.
3D Source Alpha	Used in conjunction with track motion to create 3D effects. Using 3D track motion is covered in detail in Chapter 9.
Add	Adds the colors from the track video to the underlying video tracks.
Subtract	Subtracts the colors in the track video from the colors in the underlying video tracks.
Multiply (Mask)	Multiplies the colors in the track video by the color values in the underlying video tracks. This effectively darkens the composited video. You can use the Multiply composite mode on a copied event to correct a track that is too light or washed out.
Source Alpha	Uses the alpha (transparency) mask of the track to determine the transparency of the overlay. If the overlaying track media has no alpha channel, this composite mode has no effect.
Cut	Cuts the colors of the overlaying track video from the underlying tracks.
Screen	Multiplies the inverse of the colors in the track video from the underlying tracks. This is the opposite of the Multiply composite mode, and it effectively lightens the video. You can use the Screen mode on a copied track to compensate for a track that is too dark.
Overlay	Increases contrast in the track video by applying the Multiply mode to darker colors in the underlying track video, and the Screen mode to lighter colors in the underlying track video.
Hard Light	Applies colors from the track video to the underlying track video as if a brightly focused spotlight illuminated the track video.
Dodge	Uses the track video colors to brighten the underlying tracks.
Burn	Uses the track video colors to darken the underlying tracks.
Darken	Uses the track video colors whenever they are darker than the colors in the underlying track videos.
Lighten	Uses the track colors whenever they are lighter than the underlying track video colors.
Difference	Compares the colors of the track video to the underlying track video on a pixel-by-pixel basis and subtracts the darker color from the lighter color to create a new color; or as the name implies, the difference between the colors of the track video and underlying track video.
Difference Squared	Creates a new color by comparing the video colors of the video track and subtracting the squared amount from lighter colors. This composite mode results in more striking color changes when the colors are very light.

Explore composite modes

1. Create a new project and import a video clip into the Project Media window.

2. Drop the media clip into the main window, aligning it with the beginning of the timeline.

3. Right-click the video track and choose Insert Video Track from the shortcut menu.

   Vegas creates a new video track at the top of the track list.

4. Click the Media Generators tab in the Window Docking area and then click Solid Color.

   Your Window Docking area should resemble Figure 4-17.

5. Select the Red option and drop the icon into the track you just created, aligning it with the beginning of the timeline.

   The Video Event FX dialog box appears.

6. Accept the default options and click the Close button.

   Vegas creates an event that is solid red in color and 10 seconds in duration.

7. Trim the generated media event to match the duration of your other clip.

8. Drag the Level slider in the uppermost video track to 50, as shown in Figure 4-18.

FIGURE 4-17
Choosing generated media

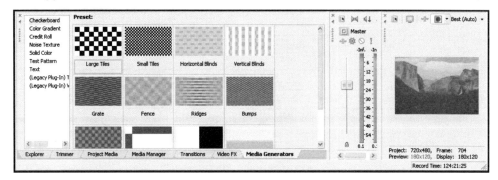

FIGURE 4-18
Adjusting a track's composite level

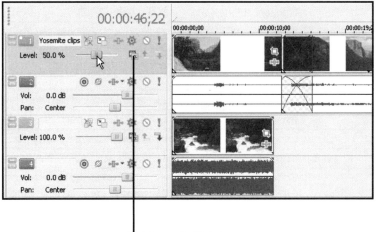

Track Composite Mode button

FIGURE 4-19

Choosing a composite mode

3D Source Alpha
Custom...
Add
Subtract
Multiply (Mask)
● Source Alpha
Cut
Screen
Overlay
Hard Light
Dodge
Burn
Darken
Lighten
Difference
Difference Squared

9. Click the Composite Mode button to reveal the menu shown in Figure 4-19.

10. Select the desired composite mode.

Each composite mode achieves a different outcome. Experiment with each composite mode to familiarize yourself with the effects each mode can add to your project.

WORK WITH EVENT
AND TRACK ENVELOPES

What You'll Do

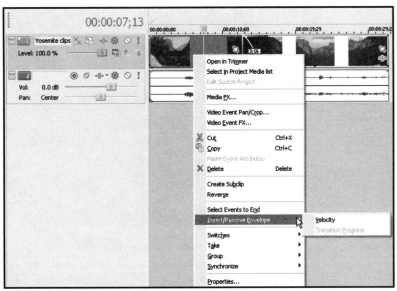

In this lesson, you learn to apply envelopes to tracks and events.

Adding Event and Track Envelopes

When you add an envelope to a track or an event, you alter certain characteristics of the track or event. You have different envelopes available for each track type, and each event type. When you add an envelope to an event or a track, you can add points to vary the effect of the envelope at various points in time. This enables you to apply frame-by-frame control over the envelopes you apply to video events, audio events, and tracks in your production. For example, if you have multiple audio tracks to mix soundtracks with audio from videos and voiceovers, you can add a Volume envelope to each audio track and then add points where you need to lower the volume of one track and raise the volume of another.

Understanding Envelope Types

You can add the following envelopes to tracks or events in your projects:

- **Mute.** This envelope is available for audio and video tracks and causes the track to be muted, which causes the track not to play. You can alternatively mute and display a track by adding points along the timeline.

- **Composite Level.** This envelope is available for video tracks and enables you to choose the composite level for the track, and vary it as needed by adding points.

- **Fade To Color.** This envelope is available for video tracks and enables you to fade a track to a color. This envelope can be used to achieve results similar to the popular fade-to-black and fade-to-white video transitions. You add points to determine where the track fades to the bottom color or the top color, or remains unchanged.

- **Opacity.** This envelope is available for video events and enables you to set the event opacity.

- **Velocity.** This envelope is available for video events and enables you to speed up or slow down a video clip. You can vary the speed during the event by adding points at desired frames in the timeline and specifying different values for each point.

- **Volume.** This envelope is available for audio tracks and enables you to set the track volume in conjunction with the track main volume control. You can vary the volume by adding points at desired frames in the timeline and specifying different DB values for each point.

- **Pan.** This envelope is available for audio tracks and enables you to control the balance of track audio between speakers. You use this envelope to augment the track main pan control. You can vary the pan by adding points at desired frames in the track timeline and then changing the balance of sound between speakers.

- **Transition Progress.** This envelope enables you to have point-by-point control over the transition from one video event to the next. Transition Progress envelopes are covered in detail in Chapter 5, "Adding Pizzazz with Transitions."

When you modify the intensity of an envelope (for example, the percentage in a Velocity envelope), you add one or more points to the track or event envelope. When one point transitions to another, the intensity fades to a different value. You determine whether the fade is smooth, linear, sharp, fast, or abrupt. To change the fade type, right-click the slope between adjacent points and select the desired fade type from the shortcut menu.

Add track events

1. Create a new project and add four video clips with embedded audio to the Project Media window.

2. Select the clips and drag them into the main window, aligning them to the beginning of the timeline.

3. Choose Insert > Video Envelopes > Track Composite Level.

   A blue line appears at the top of the event signifying that a track composite level envelope exists. By default, the composite level is set to 100 percent.

4. Drag the blue line downward.

   As you drag the marker, a tooltip appears informing you of the current composite level as a percentage, as shown in Figure 4-20. The value updates as you drag the marker.

5. Release the mouse button when the composite level is at the desired percentage.

6. Move your cursor over the Composite Level envelope marker at any point in the timeline and right-click.

   The envelope shortcut menu appears, as shown in Figure 4-21.

7. Choose Add Point.

   A blue square appears on the envelope marker.

FIGURE 4-20
Setting envelope intensity

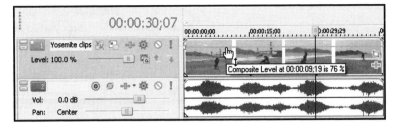

FIGURE 4-21
The envelope shortcut menu

FIGURE 4-22

A track envelope with multiple points

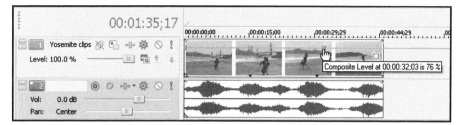

8. Right-click the envelope marker downstream from the first envelope point and choose Add Point from the shortcut menu.

   Vegas adds an additional point to the envelope marker. The video track in your project should resemble Figure 4-22. Notice that when you hover your cursor over an envelope point, a tooltip displays the current composite level and the timecode for the point. If you were actually using a Composite Level envelope in conjunction with other video tracks, you'd preview the project and add points to the envelope as needed. After adding points you'd vary the percentage of each to suit your project. You could also Composite Level envelopes to additional events to vary the opacity of each track in your project.

   ### QUICK TIP

   Right-click an envelope point and choose Set To from the shortcut menu. Enter a value in the text field to specify the desired composite level.

9. Drag the new point up or down to set the desired composite level.

   As you drag the point, a tooltip appears designating the current composite level.

   ### QUICK TIP

   Press the Ctrl key while dragging a point to change the composite level. This technique constrains the point to its current position on the timeline.

10. Release the mouse button when the composite level is at the desired percentage.

11. Right-click the video track in the track list and choose Insert/Remove Envelope > Composite to remove the envelope.

12. Keep the project open, as you'll be using it in the next objective.

> **QUICK TIP**
>
> Click the sloped line between envelope points, right-click, and then choose a fade option from the shortcut menu. Note that you also have the following commands: Flip All Points, Thin All Points, Select All, Reset All, and Delete. The Thin All Points command is reserved for automation recording and has little or no effect on manually added points.

Add the Fade to Color envelope to a track

1. Right-click the video track in the track list to reveal the video track shortcut menu.

2. Choose Insert/Remove Envelope > Fade To Color.

A red line appears in the middle of the track indicating a Fade to Color envelope has been applied to the track. Note that you can use shortcut menus to apply envelopes to tracks as well as menu commands.

3. Right-click the video track in the track list and choose Fade Colors > Top from the shortcut menu.

The Track Fade Top Color dialog box appears, as shown in Figure 4-23. By default, the Track Fade Top Color is white. You can choose a different color by entering values in the Red, Green, and Blue fields, by

dragging the R, G, and B sliders, or by dragging inside the color well. You can also set the Alpha value (transparency) for the color by entering a value in the Alpha field. Alternatively, you can enter values in the Hue, Saturation, and Luminance fields to match a known color from the HSL color model. A detailed discussion of the Sony Vegas color picker can be found in Chapter 7, "Creating Generated Media."

> **QUICK TIP**
>
> You can change the default Top Color and Bottom Color by choosing Options > Preferences. Click the Video tab and in the Default Track Fade Colors section, click the Track Fade Top, and/or Track Fade Bottom color swatch and choose a different color from the applicable dialog box.

4. Accept the default color, or specify another color, and click OK.

5. Right-click the video track list and choose Fade Colors > Bottom from the shortcut menu.

The Track Fade Bottom Color dialog box appears. This dialog box is identical to the Track Fade Top Color dialog box with the exception being the default color is black.

6. Accept the default color, or specify a different color, and click OK.

7. Move your cursor over the Fade to Color envelope marker at a frame near the end of your project, right-click, and choose Add Point from the Envelope shortcut menu.

FIGURE 4-23

The Track Fade Top Color dialog box

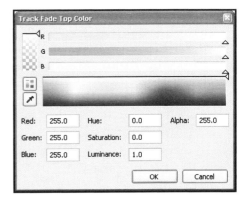

FIGURE 4-24

The volume envelope shortcut menu

Set to 6.0 dB
Set to 0.0 dB
Set to -Inf dB
Set To...
Delete
Linear Fade
Fast Fade
Slow Fade
✓ Smooth Fade
Sharp Fade
Hold
Flip All Points
Thin All Points
Select All
Reset All

8. Move your cursor over Fade to Color envelope marker at the last frame of your project, right-click, and choose Add Point from the Envelope shortcut menu.

9. Right-click the point you just created to open the Envelope shortcut menu.

When you open the shortcut menu after adding a specific envelope, commands pertinent to that envelope appear. You can use the shortcut menu to choose a preset option, or specify a specific value or setting. In the case of the Fade to Color envelope, you can choose to Set to 100 Percent Top Color (fade to the top color), Set To No Color (the track does not fade at the point), Set to 100 Percent Bottom (fade to the bottom color), or Set To. If you choose Set To, a text box appears beside the point. Enter a value between 1 and 100 to fade to the top color, or a value between −1 and −100 to fade to the bottom color.

10. Choose an option or specify a value.

> **QUICK TIP**
>
> You can select a point on any track or event envelope, and drag it up or down to set a value for the point.

11. Accept the default Fade option (Smooth Fade), or right-click the sloping line (the transition) between points and choose a different option.

12. Preview the project.

The video begins to fade to the specified color after the first point on the envelope is reached, fading to the specified color when the last point is reached.

13. Keep the project open, as you'll be using it in the next objective.

Add audio track envelopes

1. Right-click the audio track in the track list and choose Insert/Remove Envelope > Volume.

A blue line appears in the center of the track indicating an audio envelope exists.

2. Create a point near the end of the project, as outlined previously.

When you add a volume envelope to a project, you can use it to control volume between different audio tracks, or as you'll be doing here, fading out the sound at the end of your project.

3. Create a point on the last frame of your project.

4. Right-click the point on the last frame and choose Set To −Inf dB from the volume envelope shortcut menu shown in Figure 4-24.

When you choose this setting, the sound
fades away to silence. You can also choose
Set To 6.0 dB to boost the volume to 6.0 dB
above the main volume setting, choose Set
To 0.0 dB to set the volume at its original
level, or choose Set To. When you choose
Set To, a text box appears beside the point.
Enter a value between .01 and 6.0 dB to
boost the volume above the main volume
setting, or enter a value between –.01 and
–30 dB to reduce the volume below the main
volume setting. A setting of –30 will barely
be audible when the video is played.

FIGURE 4-25
The pan envelope shortcut menu

| QUICK TIP

Hover your cursor over any track or event
envelope point and a tooltip appears noting
the point's current value.

5. Right-click the audio track in the track list
and choose Insert/Remove Envelope > Pan.

A red line appears in the middle of the track
indicating a pan envelope has been added to
the track.

6. Create a point in the middle of the envelope,
as outlined previously.

7. Right-click the point and choose Set to Left
from the pan envelope shortcut menu shown
in Figure 4-25.

FIGURE 4-26

An audio track with multiple envelopes

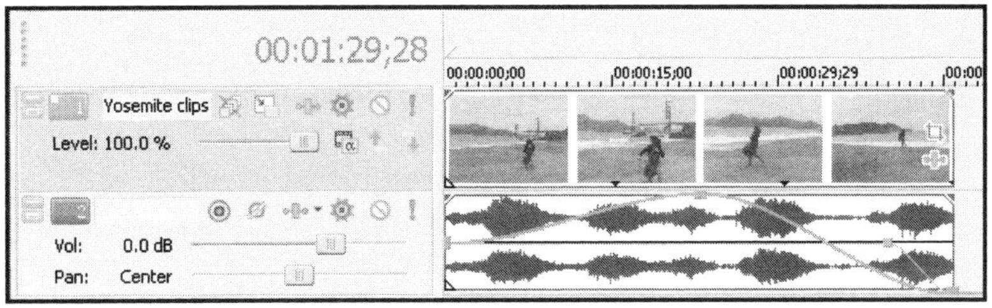

QUICK TIP

Choose Set To from the Pan Envelope shortcut menu and a text box appears beside the point. Enter a value between 1 and 100 to fade the sound towards the left speaker, or a value between −1 and −100 to fade the sound towards the right speaker. Higher positive values bias the sound toward the right speaker, whereas higher negative values bias the sound towards the left speaker.

8. Preview the project.

   As the project begins playing, the sound will begin fading to the left speaker. When the first pan envelope point is reached, all sound will emanate from the left speaker.

9. Create an envelope point on the last frame of the project.

10. Right-click the point and choose Fade to Right from the pan envelope shortcut menu.

   Your timeline should resemble Figure 4-26. The curve of the pan envelope shows that the sound will gradually pan to the left speaker in the middle of the project, and then fade to the right speaker.

Add a Velocity envelope

1. Create a new project and add a video clip to the Project Media window.

2. Drag the video clip into the main window to create a track and video event.

3. Right-click the video event and from the shortcut menu choose Insert/Remove Envelope > Velocity.

A green line appears in the middle of the event signifying a Velocity envelope has been applied to the event. You can add additional points to the envelope as outlined previously, and vary the velocity percentage by adding points at different frames in the event. You can speed the event up, slow it down, or reverse the order in which the frames play.

4. Create a point on the velocity envelope.

5. Drag the envelope point to set the desired velocity.

As you drag the line, a tooltip appears indicating the current value of the Velocity envelope. Drag the line up to increase the clip velocity, or down to reduce the clip velocity. Alternatively, you can right-click a point and choose an option from the Velocity envelope shortcut menu shown in Figure 4-27. If you choose Set To, a text box appears beside the point. Enter a value between 101 and 300 percent to speed the clip up, or a value between 1 and 99 percent to slow the clip down. Enter a value of −100 to play the event in reverse at normal speed. Enter a value between −1 and −99 to play the frames in slow motion reverse. Note that when you slow a clip down or speed it up with a Velocity envelope, you do not alter the duration of a clip. When you increase clip velocity, you shorten the duration of the frames selected from the original media clip; however, the event duration remains the same. You'll see notches in the event that signify the clip instance is looping to fill the event duration. Trim the event if you don't want the frames

FIGURE 4-27

The Velocity envelope shortcut menu

Set to 300% Forward Velocity
Set to Normal Velocity
Set to 100% Reverse Velocity

Set To...

Delete

Linear Fade
Fast Fade
Slow Fade
✓ Smooth Fade
Sharp Fade
Hold

Flip All Points
Thin All Points
Select All
Reset All

to loop. When you slow down a clip, you increase the duration of the frames selected from the original media clip and only a portion of the clip plays. To play the clip at lower speed in its entirety, increase the event duration.

QUICK TIP

To reverse an event to which you have applied a Velocity envelope, right-click the event and choose Reverse from the shortcut menu. When the event is played back, the clip will play in reverse at the speed you specified when you set the Velocity envelope.

QUICK TIP

Place your cursor at the top of a video event. When you see a tooltip that reads," Opacity = 100 %", click and drag down to insert an opacity envelope. As you drag the envelope, a tooltip appears that displays the current opacity. Release the mouse when the desired opacity is achieved. This is similar to adjusting a track's level. You cannot add points to an opacity envelope.

QUICK TIP

When you add Opacity envelopes to multiple tracks, make sure the total value of all envelopes equals 100. Otherwise, the rendered project will be too dark.

6. Add three additional points to the Velocity envelope and set different values for each point.

7. Right-click anywhere along the Velocity envelope line.

8. Choose Flip All Points from the shortcut menu.

   Vegas flips all points on the Velocity envelope. Points that had a plus value now have a minus value and vice versa.

9. Keep the project open, as you'll be using it in the next objective.

Add a Mute envelope

1. Right-click the video track title and choose Insert/Remove Envelope > Mute.

   An aqua-colored line appears at the top of the track.

2. Position your cursor over a point at which you would like the track to be muted.

3. Create a point along the envelope as outlined previously.

4. Ctrl+click the point and drag downward.

   The track is muted at that point. When the project is played back, the video from the track disappears when the point is reached. The track thumbnails from this point forward are bordered in gray, indicating the track is muted from this point forward.

5. Create an additional point downstream from the first point.

6. Ctrl+click the point and drag up.

   The track is not muted from this point forward and the gray border around the thumbnails disappears from this point forward.

LESSON 6

USE THE
TRIMMER

What You'll Do

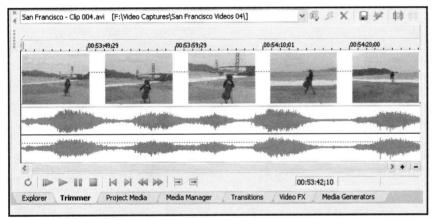

In this lesson, you learn to use the Trimmer to select desired frames from a media clip and then insert the selected frames into a track as a new event.

Trimming Video Clips with the Trimmer

As you learned previously, you can trim an event by selecting it and then manually adjusting the In and Out points by dragging the head or tail of the event. However, Vegas offers a more precise solution to trimming media clips: the Trimmer. When you open a media clip in the Trimmer, you can navigate frame-by-frame and precisely specify the In and Out points. After specifying the portion of the clip you want to insert into your project, you can add it to an existing track. If the media clip is long, you can select one portion of the clip, insert it into your project, and then define the In and Out points of another portion of the media clip and insert it as another event. Any selections you create with the Trimmer have no effect on the original media file.

Inserting a Trimmed Clip into a Track

After making a selection with the Trimmer, you can use buttons to insert the selection into a track, or you can drag and drop the selection into a track. You can also create a subclip from the selection, which will be added to the Project Media window for future use in the project.

Using the Trimmer History List

When you open multiple files in the Trimmer, they are added to the Trimmer History drop-down list. After inserting selections from one media clip into your project, you can select a different clip from the drop-down list and define the portions of the clip you want to use in your project.

You can also sort clips in the Trimmer History window, delete media from Trimmer history, and clear Trimmer history using the buttons shown in Figure 4-28. You can also save markers and regions with media clips. Markers and regions are covered in detail in Chapter 11, "Vegas Tips and Tricks" (found on the Web site). If you select the audio portion of a clip, you can

edit the clip in Sound Forge from within the Trimmer. When you're creating selections, you can zoom in or out on the media clip by using the Trimmer Zoom controls shown in Figure 4-28. They function exactly like the zoom controls in the main window.

FIGURE 4-28
The Trimmer

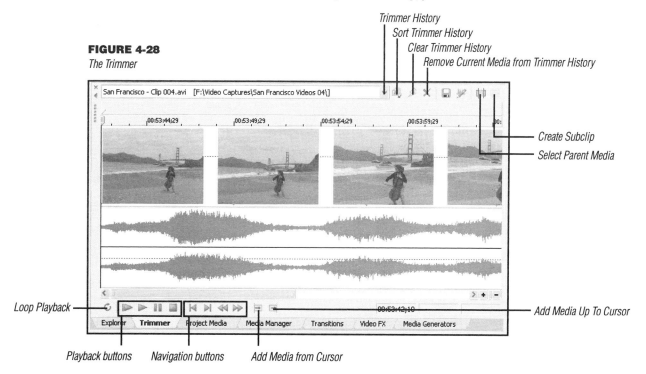

Trimmer History
Sort Trimmer History
Clear Trimmer History
Remove Current Media from Trimmer History

Create Subclip
Select Parent Media

Loop Playback

Add Media Up To Cursor

Playback buttons   Navigation buttons   Add Media from Cursor

Trim a clip

1. Launch Vegas.

2. Click the Explorer tab and navigate to the folder in which you store media clips.

3. Select three media clips, right-click, and choose Open In Trimmer from the short-cut menu.

QUICK TIP

To open media clips in the Trimmer, choose Options > Preferences and then click the General tab. Click the check box that says Double-click on a Media File Loads into Trimmer Instead of Tracks. After enabling this option, double-clicking a media clip in the Explorer, or Project Media window will open the clip in the Trimmer.

Vegas opens the last clip you selected in the Trimmer. The other clips are on the Trimmer History drop-down list. After you open a file in the Trimmer, you can use the playback controls to preview the clip and decide which portions you want to include in your project. You can then use the Navigation buttons to step forward or step backward through the clip. If you need frame-by-frame precision, you can use right and left arrow keys to advance forward or backward a frame at a time.

4. Advance the media clip to the first frame of the desired selection and press I (In) or the Left Bracket key ([ ).

   This designates the In point of the selection. Even though the Trimmer has buttons to play, pause, and stop the video clip, you must use the Navigation buttons, drag the

playhead, or press the keyboard arrow keys to advance to the In and Out points. If you use the Playback buttons, Vegas creates a region without selecting footage from the media clip. After creating a selection, you can add frames to or remove frames from the selection by dragging the In or Out selection markers left or right.

5. Advance the media clip to the frame that will be the end of the selection and press O (Out) or the Right Bracket key ( ]).

   This designates the Out frame of the clip, and the selection is highlighted, as shown in Figure 4-29.

FIGURE 4-29
Creating a selection in the Trimmer

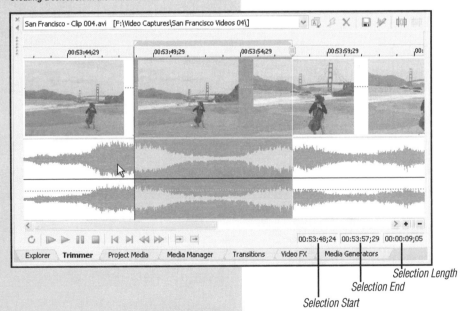

Selection Length

Selection End

Selection Start

6. Click the Add Media From Cursor button.

   Vegas creates a new track and adds the selection to the track from the current cursor position forward. The media clip is added to the Project Media window for future use.

   NOTE

   If you're using the Trimmer on a project that already has tracks, the trimmed media will be added to the currently selected track.

7. Click the triangle to the right of the Trimmer History window and choose a different media clip.

   Vegas opens the selected media clip in the Trimmer.

8. Create a selection as outlined previously and then click the Add Media to Cursor button.

   Vegas adds the selection to the track prior to the current cursor position. The media clip is also added to the Project Media window for future use in the project.

9. Position your clip between the first and second event on the track timeline. Make sure you have automatic rippling enabled.

10. In the Trimmer, select the third media clip from the Trimmer History window and create a selection as outlined previously.

11. Click the Add Media From Cursor button.

    Vegas ripples the downstream clip to insert the selection from the cursor forward. When you have multiple events on a timeline you can also insert trimmed clips before the cursor by clicking the Add Media To Cursor button. When you insert a clip before the cursor, the adjacent clip upstream from the cursor is rippled downstream from the cursor and your Trimmer selection takes its place.

12. Save the project, as you'll be using it in the next objective.

Create a subclip

1. Create the desired In and Out points on the clip you are editing in the Trimmer.

2. Click the Create Subclip button.

   Vegas displays the Create Subclip dialog box shown in Figure 4-30.

3. Enter a name for the subclip and click OK.

   Vegas adds the subclip to the Project Media window. You can use the subclip to create events as needed throughout the project. Notice there is also a Reverse check box you can click to reverse the playback of the subclip.

4. Drag the subclip from the Project Media window into the main window, aligning it to the beginning of the timeline.

   Vegas creates a new event.

5. Right-click the event and choose Open In Trimmer from the shortcut menu.

   Vegas opens the subclip in the Trimmer, complete with any regions and markers you may have added to the subclip.

6. Click the Select Parent Media button.

   In the Trimmer, Vegas replaces the subclip with the parent clip from which the subclip was created. A region surrounds the frames used to create the subclip. You can edit the In and Out points to create a new subclip.

FIGURE 4-30

Creating a subclip

SKILLS REVIEW

Working with Takes

1. Create a new project.

2. Import four clips into the Project Media window.

3. Select one clip and align it to the beginning of the timeline.

4. Select the remaining clips and add them as takes, aligning the takes to the tail of the event you previously inserted, as shown in Figure 4-31.

5. Preview each take.

6. Select the desired take.

7. Open the Delete Takes dialog box, as shown in Figure 4-32.

8. Delete the unwanted takes.

FIGURE 4-31

Adding clips as takes

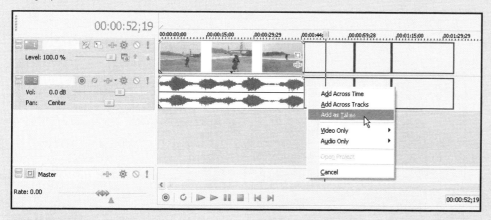

FIGURE 4-32

Deleting unwanted takes

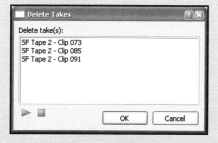

Changing Clip Opacity

1. Create a new project.

2. Import a media clip into the Project Media window.

3. Add it to the project as an event.

4. Adjust the event opacity to 50 percent, as shown in Figure 4-33.

5. Preview the project, as shown in Figure 4-34.

FIGURE 4-33
Adjusting event opacity

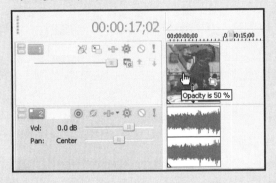

FIGURE 4-34
Previewing an event with an opacity envelope

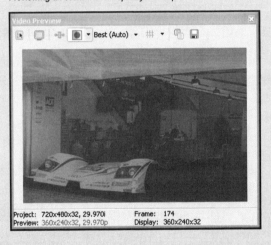

SKILLS REVIEW

Adjusting Track Properties with Envelopes and Track Controls

1. Create a new project.

2. Import four media clips with video and audio into the Project Media window.

3. Select the clips and add them to the project, aligning them to the beginning of the timeline.

4. Add a Fade To Color envelope to the video track.

5. Add one envelope point near the end of the video track, and add another on the last frame of the project, as shown in Figure 4-35.

6. Select the last envelope point and set the envelope to fade 100 percent to the bottom color.

7. Select the audio track in the track list.

8. Adjust the track volume to –2.0 dB, as shown in Figure 4-36.

9. Add a volume envelope to the audio track.

10. Add one envelope point near the end of the project, and one on the last frame of the project.

11. Adjust the last point so that the volume fades to silence at the end of the project.

12. Preview your project.

13. Keep the project open for the next skills review.

FIGURE 4-35

Adding envelope points

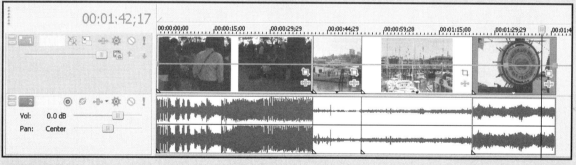

FIGURE 4-36

Adjusting track volume

Adding Event Envelopes

1. Select the second video event.

2. Add a Velocity envelope to the event.

3. Add a point to the event envelope near the middle of the event.

4. Adjust the velocity of this envelope point to 250 percent, as shown in Figure 4-37.

5. Add a point at the end of the event.

6. Adjust the velocity of this envelope point to 0 percent.

7. Trim the event so it does not repeat, as shown in Figure 4-38.

8. Reverse the event.

9. Preview the event.

FIGURE 4-37

Setting the velocity of an envelope point

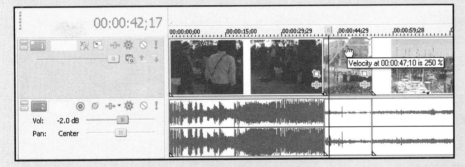

FIGURE 4-38

Adding a second envelope point

SKILLS REVIEW

Using the Trimmer

1. Create a new project.

2. Open a media clip that is longer than 20 seconds in the Trimmer, as shown in Figure 4-39.

3. Create a 10-second selection, as shown in Figure 4-40.

4. Create a subclip using the selection you just created.

5. Add the selection to the project at the current cursor position.

FIGURE 4-39
Opening a clip in the Trimmer

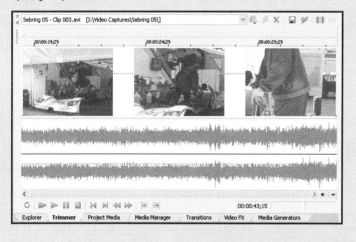

FIGURE 4-40
Creating a selection in the Trimmer

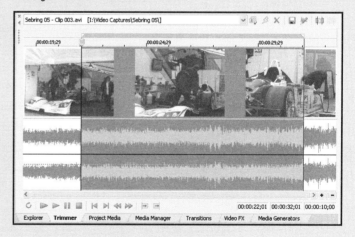

PROJECT BUILDER 1

You work for a multimedia firm. Your supervisor hands you a DVD data disc with several video clips. The clips are relatively short, less than 1 minute. You've been assigned to compile the clips as a 30-second promotion. You copy the clips to your system. Upon reviewing the clips, you see several instances where the camcorder was left running too long and unwanted footage must be trimmed before the clips can be used.

1. Create a new project.

2. Select several video clips, right-click, and choose Open In Trimmer from the shortcut menu.

3. Select the first clip from the Trimmer History window and select a usable portion of the clip, as shown in Figure 4-41.

4. Continue trimming the media clips and assemble them on the timeline to create the finished project. Your timeline should be similar to Figure 4-42.

FIGURE 4-41
Sample Project Builder 1 clip in the Trimmer

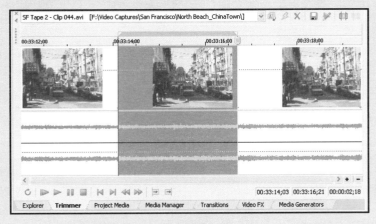

FIGURE 4-42
Sample Project Builder 1 timeline

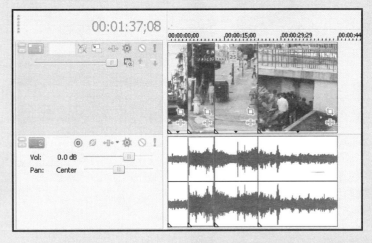

PROJECT BUILDER 2

You work in the production department for a television station. You're presented with three clips of a local politician's speech. Your staff filmed two of the clips, and an amateur videographer filmed one. The clips are different durations. Your task is to trim the clips and choose the best one for a 15-second spot on the 5:00 news.

1. Create a new project.
2. Open the three clips in the Trimmer.
3. Select 15 seconds from each clip, as shown in Figure 4-43.
4. Arrange the clips as tracks on the timeline, as shown in Figure 4-44.

5. Press the Solo button on the first track and preview the project.
6. Repeat step 5 for the second and third tracks.
7. Select the best track and delete the unwanted tracks.

FIGURE 4-43
Sample Project Builder 2

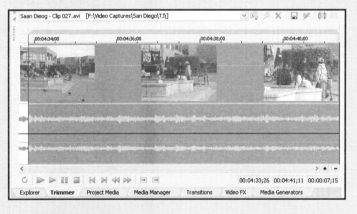

FIGURE 4-44
Sample Project Builder 2

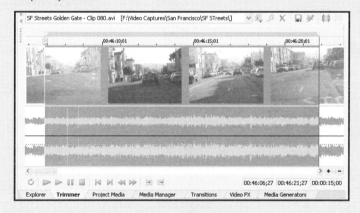

DESIGN PROJECT

You work for an ad agency that specializes in multimedia content. Your client is a rock band that wants you to create a clip of them playing their latest hit song at their last concert. They ask you to create something that is comical, yet at the same time cutting edge. Upon reviewing the footage, you decide to trim their entrance to stage from the clip, speed it up, and use it as an intro to the song.

1. Create a new project.

2. Open a clip in the Trimmer that shows people in motion.

3. Create a selection with about nine seconds of people walking at the start of the clip.

FIGURE 4-45
Design Project Sample 1

Figure 4-45 shows a sample of what you should see in the Trimmer.

4. Add the selection to the project.

5. Create a selection that shows people engaged in activity, such as talking. Your goal is to create a selection that shows motion. This will be your reasonable facsimile of the rock group on stage. If you do have footage of a musical group, by all means use it.

6. Insert the selection after the first event.

   Your timeline should resemble Figure 4-46.

7. Add a Velocity envelope to the first event.

8. Adjust the velocity to 200 percent.

9. Trim the first event so that it does not loop.

   You'll see a notch where the event begins to loop. Select the tail of the clip and drag left until the notch at the tail of the clip is no longer visible. You may find it helpful to zoom in on the timeline in order to make the notch more visible.

10. Preview your project.

    Your first event should look like something out of a Charlie Chaplin movie with very quick motion. You could augment your production by adding some footage of the band bowing after the number. Add a Velocity envelope to this event and increase the speed to finish the effect.

FIGURE 4-46
Design Project Sample 2

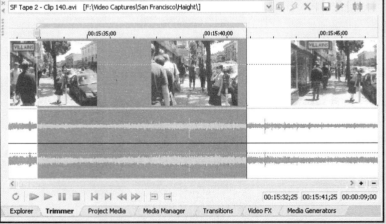

CHAPTER SUMMARY

This chapter covers advanced video editing. Slipping and sliding events alters the frames that are displayed in an event. Working with takes enables you to select the perfect footage for an event by auditioning several takes and then choosing the desired take. Composite modes determine how tracks blend with each other. You can precisely trim video clips using the Trimmer.

What You Have Learned

In this chapter, you:

- Learned to slip and slide events.
- Discovered how to choose the ideal footage for an event by auditioning multiple takes.
- Used multiple tracks to add diversity to a project.
- Gained an understanding of how composite modes blend multiple tracks.

- Learned to alter events and tracks through the use of envelopes.
- Learned to precisely trim media using the Trimmer.
- Discovered how to create a subclip in the Trimmer.

Key Terms from This Chapter

- Composite blend modes. Determines how multiple tracks are blended.
- Decibel. A unit of measure to determine the level of a sound. A decibel level above 100 is a very loud sound, whereas a decibel level of 130 is painful for humans.
- Sliding. When you slide an event that is a smaller than the original clip, the media file maintains its position in the timeline, but the event moves in the direction you drag.

- Slipping. When working with an event that is smaller than the original media, you can slip the event to determine which portion of the original footage is displayed in the event.
- Slip-trimming. When you slip-trim an event, the opposite edge of the event is unaffected and the event is trimmed from the direction you drag.
- Subclip. A portion of the original media that is created in the Trimmer. Subclips are added to the Project Media window.
- Trimmer. A device used to precisely trim a clip to the desired length.
- Velocity envelope. Used to change the speed of an event. A velocity envelope can speed up, slow down, or play an event in reverse.

5

ADDING PIZZAZZ
with Transitions

1. Create a crossfade transition.

2. Use video transitions.

3. Use the Push and Wipe transitions.

4. Change scenes with a Page Curl transition.

5. Create special effects with video transitions.

6. Create a custom transition.

7. Add a Transition Progress envelope.

chapter 5 ADDING PIZZAZZ
with Transitions

Many video editors and producers prefer the old-fashioned straight cut from one scene to the next, whereas others like to add a transition between scenes. When you insert events into a project with automatic rippling enabled, the events align head to tail by default. If you have automatic crossfades enabled, a crossfade occurs whenever you overlap two events. A standard crossfade gradually fades the tail of one event into the head of the next event. You can modify the manner in which one event fades into another by changing the crossfade curve.

Undoubtedly, you've seen the crossfade transition many times. It's a classic, and it does a great job of adding polish to a video production. However, sometimes you have footage that could benefit from a more artistic transition. For example, if there's a significant time span from when the footage in one event is shot to the next, you can use one of the **Clock Wipe transitions** to inform your audience that the hands of time are indeed ticking as the next event begins. Other types of footage will be better served with other transitions from the preset library of Sony transitions that you find in

the Window Docking area. For example, if you're editing video footage in which a subject is reminiscing or going into a dream state, one of the **Flash transitions** or **Dissolve transitions** can be used to good effect.

Vegas has hundreds of transitions from which to choose. When you choose a transition, you can choose a preset, or you can modify the transition to suit your project. You can also save a modified preset for future use.

The number of frames that events overlap each other determines the length of the transition. Some event transitions should occur quickly to create a dramatic transition, such as when you're creating a project with video clips from an automobile race. Other video footage might benefit from a transition of longer duration, such as scenery. If events are similar, you might want to use a straight cut. There's no rule that says you need to have a transition between every event in a production.

You can also change the manner in which a crossfade transition occurs. You can choose one of the preset transition curves

180

to determine how the tail of one event segues into the head of the next. If you use a transition other than a crossfade, you can apply a transition envelope for a more pronounced effect. As with other Vegas envelopes, you add points to determine how the transition acts at that point in time. With a transition envelope, you can reverse the transition momentarily or hold it before completion. For example, if you apply a Transition Progress envelope to one of the Clock Wipe transitions, you can reverse the hands of time and then move forward to the end of the transition.

Tools You'll Use

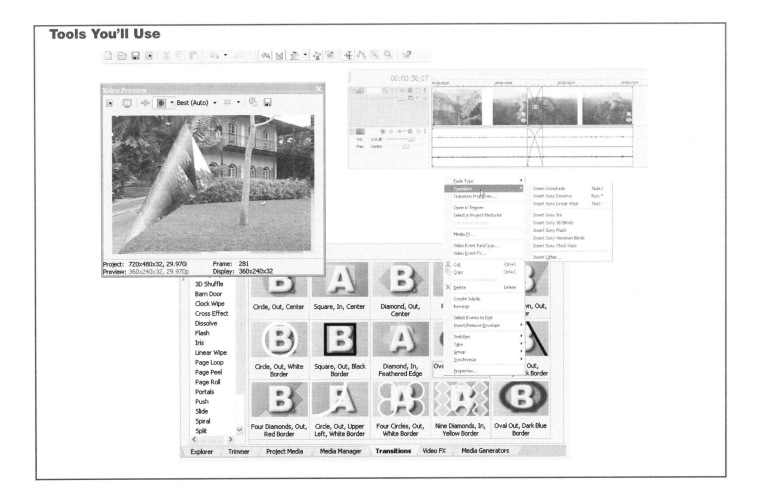

CREATE A
CROSSFADE TRANSITION

What You'll Do

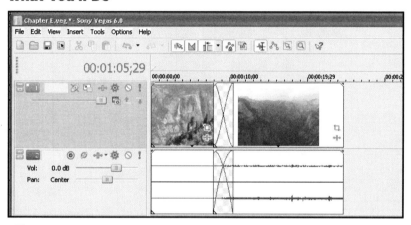

 In this lesson, you learn how to create a classic crossfade transition.

Understanding Crossfade Transitions

In every art, there's a classic. In graphic design, it's the drop shadow. In video editing, it's the crossfade transition. The crossfade transition is indeed quite popular, and you see it with about the same regularity in video productions as you see the drop shadow in graphic illustrations and Web site images. The crossfade gently segues from one event to the next by displaying a partially transparent image of each overlapping event. When the crossfade begins, you see more of the first event. As the crossfade reaches its conclusion, you see more of the last event.

Creating a Crossfade

To create a crossfade, you manually overlap two adjacent events on the same track. After you overlap the clips, you can specify the manner in which one event fades into the next. You can also slide a crossfade to trim one event while changing the In or Out point of the other event.

You can use a crossfade as needed. However, the wholesale use of crossfades when events change can be visual overkill. Use crossfades when the footage from one event to the next is different enough to warrant a crossfade. The artistic and efficient use of crossfades enables you to create a compelling video that your audience can easily follow.

FIGURE 5-1

Automatic Crossfade button

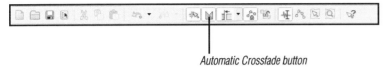

Automatic Crossfade button

FIGURE 5-2

Crossfaded events

1. Create a new project.

2. Import two video clips into the Project Media window.

3. If automatic crossfades are not enabled, click the Automatic Crossfade button on the toolbar, as shown in Figure 5-1.

   If you overlap two clips without enabling automatic crossfades, the second clip eclipses the first as soon as it plays.

4. Select the clips and drag them into the main window, aligning them with the beginning of the timeline.

   ### QUICKTIP

   To automatically overlap multiple clips when inserting them, choose Options > Preferences. Then click the Editing tab. Choose the Automatically Overlap Multiple Selected Media When Added option. If desired, type a value in the Amount field to change the default overlap of .250 seconds to one that better suits your projects.

5. Drag the second event over the first to set the desired overlap, as shown in Figure 5-2.

   If you have grid snapping enabled, you can snap the event to the ruler marks. To overlap the event with precise control, choose Options > Grid Spacing > Seconds.

6. Select the second event; then drag it to the left.

   When you drag to the left, you increase the overlap. A transition of two or three seconds works well in most instances.

7. Keep the project open. You'll be using it in the next objective.

Preview a crossfade

1. Place your cursor in the middle of the crossfade you just created; then double-click.

   Vegas creates a loop region. The loop region turns dark blue, as shown in Figure 5-3. Note that the timeline has been magnified in this screenshot so that you can see the loop region easily.

2. Click the Loop Playback button ⟳ in the Transport bar.

   This option loops a region repeatedly after you click the Play button.

3. If the Video Preview window is not displayed, choose View > Video Preview.

4. Click the Play button.

   The transition area loops repeatedly, enabling you to preview the crossfade.

5. Click the Stop button ☐ to halt the preview.

Change the fade type

1. Right-click the crossfade you just created; then choose Fade Type from the shortcut menu.

FIGURE 5-3
Insert a loop region

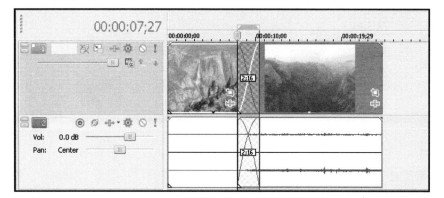

FIGURE 5-4

The Fade Type menu

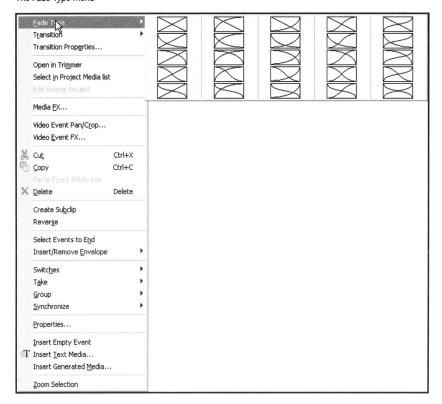

Vegas displays the Fade Type menu, shown in Figure 5-4. Each icon is a visual representation of how one event fades into the next.

> **CAUTION**
>
> You cannot apply a fade type to a transition selected from the Transitions tab. If you apply a fade type to a transition other than a crossfade, the transition reverts to a crossfade.

2. Choose the desired fade type.

3. Preview the transition, as outlined previously.

4. Choose different fade types for the transition; then preview them to see the numerous effects you can achieve by choosing various fade types.

When you choose a different fade type, the icon from the Fade Type menu is displayed where the clips overlap. You can determine which event gets emphasis and viewer attention by choosing the proper fade type. You can decipher the fade type icon by examining the crossing lines. The line that begins at the upper left of the icon shows how the first event fades out to the second, whereas the line at the lower left shows how the second clip fades in. A diagonal line signifies a linear fade, whereas a gently sloping curve designates a slow fade, and so on.

Slide a crossfade

1. Create a new project.

2. Import two media clips into the Project Media window.

3. Select the clips; then drop them in the main window, aligning them to the beginning of the timeline.

4. Overlap the events to create a crossfade.

5. If the Video Preview window is not displayed, choose View > Video Preview.

6. Position your cursor over the transition, press Ctrl+Alt, and then drag left.

    When you slip or slide an event, the Video Preview window is split into two panes. The left pane shows the Out frame of the event to the left of the transition, whereas the right pane shows the In frame of the event to the right of the transition. As you slide the crossfade, the panes update in real time.

7. When you slide a crossfade, your cursor becomes a dual-headed arrow over a rectangle with an X in the center, as shown in Figure 5-5. The X signifies the crossfade. As you drag left, you effectively shorten the duration of the left event, while increasing the duration of the right event. The duration of the transition is unaffected, but it appears at a different point on the timeline.

8. Release the mouse button when the desired duration and Out point of the left event have been achieved.

FIGURE 5-5
Sliding a crossfade

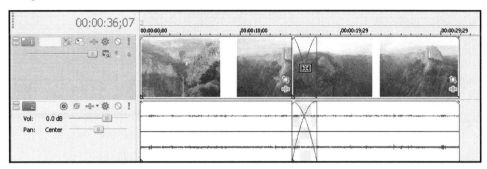

FIGURE 5-6

Trimming an event after sliding a crossfade

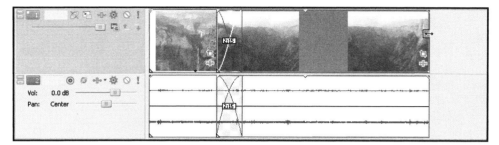

After you release the mouse button, Vegas resizes the events and moves the crossfade. When you slide a crossfade, one of the events loops. Click the head of the right event (when you slide a crossfade left), or click the tail of the left event (when you slide a crossfade to the right) and drag until you've aligned the cursor with the notch, shown in Figure 5-6. If you have automatic rippling enabled, the events ripple to fill in the gaps. If automatic rippling is not enabled, use the applicable manual rippling method, as outlined in Chapter 3, "Working with Media Events."

9. Press Ctrl+Z to undo sliding the crossfade.

10. Place your cursor over the crossfade, press Ctrl+Alt, and then drag right.

11. Release the mouse button when the desired In frame on the right event has been achieved.

When you slide a crossfade to the right, you effectively decrease the duration of the right event, while increasing the duration of the left event. After you slide a crossfade, you can trim the left event to prevent it from looping.

USE VIDEO
TRANSITIONS

What You'll Do

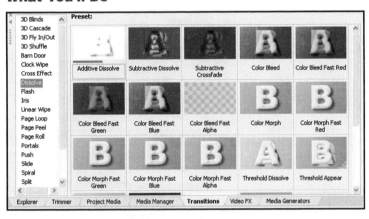

In this lesson, you learn how to work with presets from the Video Transitions tab.

Using Transition Presets

In addition to the classic crossfade transition, Vegas ships with a plethora of preset transitions that you can use to add polish and panache to your video projects. The presets run the gamut from sublime transitions that you use to gently segue the viewer from one event to the next, to the WOW transitions you can use to signify that something exciting is going to happen in the next event.

Converting a Crossfade to a Transition Preset

The first step is to create the classic cross-fade transition. After you create the cross-fade, you can choose one of the preset transitions to suit your project. When you decide to use one of the video transition presets, you can choose the preset in one of two ways. You can choose a video transition from the Transitions shortcut menu, or you can choose a video transition from the Transitions window. Doing either opens a dialog box for the selected transition, which enables you to set parameters for the transition.

FIGURE 5-7
Transition menu

FIGURE 5-8
Sony Iris transition

1. Create a new project.

2. Add two clips to the Project Media window.

3. Select the clips; then drop them in the main window, aligning them to the beginning of the timeline.

4. Create a crossfade transition, as outlined previously.

5. Right-click the transition; then move your cursor over the Transition title in the short-cut menu.

   A submenu appears listing the most popular video transitions, as shown in Figure 5-7.

6. Choose Transition > Insert Sony Iris.

   The Video Event FX dialog box opens show-ing the parameters for the Iris transition.

7. Accept the default parameters and close the dialog box.

   Vegas changes the transition to the Iris type. The preset name appears on the transition. Note that you'll only be able to see part of the preset name unless you zoom in on the transition.

8. Preview the project.

   Figure 5-8 shows the Iris transition in action.

Select a video transition from the Transitions window

1. Create a new project.

2. Import two clips into the Project Media window.

3. Select the clips; then drop them in the main window, aligning them to the beginning of the timeline.

4. Overlap the clips to create a crossfade transition, as discussed previously.

5. Click the Transitions tab in the Window Docking area; then choose Venetian Blinds.

   When you choose a transition category, thumbnails of the available transitions appear, as shown in Figure 5-9. Move your cursor over a thumbnail to see an animated preview.

6. Select a preset that suits your project; then drop it on the video transition between the two events.

   The Video Event FX dialog box appears with the parameters for the selected Venetian Blinds transition, as shown in Figure 5-10. The preset text box displays as (Untitled), even though you selected a preset from the Transitions tab. The parameters are identical to the preset you selected. However, you can modify the preset, or choose a different preset from a list.

7. Click the down arrow to the right of the preset name; then choose an option from the drop-down list.

   The parameters are adjusted to the selected preset. You can change these parameters to suit your project by dragging the sliders or by entering values in the text fields.

FIGURE 5-9
Transitions tab

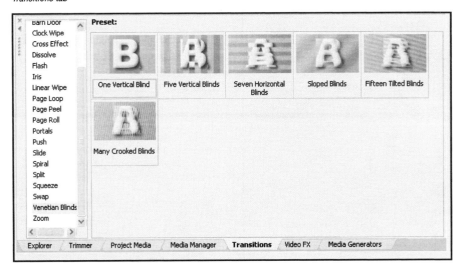

FIGURE 5-10
Venetian Blinds Transition dialog box

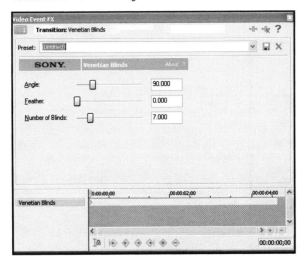

USE THE PUSH AND
WIPE TRANSITIONS

What You'll Do

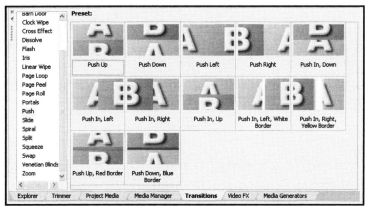

In this lesson, you learn how to add the Push and Wipe transitions to your projects.

Mastering the Art of Video Transitions

Vegas has so many cool transitions that I could easily fill three chapters with material and still not completely cover it. As with any other tool, you gain mastery through experimentation and letting your inner child run amuck, if you will. The remainder of this chapter shows you how to add some of the more popular transitions to your video projects. To learn how to harness the power of video transitions, you might want to consider creating a project with several video clips, overlap the video events to create crossfades, and then use a different transition preset for each transition to see the effects you can achieve with them. Regard your creative play as an experiment and not a finished project. When you create a project for public viewing, it's a good idea to keep your transition types to a minimum, using no more than three or four when you're creating a video that's only a few minutes long. If you use too many transition presets in a project, the effect is jarring to the viewer. When you use multiple transition presets in a project, use ones that have a similar look. Think artistically when you choose transitions for a project by selecting those that enhance the footage. Of course, you have artistic license, but you should always consider the intended audience for your project.

Selecting a Push and Wipe Preset

In this lesson, you learn to use two popular transitions: the Push and the Wipe. The **Push transition** pushes out the previous event to reveal the next event. You choose the push direction that suits your footage. You can push the event from left to right, right to left, top to bottom, and so on. The aptly named **Wipe transition** wipes out the old and reveals the new. You can determine whether the transition has a hard or soft edge, wipes in from right to left, left to right, diagonally, and so on.

Use the Push transition

1. Create a new project.

2. Import two video clips into the Project Media window.

3. Drop the clips in the main window, aligning them to the beginning of the timeline.

4. Create a crossfade transition by overlapping the events as outlined previously.

5. Click the Transitions tab; then choose Push.

   The Push transition presets shown in Figure 5-11 appear. Move your cursor over a thumbnail to see an animated preview of the preset.

6. Select a preset you like; then drop it on the transition.

   The Video Event FX dialog box appears. The dialog box lists the selected transition in the title bar and shows the parameters for the preset. You learn how to modify a transition's parameters in an upcoming lesson. Figure 5-12 shows the Video Event FX dialog box for the Push transition.

7. Accept the default parameters; then click the Close button.

   QUICKTIP

   Click the Plug-In Help button for information on how to set the transition's parameters.

FIGURE 5-11

Push Transition presets

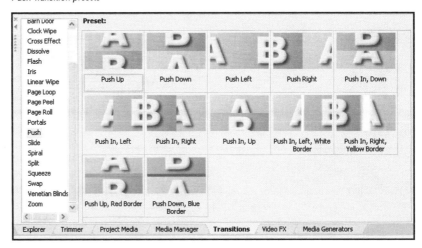

FIGURE 5-12

Push Transition dialog box

Replace Plug-in

Remove Selected Plug-in

Plug-in Help

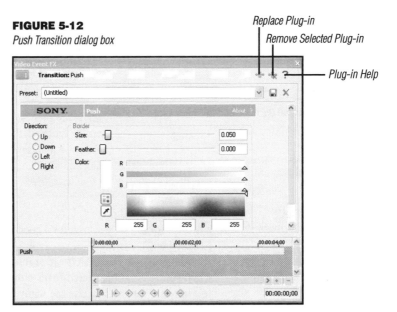

FIGURE 5-13

Push transition as previewed in the Video Preview window

8. Preview the transition, as outlined previously.

   Figure 5-13 shows the Push transition as displayed in the Video Preview window.

9. Right-click the transition; then choose Transition Properties from the shortcut menu.

   The Event FX dialog box for the Push transition appears, as shown previously in Figure 5-12.

10. Click the triangle to the right of the Preset window; then choose a different preset.

    The parameters update in the Event FX dialog box for the Push transition.

11. Click the Close button; then preview the transition.

12. Repeat steps 10–12; then try some of the other presets available with this compelling transition.

13. Keep the project open. You'll be using it in the next objective.

Use the Wipe transition

1. Right-click the transition; then choose Transition Properties from the shortcut menu.

   The Event FX dialog box for the Push transition, seen previously in Figure 5-12, opens.

2. Click the Replace Plug-In button.

   The Plug-In Chooser-Transition dialog box appears, as shown in Figure 5-14.

3. Choose Sony Linear Wipe; then click Add.

4. Click OK to exit the dialog box.

   The Video Event FX dialog box updates, showing the parameters for the Linear Wipe transition.

5. Click the Close button to exit the Video Event FX dialog box.

6. Preview the transition.

   The default Linear Wipe reveals the next event by wiping diagonally across the frame, as shown in Figure 5-15.

7. Follow the previous steps; then experiment with the other Linear Wipe presets.

FIGURE 5-14
Plug-In Chooser-Transition dialog box

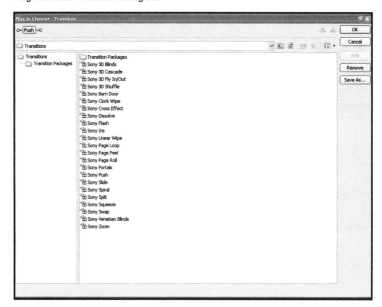

FIGURE 5-15
Linear Wipe transition as previewed in the Video Preview window

CHANGE SCENES WITH A
PAGE CURL TRANSITION

What You'll Do

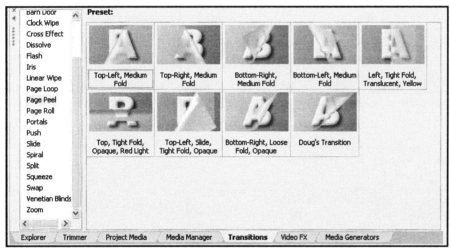

 In this lesson, you learn how to create compelling Page Curl transitions.

Exploring the Page Curl Transition

Watching a movie is like reading a book. As the movie progresses from scene to scene, it's like turning the pages of a book. A classic **Page Curl transition** is similar to the motion of turning the

pages of a book. The Page Curl begins at the top of one corner of the frame and curls diagonally to the opposite bottom corner of the frame. As the page curls, the next event is gradually revealed. The back of the page contains an opaque rendering of the previous event.

Using the Vegas Page Curl Variations

Page curls are popular. Vegas offers the classic Page Curl transitions, and much more. In the Transitions tab, you'll find three categories of Page Curl transitions: Page Loop, Page Peel, and Page Roll. Between the three categories, you have 24 presets from which to choose. And if that's not enough variety, you can modify the parameters of any preset and save the result as a custom transition, a technique you learn in this chapter's Lesson 6, "Create a Custom Transition."

Add a Page Curl transition

1. Create a new project.

2. Import two video clips into the Project Media window.

3. Drop the two clips in the main window, aligning them to the beginning of the timeline.

4. Create a Crossfade transition, by overlapping the events as outlined previously.

5. Click the Transition tab; then choose Page Peel.

   The Page Peel section of the Transitions tab is displayed, as shown in Figure 5-16. Each transition is displayed as a thumbnail. Move your cursor over a thumbnail to reveal an animated display of the preset.

6. Select the desired preset; then drop it on the transition.

   The Video Event FX-Transition dialog box appears.

7. Accept the default parameters; then click the Close button.

8. Double-click the transition to create a region; then preview the transition, as outlined previously.

   Figure 5-17 shows the Top Left, Medium Fold transition, as displayed in the Video Preview window.

FIGURE 5-16

Page Peel transition presets

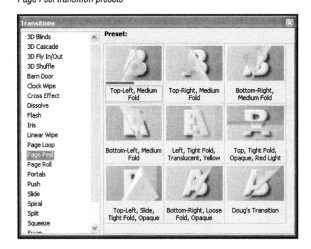

FIGURE 5-17

The Top Left, Medium Fold transition

9. Right-click the transition; then choose Transition > Change to Sony Page Loop from the shortcut menu.

The Video Event FX dialog box appears.

10. Accept the default parameters and close the dialog box.

The default Page Loop transition replaces the Page Peel transition you applied in step 6.

11. Preview the transition, as outlined previously.

The Page Loop transition looks like someone ripped a page from a book and sent it fluttering through the air. When you create transitions using one of the Page Loop presets, you can add some variety to your video by mixing in some Page Peel and Page Roll transitions. These transitions add nice variety to your video, yet are similar enough so that your video does not look like an amateur created it using every transition preset in the project except the proverbial kitchen sink.

12. Click the Transitions tab; then choose Page Roll.

13. Select one of the presets; then drop it on the transition.

The Video Event FX dialog appears.

14. Accept the default parameters; then click the Close button.

15. Preview the transition, as outlined previously.

16. Right-click the transition. Choose Transition properties from the shortcut menu; then choose a different preset from the Preset drop-down list.

If you have the time, experiment with the presets from each transition type. This short lesson should give you an example of the diversity you can add to your video projects using the Vegas variations of the classic Page Curl transition.

CREATE SPECIAL EFFECTS
WITH VIDEO TRANSITIONS

What You'll Do

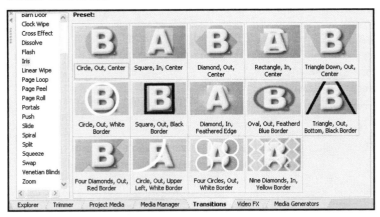

In this lesson, you learn how to add transitions to your projects that are designed to increase the "Wow" factor of your finished video.

Adding Panache to a Production with Video Transitions

You pull out all the stops and use a visually compelling transition when you want to increase viewer excitement, raise the viewer's level of expectation, or just let viewers know they're about to view

something special. In other words, you're adding the "Wow" factor to your video. Of course, everyone has his own definition of "Wow." When you factor in the intended audience, the video clips with which you're working, and your own artistic tastes, any number of the preset transitions can fit that category. In this lesson, you'll scratch the tip of the iceberg and work with a few of the more compelling transitions.

Using the 3D Fly In/Out, Flash, and Iris Transitions

You'll be using your own video clips with these transitions, which will give you an idea of which ones are best suited for your projects. You'll be focusing on three transition categories: 3D Fly In/Out, Flash, and Iris. Each category has presets with which you can experiment. When you find a transition that suits your projects well, you can always edit the transition to fine-tune it to your tastes. After you tweak a transition, you can save it as a preset for future projects.

FIGURE 5-18

3D Fly In/Out presets

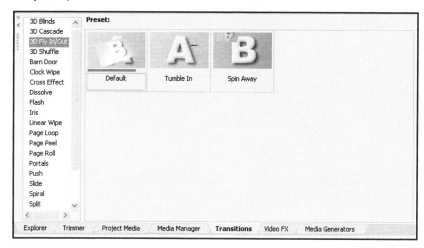

FIGURE 5-19

Video Event FX dialog box for the 3D Fly In/Out preset

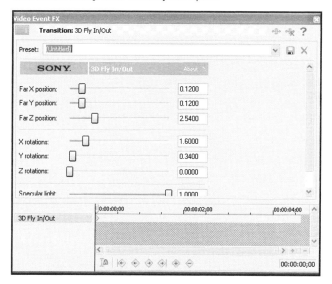

1. Create a new project.

2. Import two video clips into the Project Media window.

3. Select the clips; then drop them in the main window, aligning them with the beginning of the timeline.

4. Overlap the events to create a crossfade transition.

5. Click the Transitions tab; then choose 3D Fly In/Out.

   The 3D Fly In/Out transition group has three incredible presets. Figure 5-18 shows the thumbnail previews for each.

6. Select the Spin Away preset; then drop it on the transition.

   The Video Event FX dialog box for the 3D Fly In/Out preset appears, as shown in Figure 5-19. Notice the available parameters you can modify to fine-tune the transition.

7. Accept the default parameters; then click the Close button.

   Vegas replaces the crossfade transition with the Spin Away transition.

8. Preview the transition.

   Figure 5-20 shows the Spin Away transition at work. This eye-catching transition does a good job of letting viewers know that something special is about to unfold.

9. In the Transitions tab, click the Flash tab.

   Thumbnails are displayed for each preset, as shown in Figure 5-21. Move your cursor over each thumbnail to see an animated preview of the preset.

FIGURE 5-20

Spin Away transition as seen in the Video Preview window

FIGURE 5-21

Flash transition group presets

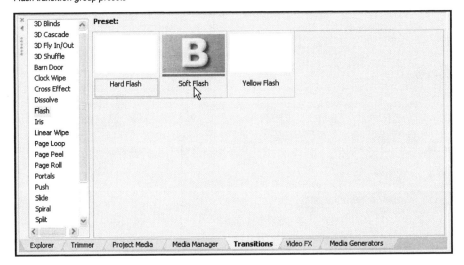

FIGURE 5-22

Event FX dialog box for the Flash transition

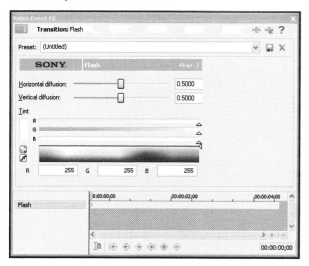

FIGURE 5-23

Flash transition, as seen in the Video Preview window

10. Select the Soft Flash preset; then drop it on the transition.

The previous transition is replaced by the Soft Flash transition, and the Event FX-Transition dialog box for the Flash transition appears, as shown in Figure 5-22. Notice that you can change the color of the flash as well as the diffusion (softness) of the transition effect vertically and horizontally.

11. Accept the defaults; then click the Close button.

12. Preview the transition.

Figure 5-23 shows the Flash transition in action.

13. Replace the current transition with one of the presets from the Iris transition, as outlined previously.

14. Preview the transition.

15. If you have time, experiment with the different presets from each transition group used in this lesson to experience the compelling effects they can add to your projects.

> **QUICKTIP**
>
> If you have prominent circular or rectangular objects in your scene, you can create a nice effect using the Iris transition. The Iris transition overlays a shape on the previous event, which acts as a window that gradually increases in size to reveal the next event in your production.

CREATE A
CUSTOM TRANSITION

What You'll Do

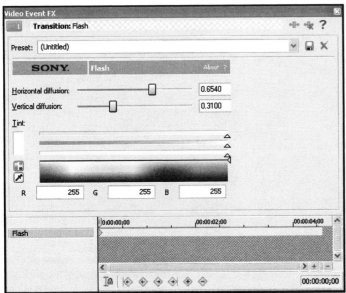

In this lesson, you learn how to edit a transition and then save it as a custom transition.

Editing a Transition Preset

If you've read this chapter in its entirety, you know that video transitions can add style and panache to your projects. You also know that each transition has its own set of parameters that you can tweak to suit the video clips in your project. After you've edited a transition that you think will be useful for other projects, you can save it. After you save an edited transition preset, it's available from the transition group's section in the Transition tab, as well as in the preset menu whenever the Event FX dialog box appears for a transition in the group from which the custom transition was spawned.

Saving Custom Transitions

Whether you create videos for profit or fun, creating a cache of custom video transitions lets you put your own stamp of originality on any project. Make it a regular practice to engage in some spirited "fun time" with Vegas. Import some video clips into the Project Media window, assemble them on the timeline, and play around with the different transitions. Tweak the parameters to suit your footage. When you stumble upon something cool (also known as a "happy accident"), save it as a custom preset for your future work.

FIGURE 5-24

Editing the Simple Blinds transition preset

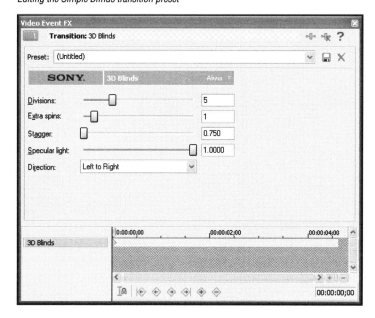

1. Create a new project.
2. Import two video clips into the Project Media window.
3. Drop the clips in the main window, aligning them to the start of the timeline.
4. Create a crossfade transition, as outlined previously.
5. Click the Transitions tab; then choose 3D Blinds.
6. Select the Simple preset; then drop it on the transition.

   The Event FX-Transition dialog box for 3D Blinds appears.
7. Drag the Divisions slider to 5.
8. Drag the Extra Spins slider to 1.
9. Enter a value of .750 in the Stagger text box.

   Your dialog box should resemble Figure 5-24.
10. Type a name for the edited preset in the Pre-set field.
11. Click the Save button, which looks like a floppy disk.
12. Click the Close button.

   The edited video transition is added to the 3D Blinds presets.

13. Preview the transition.

As you can see, the edited preset looks quite different from the original. Figure 5-25 shows the result you can expect when you apply the Simple Blinds Transition preset, modified per the previous steps, to a transition.

> **QUICKTIP**
>
> In the Video Event FX dialog box, select a custom preset that you no longer want, and then click the Delete Preset button to delete the preset. Note that you cannot delete a Vegas preset.

FIGURE 5-25

Edited preset in action

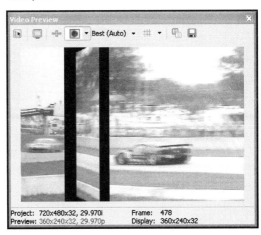

ADD A TRANSITION
PROGRESS ENVELOPE

What You'll Do

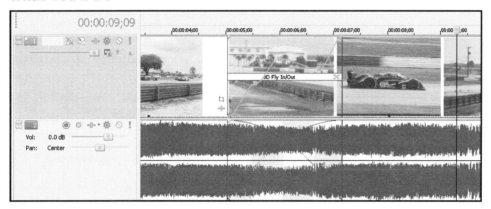

In this lesson, you learn how to add a Transition Progress envelope.

Applying a Transition Progress Envelope

When you add a transition between two events, the transition progresses from 0 to 100 percent from one event to the next. With the addition of a Transition Progress envelope, you can halt the progress of a transition, reverse a transition, or repeat a part of a transition.

Changing the Progress of a Transition

As with other Vegas envelopes, you add points to determine at which point in the transition the progress percentage is altered. The default progress envelope is a gently sloping curve from lower left (0 percent progress) to upper right (100 percent progress). By adding points and changing their positions, you transform the gently sloping curve into a curve whose shape determines how the transition progresses between events.

Create a Transition Progress envelope

1. Create a new project.

2. Import two video clips into the Project Media window.

3. Drop the clips in the main window, aligning them to the start of the timeline.

4. Create a crossfade transition, as outlined previously.

   When you're using a Transition Progress envelope, it's best to create a transition of at least two seconds in duration.

5. Click the Transitions tab; then choose Barn Door.

6. Select Vertical, In, No Border; then drop it on the transition.

   The Video Event FX dialog box appears.

7. Accept the default parameters; then click the Close button.

8. Right-click the transition; then choose Insert/Remove Envelope > Transition Progress from the shortcut menu.

   Vegas inserts a gently sloping purple curve across the duration of the transition, as shown in Figure 5-26. The timeline in this screenshot has been magnified so that you can better see the envelope.

   QUICKTIP

   When you're working with a Transition Progress envelope, use the Zoom Edit tool to zoom in on the transition.

9. Add three points to the envelope, evenly spacing them across the transition envelope, as shown in Figure 5-27.

FIGURE 5-26

Inserting a Transition Progress envelope

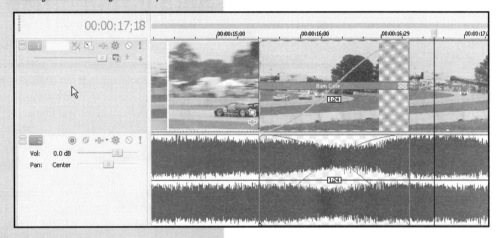

FIGURE 5-27

Adding points to the envelope

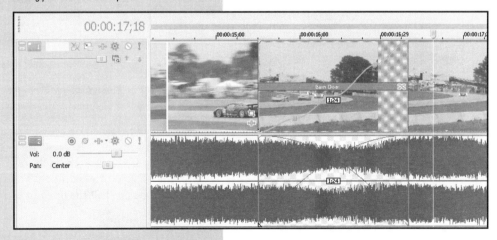

- To add an envelope point, right-click at the desired position and choose Add Point from the shortcut menu.

10. Select and drag each point on the curve; then adjust the curve so that it's similar to Figure 5-28.

QUICKTIP

Right-click a point and choose one of the transition progress options to set the point to 0, 50, or 100 percent progress. Alternatively, choose Set To and then enter the desired percentage in the text box.

Position your cursor over a Transition Progress envelope point to display the current transition progress in a tooltip.

11. Double-click the transition to create a region.

12. Preview the transition.

The barn doors begin closing in on the first event. After the envelope point, the doors reverse direction. When the second envelope point is encountered, the doors close again, revealing the second event.

13. Drag the second point so that it is level with the first point.

Your goal is to hold the transition. To precisely set the second point percentage to the first point, hold your cursor over the first point to reveal the percentage in a tooltip. Right-click the second point and choose Set To from the shortcut menu. Then enter the value of the first point in the text box.

14. Preview the transition.

The barn doors close partway and halt between the first and second points. After the third point, the doors close completely and reveal the second event.

FIGURE 5-28

Modifying the Transition Progress envelope points

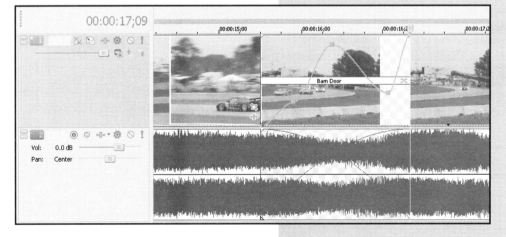

Creating a Crossfade Transition

1. Create a new project.

2. Import two video clips into the Project Media window.

3. Select the two clips and drop them in the main window, aligning them to the beginning of the timeline.

4. Create a crossfade transition, two seconds in duration, as shown in Figure 5-29.

5. Preview the transition, as shown in Figure 5-30.

6. Keep the project open for the next skills review.

FIGURE 5-29
Creating a crossfade

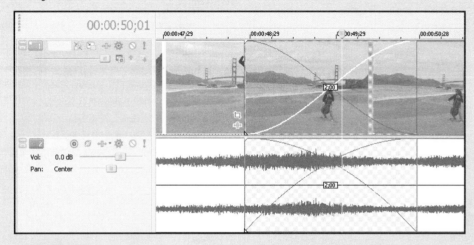

FIGURE 5-30
Previewing a transition

Applying the Iris Transition

1. Click the Transitions tab; then choose Iris.

2. Select the Circle, Out, Center preset. Then drop it on the transition to open the Video Event FX dialog box, shown in Figure 5-31.

3. Click the Close button.

4. Preview the transition, as shown in Figure 5-32.

5. Keep the project open for the next skills review.

FIGURE 5-31

Video Event FX dialog box

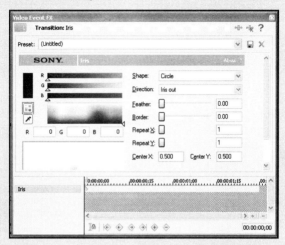

FIGURE 5-32

Circle, Out, Center Iris transition preset

Editing a Transition

1. Right-click the transition.

2. Choose Transition Properties from the shortcut menu.

3. Select the Oval Out Feathered Blue Border preset.

4. Change the color to a darker blue.

5. Change the Border value to .20.

6. Change the Feather value to 0.75.

7. Drag the small blue square to change the position from which the oval appears in the frame, as shown in Figure 5-33.

8. Close the Video FX Event-Transition dialog box.

9. Preview the transition, as shown in Figure 5-34.

10. Save the project for the next skills review.

FIGURE 5-33

Editing a transition

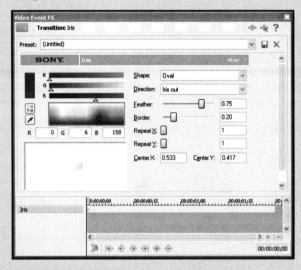

FIGURE 5-34

Previewing an edited transition

Adding Pizzazz with Transitions Chapter 5

Creating a Custom Transition

1. Right-click the transition.

2. Choose Transition Properties from the shortcut menu.

3. Click the Save Preset button.

4. Save the edited preset as Oval Out, Dark Blue Border, as shown in Figure 5-35.

5. Close the Video Event FX-Transitions dialog box.

6. Close the project.

Applying a Custom Transition

1. Create a new project.

2. Import two video clips into the Project Media window.

3. Select the clips; then drop them in the main window, aligning them with the beginning of the timeline.

4. Overlap the clips to create a crossfade transition.

5. Click the Transitions tab; then choose Iris.

6. Select the Oval Out, Dark Blue Border transition, as shown in Figure 5-36. Then drop it on the transition.

7. Preview the transition.

FIGURE 5-35

Saving a custom preset

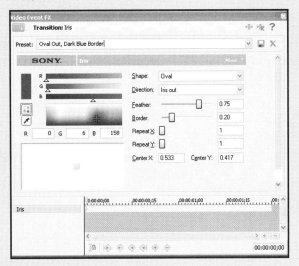

FIGURE 5-36

Selecting a custom preset

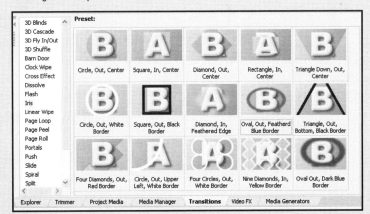

You're the head of the production department for a company that creates and distributes educational material on CD-ROMs. While you were on vacation, a member of your team compiled video footage for a historical perspective of an auto race that first ran in 1950. The clips show footage from old races that transition into clips from last year's event. The compilation is good, but there are no transitions between scenes—only straight cuts from one clip to the next. Some of the cuts are too jarring to be acceptable. You decide to augment your employee's work with the creative use of transitions in Vegas. You know that mixing too many transitions in a project looks unprofessional. Your job is to choose the best transition for the presentation.

1. Create a new project.

2. Import several clips into the Project Media window.

   If possible, choose clips of the same subject matter, but shot at different times of the day, or the same subject matter in different locales. Your goal is to choose clips that need transitions so that you can avoid a jarring segue from one scene to the next.

3. Select the clips; then drop them in the main window, aligning them with the beginning of the timeline.

4. Create a crossfade for each event.

5. Preview the project.

6. Choose what you feel is the best transition for the job.

   Figure 5-37 shows an Iris transition applied to some footage of a race car. The oval preset was chosen because its aspect ratio matches the frame size of the video and is also suited to the shape of the rapidly moving automobile.

FIGURE 5-37

Project Builder 1 sample

Even though your title is production assistant, you do most of the creative work while your boss hob-nobs with clients and staff videographers. You've been given a selection of clips of a famous author's home that will be used as part of a documentary on the author's life and works. You boss tells you to use something literary for scene transitions, which, of course, leads you to the transitions that look like pages of a book turning. Your job is to compile the clips and choose two Page Curl transitions for the scene transitions.

1. Create a new project.
2. Import several clips of a home interior into the Project Media window.

   If you have actual clips of a historic house, these are ideal.
3. Select the clips; then drop them into the main window, aligning them with the beginning of the timeline.
4. Overlap the clips to create transitions. The transition duration is at your discretion.

5. Preview the project.
6. Choose two transitions from the Page Loop, Page Peel, or Page Roll section. Choose similar transitions that won't be jarring to the viewer.
7. Preview the project.

   Figure 5-38 shows some footage of a historic home in Florida with one of the Page Loop transitions applied.

FIGURE 5-38

Project Builder 2 sample

You work for a video production company. Four videographers covered the wedding of a socialite's daughter. In addition to covering the wedding, they covered some of the bride and groom's activities prior to the wedding. After previewing the video, you see a charming scene of the couple on a remote island trail reading a map prior to moving on. Your goal is to find the perfect transition to segue to the beach scene that follows.

1. Create a new project.

2. Import two video clips into the Project Media window.

   If possible, choose one clip that focuses on two people, and another one that features scenery with no people.

3. Select the clips; then drop them in the main window, aligning them to the beginning of the timeline.

4. Overlap the clips to create a crossfade transition.

5. Preview the clips.

6. Choose what you feel is the ideal transition for the clip. If needed, edit the default transition to get the desired effect.

   Figure 5-39 shows a similar scenario to the project assignment. The sample uses the Diamond In, Feathered Edge transition to signify the upcoming wedding vows.

FIGURE 5-39
Design Project sample

This chapter covers adding an artistic touch to your productions through the use of transitions. Vegas has several transition groups from which to choose. Each transition group has presets that can be modified to suit your productions, and you can save modified presets for future use.

What You Have Learned

In this chapter, you:

- Mastered the classic crossfade transition.
- Learned to use preset video transitions in place of crossfade transitions.
- Mastered the Push and Wipe transitions.

- Used the Page Curl transitions.
- Created special effects with video transitions.
- Mastered the Transition Progress envelope.
- Created a custom transition.

Key Terms from This Chapter

- **Clock Wipe transitions.** A transition group with presets that look like the hour hand of a clock revealing the next scene.
- **Dissolve transitions.** A group of transitions that dissolves the video from the previous scene into the next scene.

- **Flash transitions.** A group of transitions that uses a flash of light to reveal the next scene.
- **Page Curl transition** A group of transitions that curls the video from one scene into the next, much like the pages of a book being turned.
- **Push transition.** A group of transitions that appears to push in the next scene.
- **Wipe transition.** A group of transitions that appears to wipe the video of one scene into the next.

chapter

6

WORKING WITH
Sound

1. Work with audio effects.

2. Edit audio events.

3. Record voice-overs.

4. Work with audio busses.

5. Mix audio and bus tracks.

chapter 6 WORKING WITH
Sound

When you create a Vegas project, audio is included by default. If the video clips you use in a project have embedded audio, Vegas creates an audio track as soon as you add a clip to the project. Of course, you can add other audio tracks above and beyond the default audio track. You can use additional audio tracks for voice-overs, music tracks, and so on. You can vary the volume and pan of each track, apply audio effects to the entire track, and adjust the master volume to determine the volume of the rendered audio tracks in your project. When you do render the video, Vegas mixes the tracks.

Each audio track has three automatable FX that you can use to compensate for deficiencies in the audio track. For example, you can use **Track Noise Gate** to eliminate hiss or low-frequency rumble in an audio track. You can add other FX plug-ins to audio tracks, and for that matter, individual audio events. And if that doesn't give you enough control over project audio, you can also use individual audio event switches to mute, lock, loop, invert phase, or normalize audio.

When you use multiple audio tracks in a project, you can create busses to which you can route the audio tracks. You can use one audio bus to control the volume of several audio tracks, another audio bus to control the volume of a musical soundtrack, and a third bus to assign a plug-in to one or more audio tracks. After you assign audio busses to your project, you control the influence of each bus by using a Level slider. You mix the busses and the main volume in the **Mixer window**, which works similarly to a mixing board in a recording studio. You then adjust the volume for the entire project by using the Main bus control in the Mixer window, or by using the controls on the Master track.

Tools You'll Use

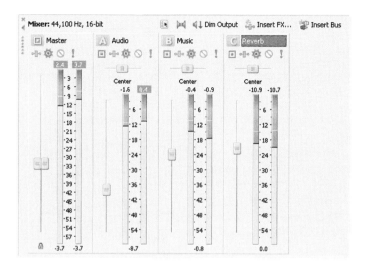

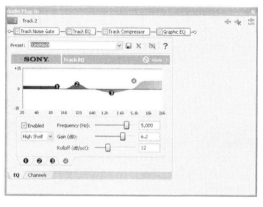

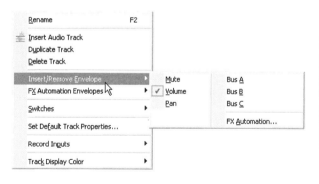

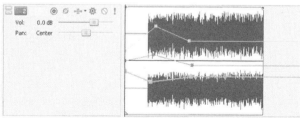

WORK WITH
AUDIO EFFECTS

What You'll Do

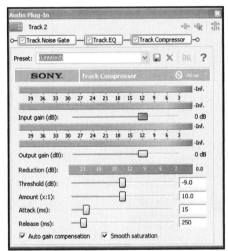

 In this lesson, you learn to modify audio tracks with the use of FX. You learn to modify the default Automatable Track FX, as well as add other FX to the track plug-in chain.

Modifying Audio Tracks with Automatable FX

When you're previewing a project, you might notice that the audio tracks need

some work. You have a number of tools at your disposal for fine-tuning the audio tracks in your project. First and foremost, you can modify the track volume and balance between speakers. If you need further control, you can use the default automatable FX that are assigned to each track. These include Track Noise Gate, Track EQ, and Track Compressor. The Track Noise Gate is used to mute any sound below a certain decibel range. You can use this plug-in to eliminate hissing noises and other anomalies, such as low-level noise that you can hear during silent sections of the audio. If the track audio is significantly louder than any low-level noise, you can effectively mask it with the Track Noise Gate. **Track EQ** gives you the capability of tweaking the tonal characteristics of an audio track. You have four frequency bands with which to work. **Track Compressor** makes it possible for you to modify the dynamics of an audio track, which you can use to make a track stand out in the mix.

Adding FX to the Plug-in Chain

In addition, you can add other automatable FX to an audio track plug-in chain. Audio FX that support automation can be controlled through the use of an envelope. You can augment the three default automatable FX with FX from the Automation folder, which is available after you click the Track FX icon.

Adding Other Audio FX Plug-ins to the Chain

Unfortunately, there are far too many FX to cover in a single chapter. You can add other FX to the plug-in chain, such as Chorus, Wah-Wah, Distortion, and so on. You use these FX to create special effects on narration tracks and music tracks. You can add as many FX as needed to a track. However, you can go overboard, applying so many FX plug-ins that the audio track is rendered to electronic noise. Of course, if that's the effect you're after, have at it.

FIGURE 6-1
Audio Track FX button

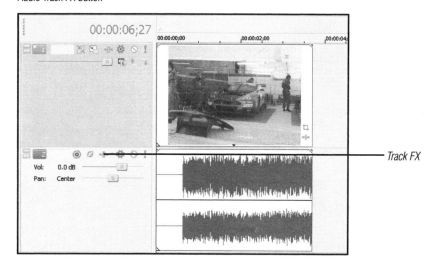

Track FX

FIGURE 6-2
Audio Plug-In dialog box

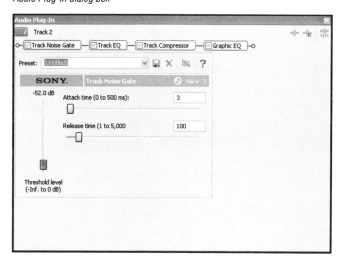

1. Create a new project.

2. Import a video file with embedded audio into the Project Media window.

3. Drop the clip into the main window, aligning it with the beginning of the timeline.

4. Click the Audio Track FX icon, shown in Figure 6-1.

   The Audio Plug-in dialog box appears. All of the default automatable FX are listed. To modify the FX parameters, click the applicable button.

5. Click the Track Noise Gate button
   ☑ Track Noise Gate .

   The Track Noise Gate parameters appear in the Audio Plug-In dialog box, as shown in Figure 6-2.

   > **NOTE**
   >
   > If the message "FX Muted" appears in the dialog box, audio for the project has been muted. To restore audio and FX, choose Options > Mute All Audio.

6. Click the Preset down arrow to display its defaults.

   Each default is designed to correct or mask a certain noise problem. Unless you have worked with sound extensively, the defaults might seem foreign to you. The easiest way to learn what each default does is to select each in turn and see what effect it has on the audio track.

7. Select a preset, but leave the dialog box open.

When you're modifying an automatable FX, you can preview the effect it will have on the track to which you're applying it.

8. Preview the project.

As you preview the project, you can hear how the Track Noise Gate affects the sound.

9. Drag the Threshold Level slider up.

Dragging the slider up sets the threshold dB at a higher level. All sound below the threshold level is muted. As a rule, most noise occurs below 40 dB.

10. Drag the Attack Time slider to the right.

As you drag the slider to the right, you increase the amount of time it takes the Noise Gate to go from 0 to 1 after the signal exceeds the threshold level.

11. Drag the Release Time slider to the right.

As you drag the slider to the right, you increase the amount of time it takes the Noise Gate to go from 1 to 0 after the signal drops below the threshold level.

12. Keep the project open. You'll be using it in the next objective.

Modify the Track EQ

1. Click the Track Noise Gate check box.

Clicking a plug-in's check box enables or disables the plug-in's effect on the plug-in chain. Temporarily disabling a plug-in allows you to fine-tune the parameters of the other plug-ins you have applied to the audio track.

When a plug-in is disabled, it still appears in the Audio Track FX dialog box, but the check mark is not visible, your indication that the plug-in is not enabled.

2. Click the Track EQ button ⌐☑Track EQ ¬.

The Audio Plug-In dialog box is reconfigured to display the default parameters for the Track EQ plug-in, as shown in Figure 6-3.

FIGURE 6-3
Modifying Track EQ parameters

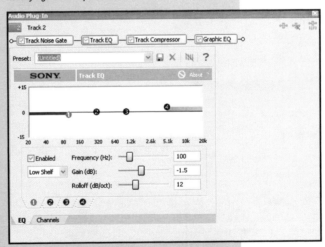

3. Click the Preset down arrow to display a drop-down list of the available presets.

Each preset is designed to cure a specific deficiency, such as removing low and inaudible frequencies.

4. Select the desired preset and begin previewing the project.

5. Click the Loop Playback button $\circlearrowright$ in the Transport Control toolbar.

This enables you to apply each preset in turn and hear the difference without having to re-cue the project. You can also create a region when previewing a project. You can create a region for an individual event, the entire project, or a selection for a desired duration.

6. Select each preset in turn.

After you preview each preset, you'll modify the parameters to see the effect each one has on the soundtrack.

QUICKTIP

Click the Channels tab; it enables you to select the channels to which you apply the Track EQ plug-in.

7. Select the band for which you want to modify the equalization settings.

The audio frequency is split into four bands. Click the number to specify the band to which the settings are applied. Alternatively, you can click the band's tab near the bottom of the dialog box.

8. Click the Band Mode down arrow, which is directly beneath the Enabled check box; then select one of the following: Low Shelf, Band, or High Shelf.

This option determines the band for which Vegas creates a bypass. Notice that the Enabled option is selected by default. Deselect this option if you do not want a band to be bypassed.

- If you choose Low Shelf, frequencies below the specified frequency will be attenuated or boosted by the specified amount. Increase the Rolloff value to use the Low Shelf band mode for high pass filtering.

- If you choose the Band filter, a range of frequencies around the center frequency are boosted or cut. You specify the Bandwidth value to determine the range of frequencies that will be affected.

- If you choose High Shelf, frequencies above the specified frequency will be attenuated or boosted by the specified amount. Increase the Rolloff value to use the Low Shelf band mode for low-pass filtering.

9. Drag the Frequency slider to set the value.

When Low Shelf or High Shelf is selected, the Frequency value determines the cutoff frequency at which the filter begins processing the audio. If you do not specify a value, the center frequency of the band is used for filtering purposes. As you change the frequency, the band's position on the EQ graph is updated to reflect the specified frequency.

10. Drag the Gain slider to set the value.

This value determines the amount of gain applied to a band. As you drag the Gain slider, the EQ graph is updated to reflect your changes.

11. Drag the Rolloff slider to specify a value.

This slider is only available if you choose Low Shelf or High Shelf for the Band Mode. The value you specify determines the number of decibels above which the filter will roll off per octave. Specify a high value for a sharp cutoff, or a low value for a gradual cutoff. The steepness of the EQ curve changes to reflect the setting you choose.

12. Drag the Bandwidth slider to specify a value.

This slider is only available if you choose Band for the Band Mode. This value determines the range of frequencies around the center of the range that will be affected by the EQ. Figure 6-4 shows the EQ Plug-In dialog box after several changes have been made to the Track EQ.

> **NOTE**
>
> There is also a Channels tab for Track EQ settings. This tab contains options for the channels in your audio track. The options determine to which channels the settings are applied. The options differ depending on whether your project is two-track stereo or 5.1 surround sound. For example, if the project is two-track stereo, your options are Enable Left and Enable Right.

13. Keep the project open. You'll be using it in the next objective.

FIGURE 6-4

EQ graph after Track EQ settings have been modified

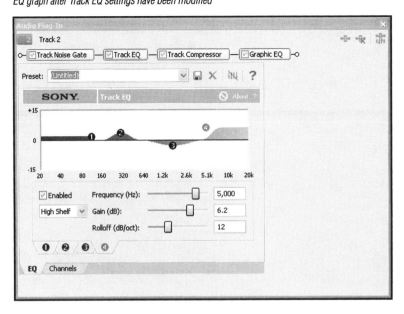

FIGURE 6-5

Track Compressor parameters

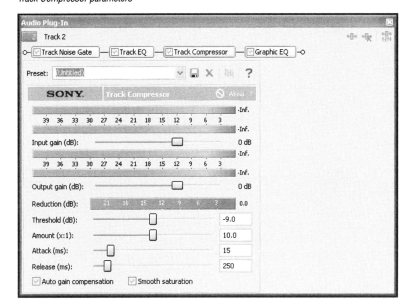

1. Click the check box in the Track Noise Gate and Track EQ buttons.

   Clicking a plug-in's check box enables or disables the plug-in's effect on the plug-in chain. Temporarily disabling a plug-in allows you to fine-tune the parameters of the other plug-ins you have applied to the audio track. When a plug-in is disabled, it still appears in the Audio Track FX dialog box, but the check marks are not visible, your indication that the plug-in is not enabled.

2. Click the Track Compressor button

   .

   The Audio Plug-In dialog box is reconfigured to show the parameters of the Track Compressor plug-in, as shown in Figure 6-5. Notice that the plug-ins you've disabled do not have check marks in the box to the left of the plug-in name.

3. Click the Loop Playback button; then begin previewing the project.

4. Click the Preset down arrow and choose a preset from the drop-down list.

   The presets limit the dynamic range of the audio track. Some of the preset names might be confusing if you are not well versed in the science of editing sound. The best way to master this plug-in is by previewing each preset on an audio track and noting the change that occurs when the preset is applied to the track. After you select a preset, you can modify the parameters to fine-tune the effect that the plug-in has on the track.

5. Select each preset in turn and note the effect each has on the audio track.

6. Drag the Input Gain (dB) slider to change the value.

   This value changes the input level of the audio track and affects the output gain level. As you drag the slider, note the difference in the Input and Output level meters. Change this value to compensate for an audio track that is too loud or too soft. Drag the slider until the Input level meter occasionally spikes into the yellow range. If the meter peaks into the red, the gain is too high, and the sound will be distorted.

   > **QUICKTIP**
   >
   > Right-click any meter to reveal a shortcut menu from which you can choose the dB range to display a different range of values. For example, you can change the Input meter so that it displays a range of −12.0 to 0 dB instead of the default −42 to 0 dB.

7. Drag the Output Gain (dB) slider to change the value.

   This value determines the output gain of the track and the volume of the audio track when rendered. Drag the slider until the Output level meter occasionally spikes into the yellow. The sound will be garbled and distorted if the meter peaks into the red. As you drag the slider, note the change in the Reduction meter. This meter shows the level to which the track is being compressed. All meters update in real time.

8. Drag the Threshold slider to specify a value.

   This value determines the level at which the Track Compressor processor begins modifying the signal. As the track signal rises above the Threshold value, compression occurs. A low value applies more compression to the track. If you specify too low a value, distortion might occur.

9. Drag the Amount (x:1) slider to specify a value.

   This value determines the actual compression that's applied to the signal. The value is a ratio that determines how many decibels above the threshold value the signal must rise to apply a 1 dB reduction in output level. For example, if you specify a value of 6, this is a 6:1 compression ratio. The signal would need to increase to 12 dB to increase the output level by 3 dB.

10. Drag the Attack slider to specify a value.

    This value determines the amount of time in milliseconds that it takes the compressor's gain reduction to reach its maximum value.

11. Drag the Release slider to specify a value.

    This value determines the amount of time in milliseconds that it takes the compressor's gain reduction to drop from its maximum value to 0.

12. Accept the default Auto Gain Compensation option, or click the check box to deselect the option.

    This option boosts the output value of the compressor by a constant value, depending on the Threshold and Ratio settings you specify.

13. If not selected by default, click the default Smooth Saturation check box to enable the option.

This option limits the amount of distortion created when applying heavy compression to an audio track. When this option is applied, the compensation level is reduced to remove any compression anomalies, such as "pumping" or "breathing."

NOTE

The Auto Gain Compensation and Smooth Saturation options will not be selected by default for certain presets, as they are not needed to achieve the preset's desired result.

FIGURE 6-6
Automatable FX

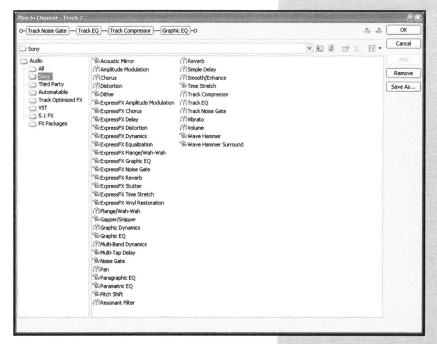

14. Click the Close button to exit the Audio Plug-In dialog box and apply the FX to the track.

QUICKTIP

After you modify a preset in any plug-in, you can save it by clicking the Save button, which looks like a floppy disk. After you save a modified preset, it appears on the preset menu. You can also delete a modified preset by selecting it and then clicking the Delete Preset button. Note that you cannot delete a Sony plug-in preset.

Add FXs to a plug-in chain

1. Create a new project; then add a video clip with embedded audio to the Project Media window.

2. Select the clip; then drop it in the main window, aligning the clip with the beginning of the timeline.

3. Click the Audio Track FX button.

The Audio Plug-In dialog box appears. The default plug-ins are displayed, as shown previously in Figure 6-2.

4. Click the Plug-In chain button.

The Plug-In Chooser dialog box appears.

5. Click the Sony folder.

The Sony FX, shown in Figure 6-6, are displayed.

6. Select the Graphic EQ plug-in; then click the Add button.

7. Click OK to exit the Plug-In Chooser dialog box.

The Graphic EQ parameters are displayed, as shown in Figure 6-7. You can modify the audio track by adding points to the graph. To add a point to the graph, move your cursor to the line until it becomes a pointing hand with a plus sign. Move your cursor along the line to select the desired frequency. As you move your cursor, the frequency is displayed in the upper-right corner of the dialog box. Click to add a point, and then click and drag the point to modify the output at the point's frequency. Alternatively, you can click the 10 Band or 20 Band tab. The 10 Band and 20 Band options enable you to modify frequency ranges by dragging sliders. If you have a graphic equalizer hooked up to your home entertainment system, these controls will be familiar to you. A complete dissertation on this plug-in is beyond the scope of this book. You can, however, get help for any plug-in by clicking the Help button, which looks like a question mark.

8. Click the Plug-in Help button that looks like a question mark to the right of the Preset field.

The Help dialog for the selected plug-in appears. In this case, the Graphic EQ plug-in is part of the XFX2 plug-ins. Click the plus sign to the left of the Using XFX 2 title to reveal a section for each plug-in. Figure 6-8 shows the Overview for the plug-ins.

FIGURE 6-7

Graphic EQ Plug-In dialog box

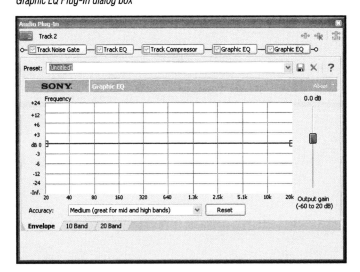

FIGURE 6-8

Plug-In Help dialog box

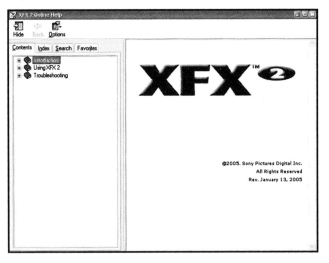

FIGURE 6-9

10 Band Graphic EQ tab

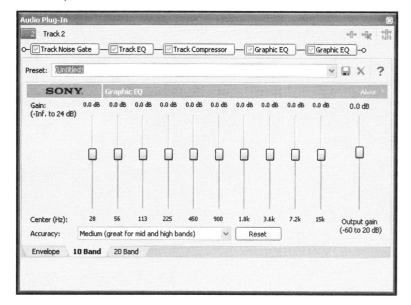

QUICKTIP

To remove a plug-in from the chain, open the Audio Plug-In dialog box and then click the Audio Track FX button. Click the button for the plug-in you want to remove, and then click the Remove Selected Plug-In button.

QUICKTIP

The quickest way to master a plug-in is to apply it to an audio track, experiment with the different presets to see the effect they have on the audio track, and then modify the parameters to see the effect that your changes render.

9. Preview the project.

10. Click the 10 Band tab at the bottom of the Audio Plug-In dialog box.

    The 10 Band tab, shown in Figure 6-9, has individual sliders that you use to set the gain for each frequency range. The sliders on the left side control the bass frequencies, whereas the middle sliders control the mid range. The sliders on the right side control the higher frequencies in the audio track. Drag a slider up to increase the frequency gain, or drag down to decrease the frequency gain.

11. Drag the sliders to modify the audio track until the sound is as desired.

12. Drag the Output Gain slider to determine the volume of the track.

    Drag the slider up to increase the volume, or drag down to decrease the volume.

13. Click the Close button to exit the Audio Plug-In dialog box and apply your changes.

14. Keep the project open. You'll be using it in the next objective.

Add an Automation FX envelope

1. Position your cursor over the audio track in the Track List window. Right-click, and then choose FX Automation Envelopes > FX Automation.

   The FX Automation Chooser dialog box opens. Notice that there is a check box for each plug-in you've assigned to the track.

2. Click the Graphic EQ button.

   The dialog box reconfigures for the selected plug-in, and the message "This plug-in does not support automation" appears. Note that not all plug-ins support Automation FX envelopes.

3. Click the Track Compressor button.

   The FX Automation Chooser dialog box reconfigures to show each option for the Track Compressor plug-in, as shown in Figure 6-10. Click a check box for each option that you want to be able to control with the envelope. Click the Select All button

FIGURE 6-10

FX Automation Chooser dialog box

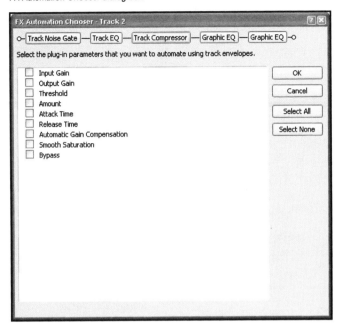

FIGURE 6-11
Track shortcut menu with a listing for each envelope that's applied to the track

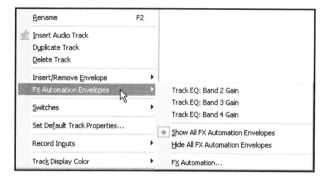

to select all parameters for the plug-in. Alternatively, you can select the parameters you want to control with the envelope. If you choose the wrong parameters, you can start from scratch by clicking the Select None button.

4. Click the Output Gain check box.

An envelope is created for each plug-in parameter that you choose.

5. Click the Track EQ button.

The FX Automation Chooser dialog box reconfigures to show each parameter for the Track EQ plug-in.

6. Click the Band2 Gain, Band3 Gain, and Band4 Gain check boxes.

7. Click OK to exit the dialog box.

An envelope is created for each plug-in parameter you selected.

8. Right-click the audio track; then hold your cursor over FX Automation Envelopes.

A separate listing for each FX Automation envelope appears, as shown in Figure 6-11. You can display or hide tracks by choosing the applicable titles. When you're initially setting up an Automation FX plug-in parameter, it's easier to work with individual envelopes. After you modify each individual Automation FX envelope for the track, you can view every envelope by right-clicking the Audio track and then choosing FX Automation Envelopes > Show All Envelopes.

9. Choose Track Compressor: Output Gain.

   A single envelope line appears in the middle of the track. You can now add points to the envelope where you want to increase or decrease output gain for the Track Compressor plug-in. To add a point, move your cursor over the envelope at the position where you want to add a point. Right-click, and then choose Add Point from the shortcut menu. This procedure is identical to adding points to a video envelope.

10. Right-click the audio track in the track list; then choose FX Automation Envelopes > Band 3 Gain.

    The envelope for the Band 3 Gain parameter of the Track EQ plug-in is displayed.

11. Preview the project; then add points where needed.

12. Drag each point to adjust the Band 3 gain to suit your project audio.

    You repeat this procedure for each plug-in parameter until the audio track plays as desired. Figure 6-12 shows an audio track to which three FX Automation envelopes have been applied. You can fine-tune any audio track through the use of FX Automation envelopes. As mentioned previously, you cannot use FX Automation envelopes with all FX plug-ins.

Work with audio event switches

1. Create a new project; then import a video clip with embedded audio into the Project Media window.

FIGURE 6-12
Audio track with multiple FX Automation envelopes

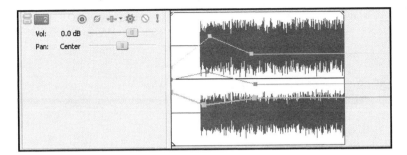

FIGURE 6-13
Audio Event shortcut menu

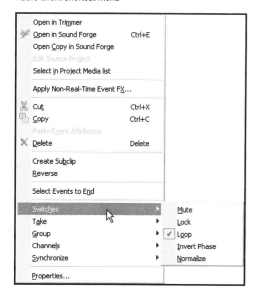

Open in Trimmer	
Open in Sound Forge	Ctrl+E
Open Copy in Sound Forge	
Edit Source Project	
Select in Project Media list	
Apply Non-Real-Time Event FX...	
Cut	Ctrl+X
Copy	Ctrl+C
Paste Event Attributes	
Delete	Delete
Create Subclip	
Reverse	
Select Events to End	
Switches ▶	Mute
Take ▶	Lock
Group ▶	✓ Loop
Channels ▶	Invert Phase
Synchronize ▶	Normalize
Properties...	

2. Drop the clip in the main window, aligning the clip with the beginning of the timeline.

3. Right-click the audio event; then hold your cursor over the Switches option.

   The Audio Event Switches menu appears, as shown in Figure 6-13. You can apply one or more of the following switches to any audio event in a project:

   - Mute. Use this switch to mute the event.

   - Lock. Use this switch to lock an event and prevent it from being edited or moved. Note that if the audio event is part of a video event, you can still move the video event when the audio event is locked.

   - Loop. This switch is selected by default. If you extend the duration of the event, the audio track loops. When a track loops, notches appear in the event to signify the point at which the track again plays from the beginning.

   - Invert Phase. This switch inverts the audio event, which in essence reverses its polarity. The results of this switch are not discernible to the ear, but can be useful when you need to match transitions when mixing audio on different tracks.

   - Normalize. Use this switch to normalize an audio event to maximum volume, without clipping the audio event during playback.

QUICKTIP

Right-click an audio track in the track list, and hold your cursor over the Switches listing to reveal the switches that are available for an audio track. Your choices are Mute, Solo, or Invert Phase. Alternatively, you can click the Mute, Solo, or Invert Phase icons at the top of the audio track. You would then select the applicable switch, for example Mute would cause the audio track to not play.

4. Select the desired audio event switch.

   If desired, you can assign multiple switches to an audio event. To learn the effect that each switch has on the audio event, I suggest you select one audio event, and then preview the project. After you preview the project, deselect the switch you just previewed, and select another.

5. Preview the project.

QUICKTIP

You can separate an audio event from the video event to which it is linked by right-clicking the audio event and choosing Group > Clear. After you clear a group, you can delete an audio event, while leaving the video event intact on the timeline. You can also move audio and video events independently of each other.

EDIT AUDIO
EVENTS

What You'll Do

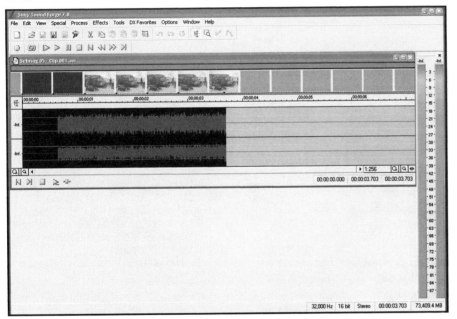

In this lesson, you learn to edit audio events and apply effects to them.

Working with Non-Real-Time Audio Event FX

Vegas provides you with some powerful tools for manipulating audio events in a project. You can use automatable FX on audio tracks, and switches on audio tracks and events, as described in the previous lesson. You can also manipulate audio events by applying a Non-Real-Time Event FX. When you apply a Non-Real-Time Event FX plug-in, you select one of the presets, or adjust the parameters based on your knowledge of the plug-in. As always, you can summon a Help dialog box for the plug-in to guide you as to what you can expect when modifying the parameters. After you apply the parameters, Vegas applies the plug-in to the event and creates a file that appears on the timeline as a take. You can create multiple takes using different plug-ins or, by using different parameters on the plug-in, you can choose to correct a deficiency in the audio event, or to apply a special effect to the event.

After you preview each take, you determine whether the take or the original file is used during the final render.

Experimenting with Non-Real-Time Audio Event FX

Vegas provides you with a plethora of Non-Real-Time Event FX from which to choose.

As with any other tool, familiarity comes with repeated use and experimentation. This lesson is by no means designed to be the authoritative reference on Non-Real Time Event FX because there are too many from which to choose. This lesson will, however, give you a solid foundation on which to build your knowledge. You learn to apply Non-Real-Time Event FX to audio events, and work with audio takes.

Another powerful feature of Vegas is its capability to edit an audio event in an audio editing application. If you own Sony Sound Forge, this is the default audio editor. You can, however, choose a different audio editor by changing audio preferences.

Apply Non-Real-Time FX to a video event

1. Create a new project; then import a video clip with embedded audio into the Project Media window.

2. Drop the video clip in the main window, aligning the clip to the beginning of the timeline.

3. Right-click the audio event; then choose Apply Non-Real-Time Event FX.

   The Plug-In Chooser-Take dialog box appears.

4. Click the Sony folder.

   The Plug-In Chooser-Take dialog box reconfigures to display Sony audio plug-ins, as shown in Figure 6-14.

5. Select the Smooth/Enhance plug-in; then click Add.

   The Smooth/Enhance plug-in is added to the plug-in chain. You can add as many plug-ins as needed to the event plug-in chain. Remember: You can also rearrange the order in which the plug-ins execute by clicking a plug-in button and then dragging it to the desired position in the plug-in chain.

6. Click OK.

   The Smooth/Enhance plug-in parameters appear in the Take dialog box, shown in Figure 6-15. Note that the name of the original clip appears in the title of the dialog box.

FIGURE 6-14
Sony Audio plug-ins

FIGURE 6-15
Smooth/Enhance plug-in parameters

FIGURE 6-16
Apply Non-Real-Time Event FX dialog box

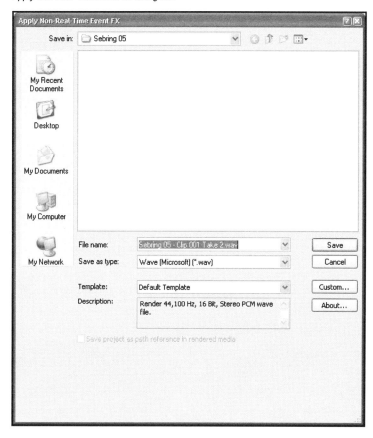

7. Click the Preset down arrow; then choose Boost High Frequencies.

   The dialog box reconfigures to the preset parameters. You can also manually adjust the parameters. Notice the Play button in the upper-right corner of the dialog box. You can use this to play the event and adjust the parameters. You will not, however, be able to view the associated video event in real time.

8. Click the Play button to preview the audio event with the plug-in applied.

   Vegas loops the audio for the event, enabling you to change the parameters until the audio is as desired.

   > **NOTE**
   >
   > Click the Loop button to the left of the Play button in the Takes dialog box to disable looping.

9. Drag the Operation slider left and right until the audio event plays as desired.

10. When plug-in parameters are adjusted as desired, click the Stop button to cease playing the audio event.

11. Click OK.

    The Apply Non-Real-Time Event FX dialog box, shown in Figure 6-16, appears.

12. Accept the default name for the track, or enter a different name.

    You can also change the format in which the sound file is saved. After you choose a file format, you can click Template down arrow and choose a preset template, or you can click Custom to open the Custom Template dialog box and modify the parameters to suit your project.

13. Click Save.

Vegas saves the take and adds it to the track. The saved take is the active take.

14. Double-click the event.

Vegas creates a time selection.

15. Press the spacebar to play the time selection.

Vegas plays the take you just saved. Listen to the take a few times.

16. Right-click the event. Choose Take from the shortcut menu, and then choose the original take from the flyout menu.

The original sound plays. You can press T to switch back and forth between takes on-the-fly. Alternatively, you can right-click and choose Take > Choose Active to open the Take Chooser dialog box, shown in Figure 6-17. You can then select a take, and preview it by clicking the Play button. Alternatively, you can select a take by clicking its name from the Take flyout menu.

17. After you preview the takes, right-click the event; then choose Take > Delete.

The Delete Takes dialog box appears.

18. Select the take you want to delete; then click OK.

> **QUICKTIP**
>
> You can add a Gain envelope to an audio event by moving your cursor toward the top of an audio event on the timeline. When your cursor icon becomes a pointing finger, click and drag down to reduce the gain of the event. As you drag, a tooltip displays the current gain of the event. Note that you cannot add points to a gain envelope.

FIGURE 6-17

Take Chooser

NOTE

If the Gain envelope is not available when you position your cursor at the top of the track, you may have to temporarily hide other envelopes you've applied to the event.

Editing an Audio Event in Sony Sound Forge

If you own a copy of Sony Sound Forge, you can edit an audio event in the application by right-clicking the event and then choosing Edit in Sound Forge from the shortcut menu. Sony Sound Forge has more sophisticated menu commands, and additional parameters you can use to fine-tune an audio event.

If you choose Open Copy in Sound Forge, your original audio event will be unaffected. When you save the edited audio event, it will be saved as a take.

If you do not own Sony Sound Forge, or you want to switch to a different audio-editing application, choose Options > Preferences. Within the Preferences dialog box, click the Audio tab. In the Preferred Audio Editor section, click the Browse button, and navigate to the directory that contains the EXE (executable) file that launches your preferred audio editing application.

RECORD
VOICE-OVERS

What You'll Do

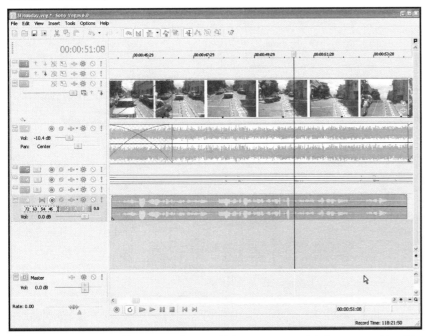

In this lesson, you'll record a voice-over. Voice-overs are useful when you need to add narration to a project, or replace less than perfect audio.

Adding Narration to a Project

Working on a video project that requires narration is easy in Vegas. You can create a simple voice-over narration, or if you have more sophisticated equipment hooked to your sound card, you can use an audio mixer to mix voice and music. If you have Microsoft Audio Mapper selected as your preferred audio device, you can specify whether a track you record is stereo, or recorded for the left or right channel.

Recording into a Time Selection

You can also record into a time selection. For example, if you've recorded a spontaneous interview using the microphone on your camcorder, your voice might be distorted, and considerably louder than the person you are interviewing. To compensate for this, you can create a time selection for the part of the audio track where your voice is heard. You can then record the exact words on another audio track. If the new recording is acceptable, you can split the original audio clip to segregate the faulty audio as an event, delete the faulty audio event, and replace it with your new recording.

Arming a Track for Recording

Before you can record, you must arm an audio track for recording. When you arm a track for recording, you specify the folder in which the recorded file will be saved. Then a level meter appears in the track that you use to monitor the volume of the recording. You can record into a new track, into an audio event, or into a time selection. After you arm a track for recording, you specify whether the recording will be full stereo, or mono record (single channel used).

Record a voice-over

1. Create a new project; then import several video clips with embedded audio into the Project Media window.

2. Drop the clips into the main window, aligning them with the beginning of the timeline.

3. Choose Insert > Audio Track. Alternatively, you can press Ctrl+Q.

4. Click the Arm for Record button, shown in Figure 6-18.

   The first time you arm a track for recording in a project, the Project Recorded Files Folder dialog box appears. This dialog box enables you to specify the folder into which the recorded sound file will be saved. You can accept the default folder (My Documents on Windows XP), or click the Browse button to specify a different folder into which the sound file will be saved.

5. Accept the default folder, or specify a different folder; then click OK to exit the Project Recorded Files Folder dialog box.

   A level meter appears in the track list. Depending on the hardware you use to record sound, a Volume slider might appear as well.

FIGURE 6-18
Recording into a track

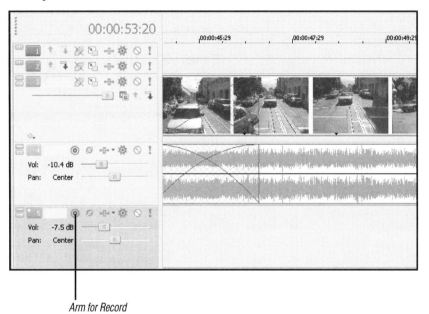

Arm for Record

FIGURE 6-19

Microsoft Sound Mapper button

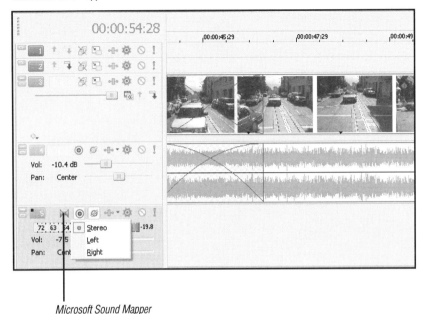

Microsoft Sound Mapper

6. Click the Microsoft Sound Mapper button, shown in Figure 6-19.

   A drop-down menu appears, giving you the option of recording in stereo (the default), or mono record (single channel used).

7. Accept the default recording method (Stereo), or choose Left or Right.

   QUICKTIP

   You can choose Options > Metronome to play a metronome while recording the track. This option is useful if you are using a MIDI device such as a keyboard attached to your computer to record into the track. Don't use the metronome while recording with a microphone; the metronome sound from your speakers will be recorded, as well as your voice.

8. Position your microphone in the optimum location for recording.

   QUICKTIP

   A headset with a high-quality microphone is ideal for recording because it enables hands-free recording. Many headset/microphone combinations are USB devices with built-in digital signal processing to cancel out background noise, enabling you to create a high-quality recording.

9. Choose View > Video Preview.

   Previewing the video while recording allows you to synchronize your narration with the video.

10. Position your cursor at the beginning of the timeline; then click the Record button on the Transport bar.

Vegas begins playing the project.

11. Begin your narration.

12. Press the spacebar to finish your recording, or click the Stop button.

The Recorded Files dialog box, shown in Figure 6-20, appears.

13. Accept the default name for the recorded file, delete the recorded file, or click the Rename button to specify a different name for the recorded file. If desired, you can also delete the file and re-record your narration.

14. Click Done to save the recorded file to disk and return to Track view.

QUICKTIP

You can record as many takes as needed. To record additional takes, move your cursor to the start of the timeline, click the Mute button on the track into which you're recording, and then record another take. After saving several tracks, click the Mute button again to enable audio. You can then preview each track using previously discussed techniques and then decide which track you will use for the final project render.

Record into an event

1. Create a new project; then import multiple video clips with embedded audio into the Project Media window. If you have any video clips with less than perfect audio that you want to replace, these are ideal.

FIGURE 6-20

The Recorded Files dialog box

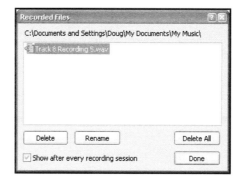

2. Drop the clips into the main window, aligning them to the beginning of the timeline.

3. Preview the project to determine which event contains audio that you want to replace.

4. Double-click the desired audio event.

   Vegas creates a time selection, as shown in Figure 6-21. When you record into a time selection, you create a new take for the audio event. You can create multiple takes for an audio event, and then preview each event to determine which one is best suited to your project.

FIGURE 6-21
Recording into an event

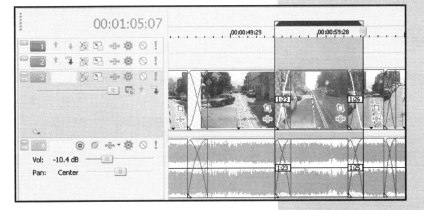

QUICKTIP

You can manually create a region of specific duration and record a voice-over for that region.

You can create punch-in and punch-out leaders for the event by dragging the begin time selection marker to the left, and the end time selection marker to the right. When you add a punch-in and punch-out point, the take you record is longer than the event. The punch-in point gives you additional time to prepare for recording. After you record the take, you can trim it to fit the event by dragging the head of the event (the **punch-in point**) to the beginning of the event, and dragging the tail of the event (the **punch-out point**) to the end of the event.

5. Click the track's Arm for Record button.

6. Click the Record button on the Transport bar.

   Vegas begins playing the region from the cursor forward.

7. Press the spacebar to stop recording.

QUICKTIP

If you refrain from pressing the spacebar when the timeline reaches the end of the region, you can record multiple takes. If you increase the duration of the region to include a punch-in and punch-out point, you'll be able to synchronize each take with the beginning of the region.

WORK WITH
AUDIO BUSSES

What You'll Do

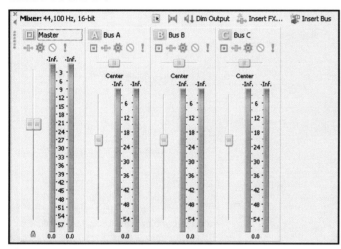

In this lesson, you learn how to add audio busses to your project. Adding audio busses enables you to control multiple audio tracks.

Using Busses with Multiple Audio Tracks

When you have a project that has multiple audio tracks, you can control the volume and pan of each track by using the Master Track control in the Window Docking area, by using the volume control in the Master track, or by inserting a volume or pan envelope on each track. However, when you have multiple tracks, setting the controls for each track is time-consuming. You can simplify this task through the use of audio busses. You can route several tracks into a bus and then use the bus sliders to control the output of the bus. For example, if you have three tracks for video events that contain audio, and two tracks for musical soundtracks,

you can route the video event audio tracks volume to one bus and the soundtrack audio tracks volume to another bus. If you decide to add an effect such as reverb, you can create a separate bus and apply the effect to the bus and then assign the bus to one or more audio tracks. You can then adjust the volume of each bus to determine the sound mix, and then adjust the Master volume to determine the output for the mixed soundtracks.

Using Audio Busses on Simple Projects

Audio busses are desirable even when you have a simple project with only two audio tracks. Because each audio bus has a level meter, you can ensure that the volume for each audio track is not clipped. Without audio busses, you have to solo each audio event to determine whether the audio is being clipped, and then preview the entire project to adjust the Master volume, which means auditioning the project three times.

If you're creating a project that is longer than a minute, auditioning each track is a time-consuming process. Previewing the entire project while adjusting the bus Level sliders is a more efficient method of working. As soon as you notice that a track is being clipped, you can adjust the slider to lower the output.

You can also use busses to route audio tracks to external hardware such as an external processor or an external mixer. The setup varies depending on your system and components. When you route busses to external hardware, they are not included in the mix when you render the project to a single video file.

In this lesson, you focus on creating busses to control multiple tracks. You don't always work with multiple tracks in a project, but when you do, audio busses help simplify mixing. You can have up to 26 individual busses in a project.

Set up a project with multiple busses

1. Create a new project.

2. Import several video clips with embedded audio into the Project Media window.

3. Import two audio files into the Project Media window.

   If you don't have audio files saved on your system, insert a music CD into your CD drive, and click the Extract Audio from CD button in the Project Media window to extract two files from the music CD.

4. Drop three video clips in the main window, aligning them to the beginning of the timeline.

5. Drop the remaining clips in the main window, inserting them below the existing tracks and aligning them to the end of the clips in the previous tracks.

6. Create two audio tracks for the music you imported or extracted from your CD drive.

7. Add one audio clip to the audio tracks you just created.

8. Trim and overlap the audio clips.

   You'll use volume envelopes to fade one track into the other. Your timeline should resemble Figure 6-22. Notice that each track has been named.

QUICKTIP

Double-click the default track name to reveal a text box. Then type the desired track name.

FIGURE 6-22

Setting up a multiple bus project

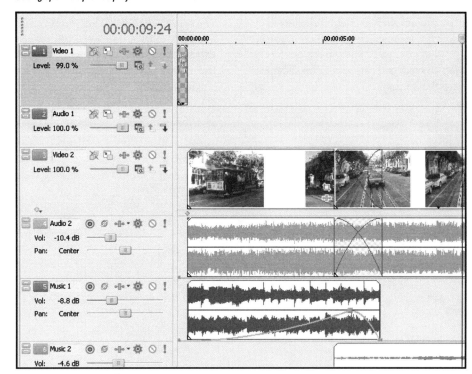

Working with Sound   Chapter 6

FIGURE 6-23

Inserting audio busses

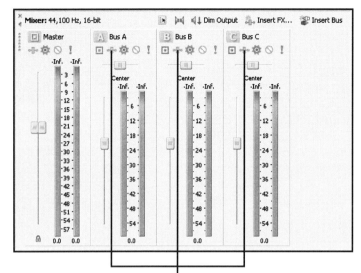

Insert Bus FX button

8. Keep the project open. You'll be using it in the next objective.

Add Audio Busses

1. If the Mixer window is not currently displayed in the workspace, choose View > Mixer. Alternatively, you can press Alt+3.

2. Click the Insert Bus button in the Mixer window three times.

   Vegas adds three busses to the project. Each bus has a button to insert bus FX as shown in Figure 6-23. Note the level controls for mixing the busses. Also note that each bus has been named. Naming busses helps you ascertain what each bus does. This is especially important when you're dealing with several busses. For the purpose of this figure, the Mixer window has been floated in the workspace.

   ### QUICKTIP

   When you're mixing a project with multiple busses, it's convenient to float the Mixer window in the workspace so that you can view each bus and the mixer controls.

3. Right-click the first audio track in the Track List window; then choose Insert/Remove Envelope > Bus A.

4. Right-click the first audio track in the Track List window; then choose Insert/Remove Envelope > Volume from the shortcut menu, shown in Figure 6-24.

   The previous two steps created a volume envelope and assigned it to Bus A.

5. Repeat steps 3 and 4 for the second audio track in the List window.

6. Right-click the first music soundtrack audio track (if you've set up your project as outlined in the previous objective, this will be track 5) in the track list; then choose Insert/Remove Envelope > Bus B from the shortcut menu.

7. Right-click the first music soundtrack audio track in the track list; then from the shortcut menu, choose Insert/Remove Envelope > Volume.

   The previous two steps created a volume envelope for the soundtrack and assigned it to Bus B.

8. Repeat steps 6 and 7 to assign a volume envelope to Bus B for the remaining music soundtrack audio track in the project.

9. In the Mixer window, click the Bus FX button in Bus C.

   NOTE

   Your available plug-ins might differ depending on which Sony applications you have installed on your machine. If you don't have the Reverb plug-in, delete Bus C from the project and skip steps 9–15.

FIGURE 6-24
Assigning volume to a bus

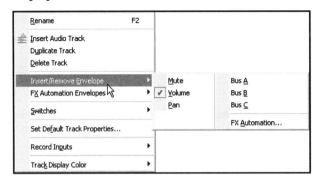

FIGURE 6-25

Audio Plug-In dialog box

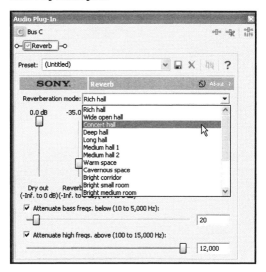

FIGURE 6-26

Assigning an audio bus to a track

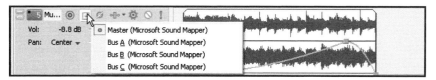

The Plug-In Chooser Bus C dialog box opens.

10. Select the Reverb plug-in from the Sony folder; then click Add.

11. Click OK to exit the Plug-In Chooser dialog box.

The Audio Plug-In dialog box appears.

12. Choose Concert Hall from the Preset field's drop-down list, shown in Figure 6-25.

You can choose any preset to suit your project. You can also modify the preset by changing its parameters.

13. Close the Audio Plug-In dialog box.

The Reverb plug-in is assigned to Bus C. Note that you can assign any plug-in to a bus track and then assign the bus track to the audio tracks you want it to control, as outlined in the next step. For that matter, you can add multiple plug-ins to a bus and adjust the plug-in parameters as desired to control the sound of individual tracks in your project.

14. Click the Master button for the first music soundtrack audio track; then choose Bus C from the drop-down list, shown in Figure 6-26.

This assigns the plug-in from Bus C to the audio track. You've already assigned the track volume to Bus B. When you mix the project in the next lesson, you determine how much each bus affects the project soundtrack.

15. Repeat step 14 for the last music soundtrack audio track.

16. Preview the project.

QUICKTIP

Double-click the default audio bus name in the Mixer window to display a text box. Type a unique name, such as **Audio Trax**, to reflect what the bus does. Note that you'll have to enter a short name; otherwise, the name will be truncated in the Mixer window.

The meters for each track are moving in synch with each track's sound. The overall mix, however, is probably far from desired. In the next lesson, you learn to mix the tracks in this project.

17. Keep the project open. You'll be using it in the next lesson. Save the project as **Chapter6_mixAudio** if you're not going to read the next lesson right away.

MIX AUDIO AND
BUS TRACKS

What You'll Do

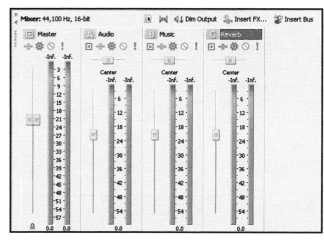

In this lesson, you learn to mix audio tracks and busses.

Mixing a Project

After you create a project with multiple soundtracks or busses, your next step is to mix the tracks to create a pleasing soundtrack that is not clipped. If you create a project with only one audio track and one music soundtrack, you can easily mix the tracks by using the track volume controller, as outlined previously. After you mix each track, you adjust the Master Volume in the Mixer window, as outlined in this lesson. Adjusting the volume of each track is fairly straightforward. The emphasis of this lesson is mixing a project with multiple audio tracks and multiple audio busses.

Mixing a Project with Audio Busses

You mix a project with multiple tracks and busses by adjusting the various level sliders in each bus track in the Mixer window. If you've applied volume envelopes to overlapping tracks in a project, as you did in the previous lesson, you'll add points to the tracks and adjust the volume to fade one track into the next.

Mix a track

1. Preview the project.

   As you preview the project, pay careful attention to the level meters in the master track and each bus track. You might notice that some of the tracks bounce into the yellow or red, as shown in Figure 6-27. When this happens, the audio is distorted, or as sound engineers refer to it, clipped.

2. Right-click the Volume envelope and choose Add Point from the shortcut menu to add points to the end of the first music soundtrack event and the beginning of the second music soundtrack event. The points should be in approximately the same position, where the two tracks overlap. Adjust the points so that the first music soundtrack audio track fades to infinity, while the second music soundtrack audio event fades from infinity to 0.0 dB, as shown in Figure 6-28. The timeline has been magnified in this figure to better illustrate the points.

3. Preview the project again while adjusting the volume of Bus A.

   Audio mixing is largely subjective. The volume of each track determines the emphasis of each track in the project. The role that the audio track plays in each project depends on the type of project you're creating. If the audio track is background chatter or the sounds of nature, reduce the volume so that the music soundtrack has emphasis.

4. While the project is playing, adjust the volume of Bus B by adjusting the sliders in the Mixer window.

FIGURE 6-27

Previewing the mix

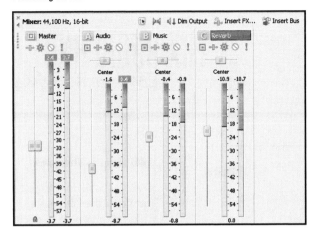

FIGURE 6-28

Modifying the volume envelopes

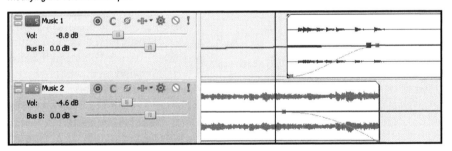

The volume of this project bus determines how much weight the music soundtrack carries in the project. As you adjust the volume, notice the effect the bus has on the overall mix, as well as the effect on the Master level meters.

QUICKTIP

Create a region for the entire project, and click the Loop Playback button in the transport bar. This enables you to preview the project repeatedly while fine-tuning the levels of each Bus slider and the Master slider.

Click the Unlock Fader Channels button at the bottom of a Bus track or the Master track to control the volume of each channel independently.

5. Adjust the volume of Bus C.

The volume of this project bus determines how much audio reverb is applied to the music soundtrack. Adding plug-ins to a bus track is an excellent way to fine-tune a soundtrack to suit a project.

6. Adjust the volume of the Master slider.

After you mix the other tracks in your project, the Master track might be too loud or too soft. Adjust the level sliders so that the sound does not peak repeatedly into the yellow or red levels. If your audio peaks repeatedly into these levels, the audio will be clipped, which makes it sound muffled and distorted, regardless of how much the viewer lowers the volume on the device on which the video is played back. Figure 6-29 shows the Mixer window after adjusting the volume of project busses and the Master track volume. Adjusting each track separately is a time-consuming task for a lengthy project to which you've applied several busses. With experience, you can adjust the mix in one preview by changing each Bus slider when you notice that clipping occurs.

FIGURE 6-29
Mixing the tracks

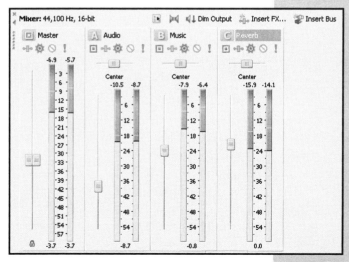

SKILLS REVIEW

Applying an Automatable FX Preset

1. Create a new project.

2. Import two video clips with embedded audio into the Project Media window.

3. Drop the clips into the main window, aligning them to the beginning of the timeline.

4. Preview the project to audition the audio.

5. Click the audio track, Track FX button in the Track List window to display the Audio Plug-In dialog box, shown in Figure 6-30.

6. Click the Track EQ button.

7. Choose the Hiss Cut preset, as shown in Figure 6-31; then click the Close button.

8. Preview the project.

9. Keep the project open for the next skills review.

FIGURE 6-30
Modifying the Track EQ

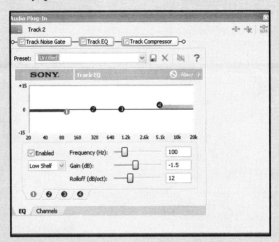

FIGURE 6-31
Using the Hiss Cut preset

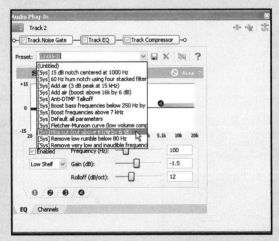

Adding an FX Plug-In to the Plug-in Chain

1. Click the Audio Track FX button in the Track List window.
2. Click the Plug-In Chain button in the Audio Plug-In dialog box to open the Plug-In Chooser dialog box.
3. Select Reverb from the Sony folder; then click the Add button.
4. Click OK to exit the Plug-In Chooser dialog box and add the plug-in to the chain.
5. Click the Preset down arrow; then choose Long Hall, as shown in Figure 6-32.
6. Close the Audio Plug-In dialog box.
7. Preview the project.
8. Keep the project open for the next skills review.

Recording a Voice-Over

1. Create a new audio track.
2. Click the Arm for Record button.
3. Specify the folder in which to save the voice-over track, as shown in Figure 6-33; then click OK.

FIGURE 6-32
Reverb FX Long Hall plug-in

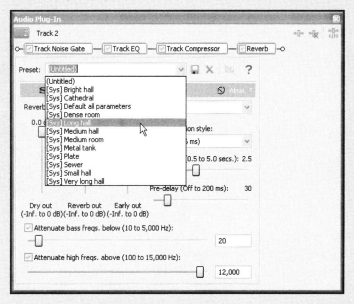

FIGURE 6-33
Specifying the folder for the voice-over recording

4. Prepare your microphone for recording.

5. Click the Record button in the Transport bar.

6. Record the voice-over, as shown in Figure 6-34.

7. Preview the project.

8. Keep the project open. You'll be using it in the next skills review.

Adding a Music Track and Audio Busses

1. Delete the voice-over track.

2. Import a music file into the Project Media window.

3. Create an audio track for the music file; then drop the music file into the track, aligning it with the beginning of the project timeline, as shown in Figure 6-35.

FIGURE 6-34
Recording a voice-over

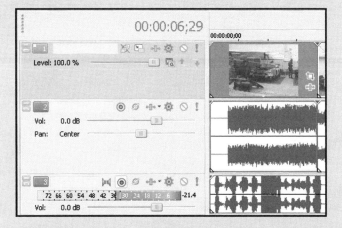

FIGURE 6-35
Adding a soundtrack to a project

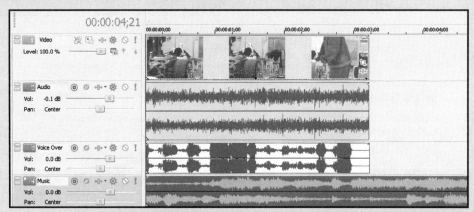

4. Trim the music soundtrack to fit the project.

5. Add a volume envelope to the music soundtrack audio track; then add points to the envelope to fade the soundtrack at the end of the project.

6. Create an audio bus to independently control the volume of each audio event.

7. Create a third audio bus.

8. Assign the Reverb plug-in to the third audio bus.

9. Choose the desired Reverb preset.

10. Assign the third audio bus to the music soundtrack.

11. Preview the project.

12. Mix the busses as desired, being careful not to clip the audio on any bus, as shown in Figure 6-36.

13. Adjust the Master volume.

14. Preview the project.

FIGURE 6-36

Mixing project audio with busses

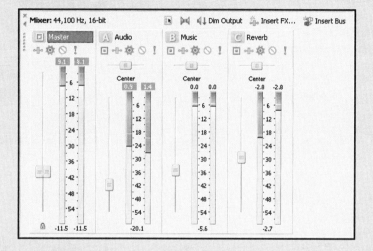

PROJECT BUILDER 1

You work in the production department for a major television station. Your ace reporter recorded a report in the field, but the audio was garbled because of ambient wind. Your production supervisor has given you the assignment of replacing the audio. You preview the video clip and transcribe the reporter's words. Fortunately, the reporter was far enough from the camera so as not to cause a problem with lip-synching the voice-over to the video. After you prepare a script, the reporter shows up to record the voice-over.

1. Create a new project.

2. Import a video clip with embedded audio into the Project Media window.

3. Drop the clip in the main window, aligning it to the beginning of the timeline.

4. Double-click the audio event to create a region.

5. Arm the track for recording.

6. Record a voice-over.

7. Record a second take.

8. Preview the takes.

9. Delete the undesirable take, as shown in Figure 6-37.

   Your timeline should resemble Figure 6-38.

FIGURE 6-37
Project Builder 1 sample 1

FIGURE 6-38
Project Builder 1 sample 2

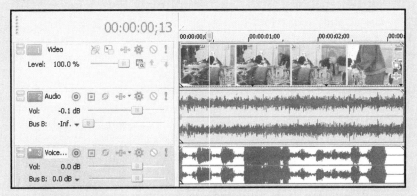

PROJECT BUILDER 2

You work for the production department of a company that creates DVDs. Your client is a baroque ensemble. Your production manager has presented you with video of the ensemble that was recorded at an outdoor concert at a medieval festival. The concert footage is wonderful, but the audio is lacking. You decide to augment the audio by adding some reverb.

1. Create a new project.

2. Import a video clip with embedded audio. If possible, import a video clip of a musical performance. If you don't have a video clip of a musical performance, delete the audio track for the video, create a new audio track, and add a music file to the audio track. Trim the music file to fit the video clip.

3. Create an audio bus to control the volume of the track.

4. Create a second audio bus.

5. Assign the Reverb plug-in to the second audio bus, as shown in Figure 6-39.

6. Assign the second audio bus to the audio track.

7. Preview the project.

8. Mix the tracks.

   Your Mixer window should resemble Figure 6-40.

FIGURE 6-39

Project Builder 2 Sample 1

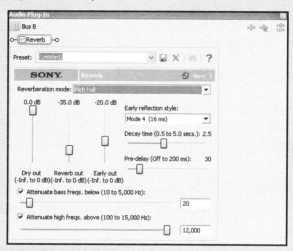

FIGURE 6-40

Project Builder 2 sample2

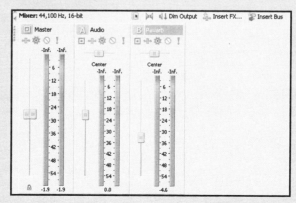

DESIGN PROJECT

Design Project

You work in the production department of a company that creates educational DVDs. You're in charge of a project to create video for a DVD that features the history of New England. You're editing footage shot on a quiet day in Salem, Massachusetts. Other than the occasional faint murmur of distant traffic, the audio consists of people talking and birds chirping. You hire a local actor with an English accent to record a voice-over for the piece, which you'll augment with a classical music soundtrack.

1. Create a new project.

2. Import video clips with embedded audio into the Project Media window. If possible, import clips of scenery with background audio that contains the sounds of nature.

3. Drop the first media clip into the main window; then align it to the beginning of the timeline.

4. Arrange the other clips on the timeline as desired.

5. Create a new audio track.

6. Arm the new audio track for recording.

7. Record a voice-over.

8. Create a new audio track.

9. Import a music file into the Project Media window; then add it to the new audio track, aligning it to the beginning of the timeline, as shown in Figure 6-41.

10. Trim the music audio event to the project duration.

11. Create three audio busses to control the volume of each track.

12. Add points to the end of each bus envelope to fade each track to –inf dB at the end of the project.

13. Mix the busses as desired, giving emphasis to the voice-over. Make sure you don't clip any tracks while setting the bus level.

14. Set the Main volume for the project.

Your Mixer window for the project should resemble Figure 6-41. Notice that each bus is labeled to signify which track it controls.

FIGURE 6-41
Design Project sample 1

FIGURE 6-42
Design Project sample 2

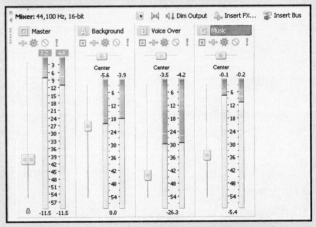

CHAPTER SUMMARY

This chapter covers the sophisticated Vegas features you use to control audio in your project. Busses are used to control audio tracks. You can assign up to 26 busses to a project. You can also assign plug-ins to busses. You use project busses to mix the sounds and then use the Master controller to determine the sound level of the rendered project.

What You Have Learned

In this chapter, you:

- Used Audio Track FX to modify audio tracks.
- Edited audio events through the use of audio plug-ins.
- Recorded voice-overs for project narration.
- Added audio busses to your projects.
- Mixed audio in the Mixer window.

Key Terms from This Chapter

- **Mixer window.** A device in the Window Docking area that is used to mix project audio.
- **Punch-in point.** A point on the timeline where you begin recording.
- **Punch-out point.** A point on the timeline where you stop recording.
- **Track Compressor.** A plug-in used to limit the dynamic range of an audio track.
- **Track EQ.** A plug-in used to equalize an audio track.
- **Track Noise Gate.** A plug-in that is used to correct deficiencies in audio tracks such as background noise and hiss.

chapter

7

CREATING GENERATED
Media

1. Use the color picker.

2. Create a scrolling text credit.

3. Create a timed sequence credit.

4. Use checkerboard and gradient backgrounds.

5. Create text overlays.

6. Animate generated media.

7. Create custom titles, credits, and other media.

chapter 7 CREATING GENERATED Media

In addition to being one of the best video-editing applications on the planet, Vegas enables you to create compelling media. Nothing adds more polish to a product than an impressive title to introduce your production to your audience. And, of course, you want to give credit where credit is due at the end of your production by adding ending credits.

You use generated media to create titles, ending credits, and eye candy, such as backgrounds and gradients. When you add generated media to a project, you can begin with a Vegas preset, and then modify it to suit your project. If you don't like some of the preset parameters, such as font size, color, and so on, you can change them to suit your project. And if you like what you create, you can save the modified preset for future use.

The tools you need to create **generated media** reside in the Media Generators window of the Window Docking area. The Media Generators window is similar to the Transitions window in that you'll find several classes of generated media from which to choose. When you choose a group, you see a thumbnail of each

preset. To add a preset to your project, you drop it at the desired point on the timeline of the desired track. This opens the dialog box for the preset, which contains several parameters that you can modify to tailor the preset to your project.

The parameters you can modify vary depending on the type of preset with which you're working. Many of the media contain so many parameters that they're divided into tabs. For example, when you add text to a project, you have one tab to edit the text, one tab to determine where the text is placed, one tab for text properties, and one tab for effects. In contrast, when you add media such as a background or color gradient to a project, all the parameters are within a single dialog box with no tabs.

As mentioned previously, when you work with generated media, you modify parameters to determine how the media looks in your project. One of the parameters you work with is color. You specify the color for text, backgrounds, gradients, and more. You choose color using the **color picker**. You can manually enter values to match a known color, drag a slider to determine the value of each component, or drag inside a color well to choose the desired color. You can also modify the alpha value (opacity) for a color that you mix.

One way that you can add viewer interest to a project is by animating media. When you add media to a project, it is displayed for a preset duration. You can modify the duration to suit your needs. Each media has a timeline to which you can add keyframes. You can change the parameters at each keyframe to make the media change over time. Vegas blends the in-between frames to create a transition from one keyframe to the next. For example, if you want the color of a background to change from red to green as the video plays back, you can do so easily by adding keyframes at the desired points within the Media dialog box, selecting the keyframe, and then changing the color. You can also determine the manner in which the transition between keyframes occurs.

Tools You'll Use

USE THE COLOR PICKER

What You'll Do

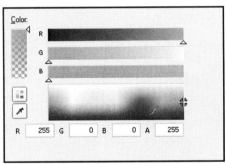

In this lesson, you learn how to use the color picker, shown in Figure 7-1, to specify colors for the media you generate. You learn to match a color to known values, as well as mix a color from the color well.

Selecting a Color

When you add color to a background or select color for media, such as a title or gradient, you have different methods for selecting the desired color. If you know the values of the color, you can type them in text fields. Color for video is a mixture of red, green, and blue hues. Each hue is composed of 256 values which, when combined, are capable of generating the millions of colors that are visible to the human eye. Modern computer monitors with a display bit-depth of 24 or 32 bits are capable of displaying millions of colors as well.

Working with a Color Model

When you specify colors for generated media, or text objects, you specify a mixture of red, green, and blue as discussed previously. The **RGB color model** is the color model for video. This color model is also used for specifying colors for Web sites. When specifying color using the color picker, you can use the default RGB color model, or you can switch to the HSL **color model**.

FIGURE 7-1

Color picker

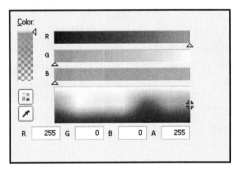

FIGURE 7-2

Media Generators window

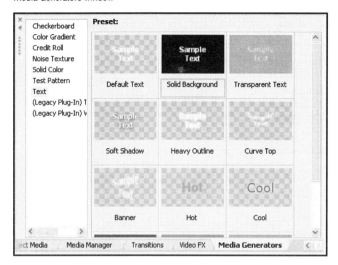

FIGURE 7-3

Solid Color presets

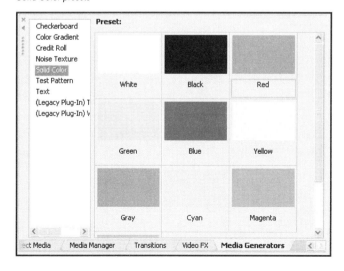

1. Create a new project.
2. Click the Media Generators window.

   Vegas displays the categories of generated media, as shown in Figure 7-2.
3. Click the Solid Color title on the left side of the tab.

   Vegas displays the Solid Color presets, shown in Figure 7-3.

Lesson 1   Use the Color Picker

4. Select the Black preset; then drop it into the main window, aligning it with the beginning of the timeline.

Vegas displays the Video Event FX dialog box, shown in Figure 7-4.

> **NOTE**
>
> The size of the color picker varies, depending on the dialog box in which the color picker resides.

5. Drag your cursor inside the color well.

As you drag your cursor, the color sample updates in real time. You might notice an information icon and a small color swatch to the left of the color well, as shown in Figure 7-5. This indicates that you have selected a color that is out of gamut for **NTSC** (National Television System Committee) and **PAL** (Phase Alternating Line) television devices. When a color is out of gamut, it does not display properly on the associated device; for example, an NTSC television set. Click the color swatch to snap the color to an NTSC and PAL safe color.

> **NOTE**
>
> This is also a warning icon when the color you select is out of gamut for PAL video. This warning icon is the same shape as the icon in Figure 7-5, but it contains a capital P.

6. Release your cursor to select the desired color.

FIGURE 7-4
Video Event FX dialog box

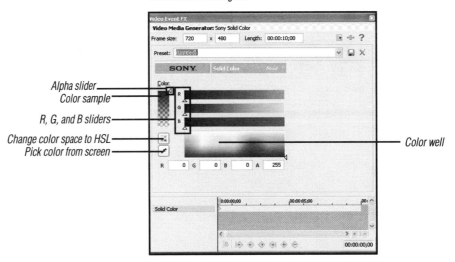

Alpha slider
Color sample
R, G, and B sliders
Change color space to HSL
Pick color from screen

Color well

FIGURE 7-5
Out of Gamut warning icon

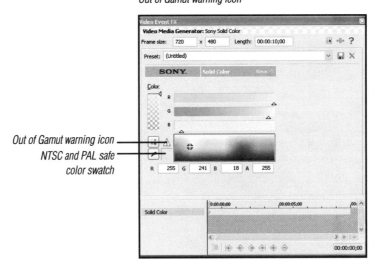

Out of Gamut warning icon
NTSC and PAL safe
color swatch

FIGURE 7-6

Matching a known color value

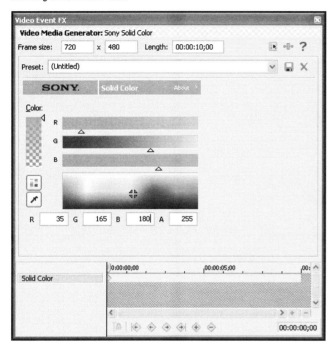

7. Drag the Alpha slider to determine the opacity of the color.

   The color sample is graduated from a value of 255 (fully opaque) to 0 (completely transparent).

8. Click the Close button.

   The specified color is applied to the generated media.

9. Keep the project open. You'll be using it in the next objective.

Match a known color value

1. Move your cursor toward the icon that looks like a filmstrip in the upper-right corner of the generated media event.

2. Click the filmstrip icon.

   Vegas displays the Video Event FX dialog box, shown previously. Depending on the size of your desktop, the entire dialog box might not be visible. If this is so, use the scroll bar on the right side of the dialog box to scroll until the R, G, B, and A text boxes are visible. Alternatively, you can click and drag any border to resize the width or height of the dialog box, or you can drag the corner to resize both width and height.

3. Enter the following values in the R, G, B, and A text boxes: **35**, **165**, **180**, and **255**, as shown in Figure 7-6.

   The color sample should be a light aqua blue that is completely opaque.

4. Click the Close button.

Vegas applies the new color to the generated media.

> **TIP**
>
> If you're matching a color with values from the Hue, Saturation, and Luminosity (HSL) color model, click the Change Color Space to HSL button to change the R, G, B sliders to H, S, L sliders, as shown in Figure 7-7. You can then type values in the text boxes to match the known color. Alternatively, you can work with the HSL color sliders or drag inside the color well.

Match a color from a video clip

1. Create a new project.

2. Add a video clip to the Project Media window.

3. Select the video clip; then drop it into the main window, aligning the clip with the beginning of the timeline.

4. Click the Media Generator tab; then click Solid Color.

5. Select the Black preset; then drop it into the video track, aligning it with the beginning of the timeline.

The Video Event FX dialog box, shown previously, appears.

FIGURE 7-7

Choosing a color from the HSL color space

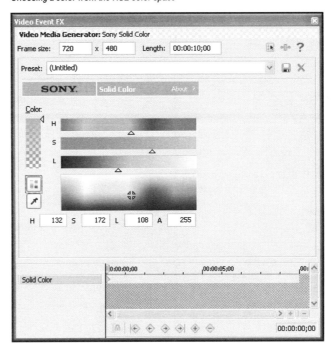

6. Accept the default parameter; then click the Close button.

   If you have Auto Ripple enabled, Vegas moves the video event to the right to make room for the generated media. If you do not have Auto Ripple enabled, press F to ripple the track timeline.

7. If the Video Preview window is not displayed in the workspace, choose Video Preview.

8. Position your cursor at the start of the video event; then press the spacebar.

   Vegas plays the project in the Video Preview window.

9. Press Enter to stop the preview when you see a frame that contains a color that you want to match to the background.

10. Click the icon that looks like a filmstrip in the upper-right corner of the generated media video event.

    Vegas displays the Video Event FX dialog box.

11. Click the Pick Color from Screen button, which looks like an eyedropper.

12. Drag your cursor into the Video Preview window; then click the color you want to sample, as shown in Figure 7-8.

TIP

It is often beneficial to dock one window with another when performing tasks such as picking a color from the Video Preview window. To dock a window with a dialog box, drag it from the Window Docking area and drop it in the desired dialog box, as shown in Figure 7-8.

The color sample in the Video Event FX window updates to match the color you sampled from the Video Preview window.

QUICKTIP

You can sample a color from anywhere inside the Vegas workspace—even the interface.

13. Click the Close button.

    The solid color background is now a perfect match for the color you sampled from the video event. Sampling a color is a wonderful way to create a background for a title clip that matches a color from the first video event in your production.

FIGURE 7-8

Matching a color

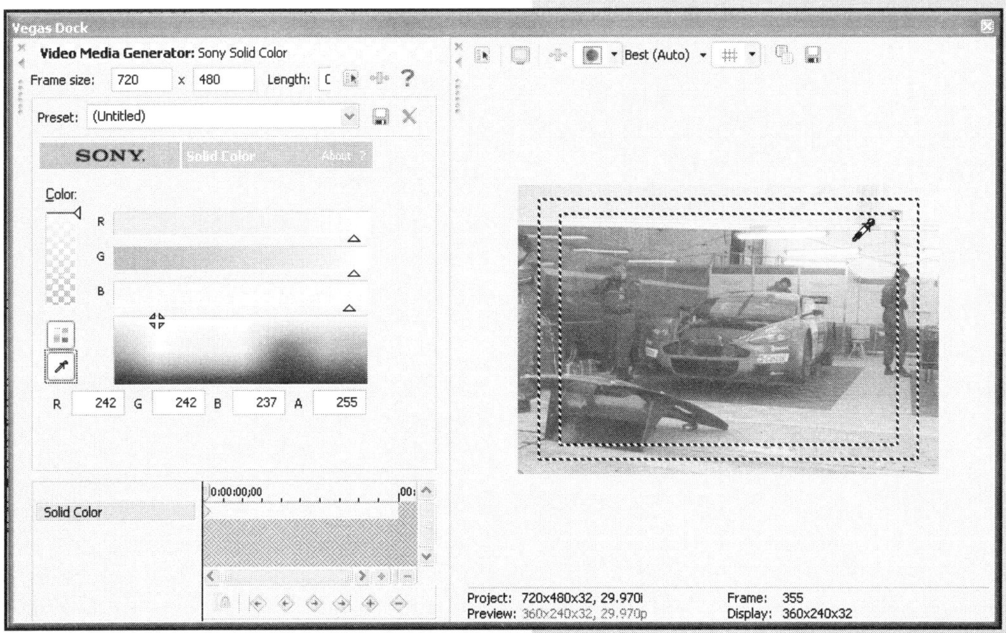

CREATE A SCROLLING
TEXT CREDIT

What You'll Do

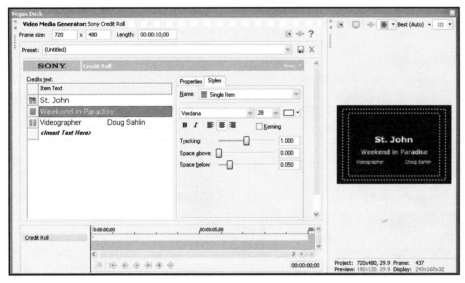

 In this lesson, you learn to create titles for your productions. You also learn to modify the parameters for the title presets.

Adding Credits to a Project

You add an obvious level of professionalism when you add title and ending credits to a production. When you decide to do so, you can choose from a wide variety of presets in the Credits section of the Media Generators window. Each preset is customizable to suit your project. You begin with a preset, and then modify the parameters to suit it.

Modifying a Preset

After you choose a preset, you can have two tabs with which to work: Properties and Styles. In the Properties tab, you'll find properties to specify the type of animation applied to the credit, specify the position of the text, and specify the effect parameters. In the Styles tab, you'll find parameters to specify background color, text color, and font parameters and styles.

Working with Text

Credits always have text of some sort. You can have a simple opening credit with a single line of text that's stationary over a solid background, or you can have multi-line text scroll in or fade in over the background of your choice. When you create a credit with multiline text, you can begin the credit with bold text, also known as a header. You can follow this up with secondary text to display other information about your project. If you are giving credit to actors, videographers, directors, and so on, you can follow up the subitem text with side-by-side text.

You can add as many lines of text as needed to display the desired information for your title and ending credits. Text for credits is divided into three categories: **Header**, **Single Item**, and **Dual Item**. You can choose different font attributes for each category, as well as the spacing, tracking, and kerning for the category text. If you display side-by-side credits, you can specify the spacing between columns, and whether to display a blank space between columns or connect them with a graphics element, such as dashes or dots. Figure 7-9 illustrates a credit preset in the Video Preview window.

FIGURE 7-9
Title credit

Create a scrolling credit

1. Create a new project.

2. Click the Media Generators tab; then choose Credit Roll.

   Vegas displays the credit presets, as shown in Figure 7-10.

3. Position your cursor over a preset.

   Vegas animates the thumbnail, which gives you an idea of how the preset will look in your production.

4. Select the Plain Scrolling on Black preset; then drop it in the main window, aligning it with the beginning of the timeline.

   Vegas creates a track for the event, and the Video Event FX dialog box appears, displaying the parameters for the Plain Scrolling on Black preset. The default text is selected, as shown in Figure 7-11.

   ### TIP

   The default duration for generated media is nine seconds, 29 frames. You can specify a longer or shorter duration for a generated media event by typing the desired duration in the Length text box, shown in Figure 7-11. Note that you must enter the duration in the following format: HH:MM:SS;FF, where HH is hours, MM is minutes, SS is seconds, and FF is frames. For example, to set a media event duration at 15 seconds, you would type 00:00:15;00 in the Length text field.

5. Enter the desired text.

6. Click the next text item.

7. Enter the desired text.

FIGURE 7-10

Credit presets

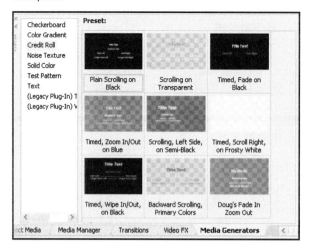

FIGURE 7-11

Plain Scrolling on Black credit parameters

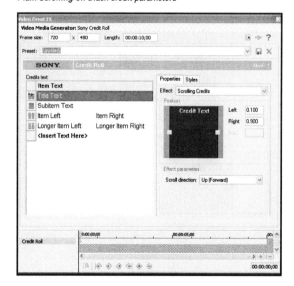

FIGURE 7-12
Previewing a credit in the Video Preview window

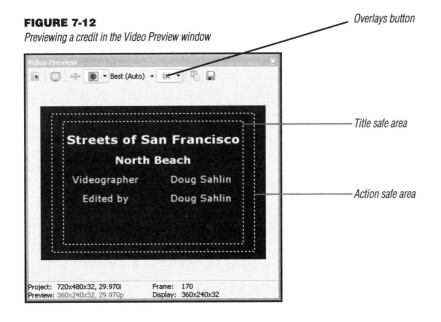

Overlays button

Title safe area

Action safe area

8. Repeat steps 6 and 7 for the remaining text items.

9. Keep the project open. You'll be using it in the next objective.

Specify credit properties

1. If the Video Preview window isn't displayed in the workspace, choose View > Video Preview.

2. Position your cursor over the middle of the media event you just created.

   Your credit text is displayed in the Video Preview window, as shown in Figure 7-12.

3. In the Properties tab of the Video Event FX dialog box, drag the left or right handle in the Position section.

   This sets the boundary for the text. Alternatively, you can type a value in the Left text box to set the left boundary for credit text, or the Right text box to set the right border for the credit text. The default values will keep the text within the title safe boundary, which is important if your project will be rendered for viewing on a television screen. If you move the text boundaries outward, the text might not display properly on a television screen. When you're working with text for a project that will be rendered for television display, it's a good idea to display safe areas in the Video Preview window. This provides a visual display of the action and title safe areas, as shown previously in Figure 7-12. To display safe areas, click the triangle to the right of the Overlays button and choose Safe Areas from the drop-down list.

4. Click the Scroll Direction down arrow; then choose a preset from the drop-down list.

Your choices are Up (Forward) or Down (Backward).

TIP

If you can't see the Scroll Direction down arrow, drag the scroll bar to reveal the bottom of the dialog box. Alternatively, you can resize the dialog box to reveal every parameter.

QUICKTIP

If you decide to change a credit from scrolling text to a timed sequence, click the Effect down arrow and choose Timed Sequence from the drop-down list.

5. Position your cursor at the beginning of the timeline; then press the spacebar.

The title credit begins playing in the Video Preview window. At this point, you might notice that your text is too small, or that it exceeds the boundary of the video frame or the title safe area. You can rectify either problem by modifying the default styles to suit your project.

6. Keep the project open. You'll be using it in the next objective.

Specify credit styles

1. Click the Styles tab.

The Video Event FX dialog box is reconfigured, as shown in Figure 7-13.

2. Select the line of text you want to edit.

Vegas highlights the text.

3. Click the Name down arrow; then choose a preset from the drop-down list.

Choose this option if you want to change the type of text. For example, you can change from Header to Single Item. When you change the type of text, the other parameters in the dialog box change as well.

4. Click the down arrow to the right of the currently selected font type; then choose the desired font type from the drop-down list.

The drop-down list displays all the fonts that are registered on your system. If you have Adobe applications such as Adobe Photoshop, the stylized Adobe fonts will not be available in Vegas, or for that matter, any application other than Photoshop.

5. Click the Font Size down arrow; then choose a preset from the drop-down list.

Alternatively, you can type a value into the text field. After you specify a value, look at the Video Preview window to make sure your text does not exceed the title safe area or the boundaries of the video frame.

6. Accept the current font color, or click the color swatch and choose a color from the color picker.

FIGURE 7-13

Modifying credit styles

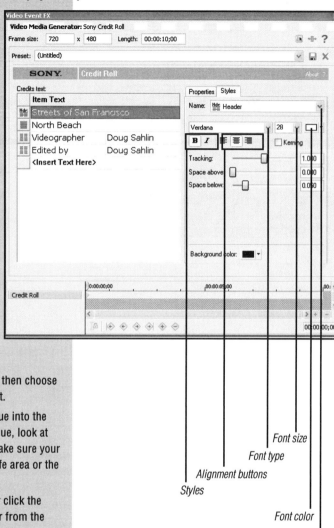

Font size
Font type
Alignment buttons
Styles
Font color
Text type drop-down

If your project will be rendered as an NTSC video, you must choose an **NTSC safe color**. To choose an NTSC safe color, type a value between 16 and 234 in the R, G, and B fields.

7. If desired, choose a different font style option.

   You can boldface or italicize credit text.

8. Select the desired alignment option.

   Your options are Align Left, Align Center, and Align Right.

9. Click the Kerning check box to automatically adjust the spacing between letters.

   The kerning depends on the font you select. Some fonts contain no kerning information.

10. Drag the Tracking slider to determine the spacing between letters.

    Drag the slider to the right to expand spacing between letters, or to the left to space letters closer together. Alternatively, you can type a value in the Tracking text field.

11. Drag the Space Above slider to determine the amount of space above the text.

    Alternatively, you can type a value in the Space Above field.

12. Drag the Space Below slider to determine the amount of space below the text.

    Alternatively, you can type a value in the Space Below field.

NOTE

If you're specifying styles for dual item text, the Styles tab also has a Center Width slider that you drag to determine the width between columns, as well as a Connect Sides With option. The Connect Sides With drop-down list contains options that determine how the text between columns is connected. You can choose a graphics element, or display nothing between columns. Click the Connect Sides With down arrow and choose the desired option from the drop-down list.

13. Accept the default background color, or click the color swatch to choose a color from the color picker.

    If your project will be rendered as NTSC video, remember to pick a color that is NTSC safe. Also, be on the lookout for the NTSC/PAL **Out of Gamut** warning, or the PAL Out of Gamut warning if you drag your cursor inside the color well to specify background color. Remember: You can also click the Pick Color from Screen button and click the eyedropper on any color in the workspace or Video Preview window.

    As you preview the credit, make sure none of the credit text exceeds the title safe area or the width of the video frame.

TIP

You can edit a generated media event at any time by clicking the Generated Media icon, which looks like a filmstrip in the upper-right corner of the event. Alternatively, you can right-click the generated media event and choose Edit Generated Media from the shortcut menu. Either option opens the Video Event FX dialog box.

CREATE A TIMED
SEQUENCE CREDIT

What You'll Do

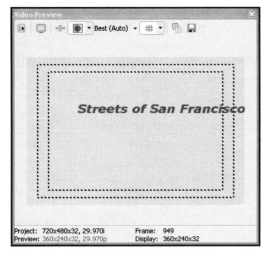

 In this lesson, you learn to add a timed sequence to a project. You also learn to modify the parameters for the title presets.

Using a Timed Sequence Preset

Sometimes a scrolling text credit isn't just what the doctor ordered. Granted, it's a tried-and-true classic, just like the drop shadow in graphics, but you have other options in Vegas. You can display credits with a timed sequence credit. You can fade the text in and out, scroll the text from right to left (or left to right), scroll the text from top to bottom (or bottom to top), zoom the text in, or wipe the text in.

Modifying Preset Parameters

You also have several options for displaying the timed sequence. You can display a single line at a time, display up to the next text header, display a text header and single subitem, or display up to the next header or single subitem.

Modifying Credit Text Attributes

In addition, you can modify the text attributes to suit your project, as discussed in the previous lesson. Perhaps this brief description will give you an idea of the versatility of a timed sequence credit. If not, the upcoming lesson certainly will.

Create a timed sequence

1. Create a new project.

2. Click the Media Generators tab; then choose Credit Roll.

3. Pause your cursor over each preset that is preceded by Timed to get an idea of the diversity you have available.

4. Select Timed, Zoomed In/Out on Blue, and drop it in the main window, aligning the media with the beginning of the timeline.

   Vegas creates a media event, and the Video Event FX dialog box opens, displaying the parameters for the credit preset, as shown in Figure 7-14.

5. Set the position for the credit text, as outlined in the previous lesson.

6. Accept the default In parameter, or click the In down arrow and choose an option from the drop-down menu.

   This option determines how the text is displayed in the first part of the timed sequence. The options are self-explanatory. If you want the text to be stationary when the credit begins, choose None.

7. Accept the Out parameter, or click the Out down arrow and choose an option from the drop-down list.

   This option determines how the text is displayed for the last half of the timed sequence. If you want the text to be stationary when the credit ends, choose None.

8. Accept the default Display parameter, or click the Display down arrow and choose an option from the drop-down list.

   This option determines how multiline credits are displayed. For example, if you choose Up to Next Header or Single Item, the first header or single item is displayed, followed by the subsequent lines of text, and then the next header or single item is included in the credit.

9. Click the Styles tab; then set the text and background styles, as outlined in the previous lesson.

10. Close the Video Event FX dialog box, then preview the credit.

11. Before proceeding to the next lesson, edit the generated media and experiment with the different In, Out, and Display parameters to get a feel for this compelling credit.

FIGURE 7-14

Parameters for the Timed, Zoomed In/Out on Blue credit preset

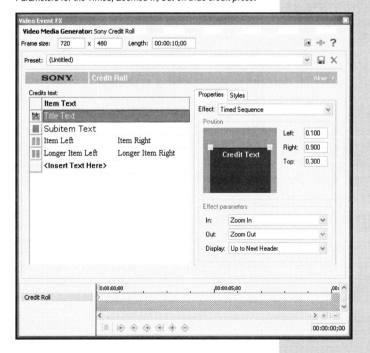

USE CHECKERBOARD AND
GRADIENT BACKGROUNDS

What You'll Do

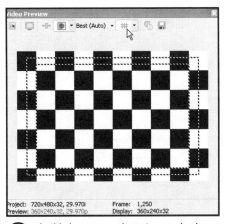

In this lesson, you learn to use checkered and gradient backgrounds to spice up your projects. You learn to work with the presets and modify them to suit your projects.

Experimenting with Generated Media

When you first start experimenting with generated media, you might feel like a kid in a candy store. There are more than enough choices to suit any creative video editor. Used on their own, backgrounds add interest to a production. However, that's just the beginning. You can mix and match backgrounds on different tracks, and vary the level and blending method for each track on which you have generated media. To add more interest to the mix, you can use track motion to have one track move across a stationary one. Mixing and matching different backgrounds can add an extra touch of panache to an already compelling production.

Mixing Backgrounds with Text

You can mix backgrounds with animated text to create your own custom titles. Backgrounds can be used when you have a project in which video events are moving or cropped to different sizes. In projects like this, the background serves as an unobtrusive (or if you so desire, obtrusive) backdrop for your moving video events.

Using the Checkerboard and Gradient Backgrounds

The backgrounds with which you'll be working in this lesson are from the checkerboard and gradient categories. Both categories contain a wide variety of presets. You can add anything from a simple black-and-white checkerboard to evoke a nostalgic art-deco feeling, to a complex background that looks like a barbed wire fence. Gradient presets run the gamut from a simple blend from white to black, to an effect that resembles a sunburst.

Creating Eye-Catching Gradient Backgrounds

If you've worked with gradients in vector applications or image editing applications, you already have an idea of the compelling effects you can achieve. Gradients in Vegas are no different. You can use multiple colors to create a rainbow gradient. You determine where each gradient control point appears, and what color is displayed at that control point. Vegas does the black magic of blending one control point into the next.

FIGURE 7-15

Checkerboard media presets

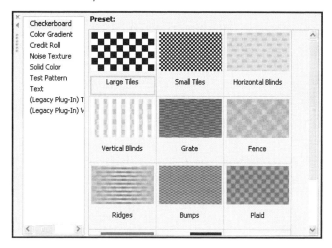

FIGURE 7-16

Parameters for the Large Tiles Checkerboard background preset

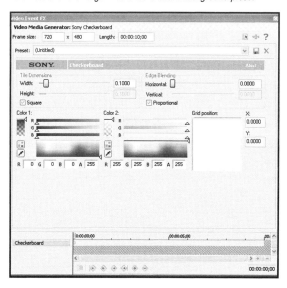

1. Create a new project.

2. Click the Media Generators tab; then choose Checkerboard.

   Vegas displays thumbnail previews of each checkerboard preset, as shown in Figure 7-15.

3. Select the Large Tiles preset; then drop it into the main window, aligning it with the beginning of the timeline.

   Vegas creates a new media event, and the Video Event FX dialog box opens, displaying the parameters for the Large Tiles preset, as shown in Figure 7-16.

4. If the Video Preview window is not displayed in the workspace, choose View > Video Preview.

   You'll be able to see the effect of each parameter change you make in the Video Preview window.

5. Position your cursor in the middle of the media event that you just created.

6. In the Tile Dimensions section of the Video Event FX dialog box, drag the Width slider to the right.

   This increases the width and height of the tile squares. Alternatively, you can enter a value in the Width text field.

7. Click the Square check box.

By default, a checkerboard background has square tiles. When you deselect this option, the Height slider becomes available, and you can enter different values in the Width and Height files to create rectangular tiles for the background.

8. In the Edge Blending section, drag the Horizontal slider to determine how the edges of the tiles blend together.

By default, this value is 0, and there is no blending of tiles. As you drag the slider, the edges of the tiles are blended. If you deselect the Proportional option, a Vertical slider becomes available, and you can specify different blend values for each axis.

9. In the Color 1 section, accept the default color, or specify a different color.

This sets the color for the first tile and every other tile in the grid. If you need a refresher on the color picker, refer to the first lesson in this chapter.

10. In the Color 2 section, accept the default color, or specify a different color.

This sets the color for the second tile and every other tile in the grid.

QUICKTIP

If you're displaying a checkerboard background on top of a video track, set the alpha value for one color to a value of 0 (transparent), and set the alpha value of the other color to a value of 255 (opaque). Every other square will display the underlying video.

Add a gradient background

1. Create a new project.

2. Click the Media Generators tab; then choose Color Gradient.

Vegas displays thumbnail previews of each color gradient preset, as shown in Figure 7-17.

3. Scroll through the presets to see the different effects you can achieve with this media.

4. Select the Linear White to Black preset and drop it in the main window, aligning it with the beginning of the timeline.

FIGURE 7-17
Color gradient presets

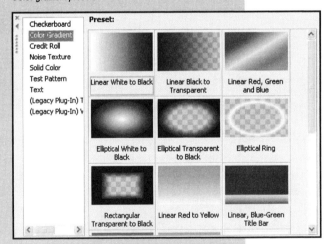

FIGURE 7-18

Parameters for the Black to White, Color Gradient preset

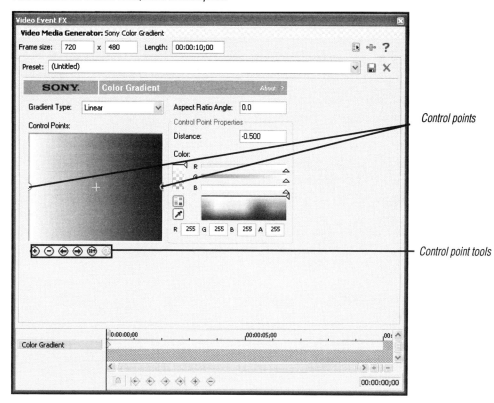

Control points

Control point tools

Vegas creates a media event, and the Video Event FX dialog box appears, displaying the parameters for the preset, as shown in Figure 7-18. In the center of the Control Points window is a plus sign that you can use to shift the positions of the control points. Also notice the two numbered circles. These are the control points that define the colors of the gradient, and the points at which they appear in the gradient. At the bottom of the Control Points window are the Control Point tools that you can use to add and delete control points, as well as navigate to the next or previous control point.

5. If the Video Preview window is not displayed in the workspace, choose View > Video Preview.

6. Position your cursor in the middle of the media event.

   This enables you to view the gradient in the Video Preview window.

7. Select the first control point; then drag it to the right and then up.

   When you drag a control point, you change the position in which the control point color appears in the gradient. Alternatively, you can type a value in the Aspect Angle Ratio text field to control the gradient offset from horizontal. A value of 90 tilts the gradient 90 degrees clockwise, a value of 180 flips the gradient horizontally, and so on. You can also type a value in the Distance text field. This value determines how far the control point is offset from the center of the video frame. A value of 0 places the control point in the middle of the gradient, a value of −.50

places the control point at the left border of the video frame, and a value of .50 places the control point on the right border of the video frame. As you change the control points, notice that the preview in the Control Points window updates, as does the Video Preview window.

8. Click the button that looks like a plus sign to add a **control point** to the gradient.

   Vegas adds a control point to the gradient and assigns the control point the next available number. The control point is placed near the currently selected control point. After you add a control point, you can move it as needed, or change the color. You can add as many control points as you want to define the look of your gradient. However, when you have many control points, it can become difficult to select a point, and the video will take longer to render.

9. In the Color section, change the color of the control point using the methods outlined earlier in this chapter. Remember: You can also use the Pick Color from Screen tool to sample a color from a video event in the project, or sample a color from anywhere in the workspace.

10. Select the first control point.

11. Click the Select Next Gradient Control Point button, which looks like a right-pointing arrow.

   This button selects the next control point in the gradient. The button is dimmed if you're at the last control point in the gradient.

12. Click the Select Previous Gradient Con-

trol Point button, which looks like a left-pointing arrow.

This button selects the previous control point in the gradient.

13. Select the second gradient control point; then click the Increase Gradient Control Point Position Number button.

   This increases the number of the control point by one. It has no effect on the look of the gradient, but it does affect the order in which the control points are selected when you use one of the gradient control point selection tools. If the selected control point is the last number in the gradient, this tool is dimmed. You can also decrease the number of a selected control points by clicking the Decrease Gradient Control Point Position Number button. This tool is dimmed if you have the number one control point in a gradient selected.

14. Click the Gradient Type down arrow; then choose an option from the drop-down list.

   Your choices are Linear, which blends the gradient control points in a straight line; Elliptical, which blends the control points in a circular manner, and Rectangular, which blends the control points in a rectangular manner from center outward.

15. After you edit the gradient, click the Close button.

   Vegas applies your changes to the preset.

16. Before you move on to the next lesson, create generated media using one or two of the other presets. Then edit them to see the effects you can achieve with a color gradient.

CREATE TEXT
OVERLAYS

What You'll Do

 In this lesson, you add text to a project. You learn to create text over a solid background, and text that overlays video on a track.

Displaying Text in a Project

When you need to display text in a project, you're not limited to scrolling credits and timed sequences. When it suits a project, you can add static text to display a message or to announce a new scene. Even though the text is static, it's still compelling. When you add static text to a Vegas project, you can choose a preset that you like, and then modify the preset to suit your project. Although text initially starts out as static, you can animate text using the options discussed in the upcoming "Animate Generated Media" lesson.

Displaying Text Over a Background

The text you add to a project can appear over a solid background, a transparent background, or a partially transparent background. Text over a transparent background is useful when you need to create the equivalent of a subtitle, or create a custom title that displays over a video clip, or a static image. You also have complete control over the font type, size, and other text attributes.

Modifying Text Parameters

Your creative latitude doesn't stop with text attributes, though. You can position the text using one of the preset options, or manually position the text to suit the video over which the text is being displayed. Other options you have available are effects. In fact, there are so many effects that there's a tab devoted to them. From within the Effects tab, you can add an outline to the text, create a drop shadow for the text, and deform the text.

Add text to a project

1. Create a new project.

2. Click the Media Generators tab; then click the Text title.

   Vegas displays the text presets, as shown in Figure 7-19.

3. Scroll through the presets to get an idea of the type of text you can add to a project.

   You can modify each preset to suit your project.

4. Select the Solid Background preset and drop it in the main window, aligning it with the beginning of the timeline.

   Vegas creates the media event, and the Video Event FX dialog box appears, showing the parameters for the preset, as shown in Figure 7-20.

5. Select the sample text; then type the desired text.

   The sample text is a placeholder for the text you want to display in the project.

6. Click the down arrow to the right of the current font type; then select the desired font type from the drop-down list.

   The drop-down list shows every font that's currently registered on your computer, with the exception of Adobe fonts.

7. Click the Font Size down arrow; then select the desired size from the drop-down list.

   After you choose a font size, the text is updated. This shows you whether the text will fit in the video frame with the current font size.

FIGURE 7-19

Text presets

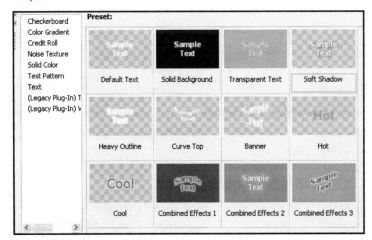

FIGURE 7-20

Solid Background Text preset parameters

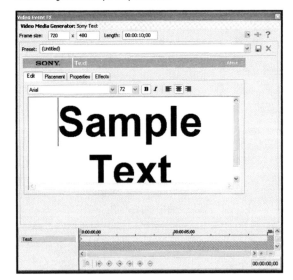

FIGURE 7-21

Text placement options

8. Choose a font style.

   You can boldface or italicize the text by clicking the applicable button.

9. Choose an alignment option.

   You can align the text to the left, center, or right by clicking the applicable button. These buttons look the same as those you'll find in most popular word processing applications.

10. Click the Placement tab.

    The Video Event FX dialog box is reconfigured, as shown in Figure 7-21.

11. Select the text and drag it to the desired location.

    When you move your cursor over the text, the pointer changes to a hand. If you click the text, the pointer becomes a closed hand. Alternatively, you can click the down arrow to the right of the current text placement option (Free Form by default), and select an option from the drop-down list. Another option is to type values in the X and Y text fields. A value of 0 in each field places the text in the center of the video frame, whereas a value of 1 or –1 moves the text out of the frame. Notice the rectangle inside the border of the Text Placement preview window. This is the title safe area. If you're creating text for a project that will be viewed on a television screen, keep your text within the safe area.

12. Keep the project open. You'll be using it in the next objective.

Modify text properties

1. Click the Properties tab.

The Video Event FX dialog box is reconfigured, as shown in Figure 7-22.

2. Accept the default text and background colors, or modify them using the applicable color picker, as outlined earlier in this chapter.

3. Drag the Tracking slider to determine the spacing between letters.

4. Drag the Scaling slider to determine the scale of the text.

The default setting (a value of 1, or 100 percent) leaves the text unaltered. Dragging the slider to the right increases the scale of the text, whereas dragging the slider to the left decreases the scale of the text. If you have the Video Preview window open and your cursor was positioned within the event before the Video Event FX dialog box gained focus, you'll be able to preview the results as you drag the slider. You can also enter a value in the Scaling text box to increase or decrease the scale of the text.

FIGURE 7-22

Configuring text properties

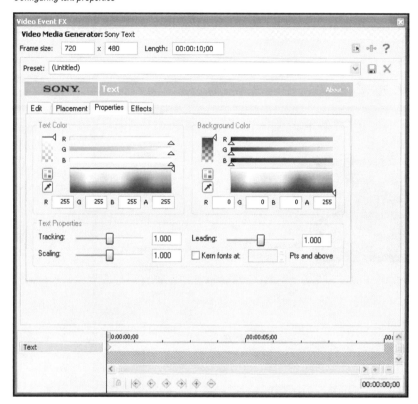

FIGURE 7-23

Modifying text effects

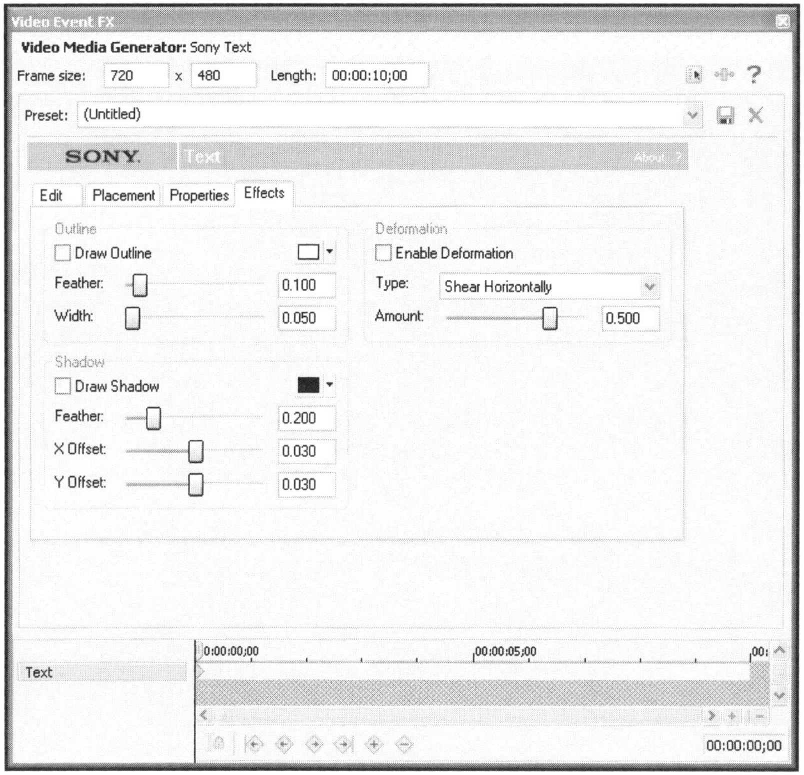

5. Drag the Leading slider to determine the spacing between lines.

Alternatively, you can enter a value in the Leading text box to set line spacing. Enter a value larger than 1 to increase spacing, or a value less than 1 to decrease spacing. You'll be able to view the results of changing text leading if you have the Video Preview window open.

6. Click the Kern Fonts At check box to kern text above a specific size.

When you choose this option, the default value is 12 points. All text at this font size and larger will be kerned using the information that's built into the font. You can type a different value in the Kern Fonts At text box, or use the spinner buttons to specify a different value.

7. Leave the Project open. You'll be using it in the next objective.

Modify text effects

1. Click the Effects tab.

The Video Event FX dialog box is reconfigured, as shown in Figure 7-23.

2. Click the Draw Outline check box to place an outline around the text.

3. Accept the default outline color, or click the color swatch to reveal the color picker. Then select the desired color as outlined previously in this chapter.

4. Drag the Feather slider to determine how the text outline blends into the background.

Alternatively, you can enter a value of 1 or less in the Feather text box. This value determines how the outline is feathered into the surrounding pixels of color. A value of 0 does not feather the text into the background, while a value of 1 totally blends the outline into the background, rendering it invisible. You'll be able to preview the results of this setting if you have the Video Preview window open and your cursor was positioned within the media event before the Video Event FX dialog box gained focus.

5. Drag the Width slider to determine the width of the outline.

Alternatively, you can enter a value in the Width text box.

6. Click the Draw Shadow check box to add a drop shadow to the text.

7. Accept the default drop shadow color, or click the color swatch to reveal the color picker. Then select the desired color.

8. Drag the X and Y sliders to determine how far the shadow is offset from the text.

Alternatively, you can type a value in either field.

9. Click the Enable Deformation check box to add a deformation preset to the text.

10. Accept the default deformation option, or click the Deformation down arrow and choose an option from the drop-down list, shown in Figure 7-24.

FIGURE 7-24

Choosing a deformation option

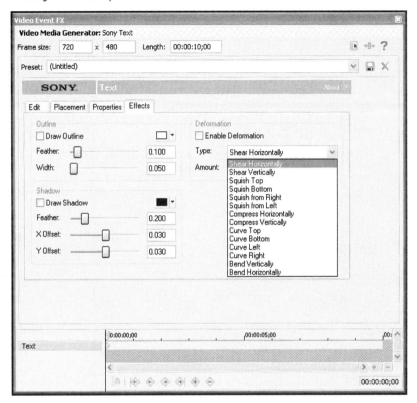

11. Drag the Amount slider to determine the level and direction of the deformation.

Alternatively, you can enter a value in the Amount text field. The effect of changing the Amount value will differ, depending on the deformation method you chose in step 10.

12. Click the Close button to exit the Video Event FX dialog box.

Create a text overlay

1. Create a new project.

2. Import an image or video clip into the Project Media window.

An image or video clip over which a text overlay has been placed is an excellent way to create a unique opening credit for a production. If you use this technique to open a production, choose an image or video clip that is approximately 10 seconds long. Remember: You can always trim the video event, or adjust the duration of the text media event.

3. Select the video clip and drop it in the main window, aligning it with the beginning of the timeline.

4. Select the video event in the track list, right-click, and then choose Insert Video Track from the shortcut menu.

Vegas creates a new video track on top of the video track you first created. Alternatively, you can choose Insert > Video Track.

5. Click the Media Generators window; then choose Text.

6. Select the Default Text preset; then drop it into the video track you just created, aligning the media event with the beginning of the timeline.

Vegas adds a media event to the project, and the Video Event FX dialog box appears, displaying the parameters for the Default Text preset. If you have Auto Ripple enabled, the video event will rippled downstream on the timeline to accommodate the generated media. If so, select the video clip, and align it to the beginning of the timeline.

7. If the Video Preview window is not displayed in the workspace, choose View > Video Preview.

8. Position your cursor in the middle of the media event.

When you're creating a text overlay, you can preview a frame of the video event and the generated media in the Video Preview window, as shown in Figure 7-25.

9. In the Video Event FX dialog box, type the desired text in the Edit window.

10. Accept the default font; then specify a font size of 24.

The font size you specify depends on what you want to accomplish with the text. When you're creating a title over a still or moving image, choose a font size that can easily display your text within the title safe area. When you're creating text that will serve as a subtitle, as you're doing here, choose a font size of 24 points or greater. A smaller font size will be hard to read.

11. Click the Placement tab.

FIGURE 7-25

Previewing a text overlay

The Video Event FX dialog box is reconfigured to display placement options.

12. Select the text and drag it so that it is just above the title safe rectangle.

> **QUICKTIP**
>
> You can also move the text in the desired direction by pressing the applicable arrow key repeatedly until the text is positioned as desired.

13. Type a value of **0** in the X text field to center the text.

At this point, your project should resemble Figure 7-26, which shows the Video Event FX dialog box side by side with the Video Preview window. If the images in your project video clip are brightly colored, you might have to choose a different color for the text.

> **QUICKTIP**
>
> When you're creating subtitle text, choose a duration of no longer than three seconds.

14. Close the Video Event FX dialog box; then preview your project.

FIGURE 7-26

Text displayed over a video event

ANIMATE GENERATED
MEDIA

What You'll Do

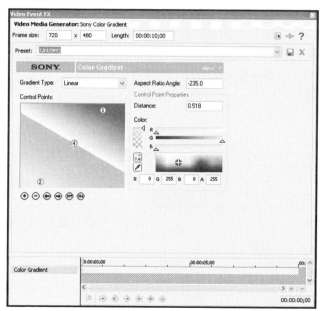

In this lesson, you learn to animate a media preset.

Animating Media with Keyframes

When you want to take a video production to the next level, you can choose a Vegas media preset that suits your project. When you edit the preset parameters, you can cause the parameters to change during the duration of the preset. You do this by adding keyframes to the media event timeline in the Video Event FX dialog box. At each keyframe, you modify the parameters to get the desired effect. For example, if you want the size of text in a media event to change, you can create a keyframe in the middle and end of the media event, and then specify a different font size at

each keyframe. When the video project is previewed, or played back after being rendered, the text will gradually change size between keyframes. Vegas extrapolates the text size on all frames between the keyframes you create.

Choosing a Keyframe Transition

When you animate a media event, you can also specify how Vegas extrapolates the transition between keyframes. You can choose the following transition types: Linear, Fast, Slow, Smooth, Sharp, or Hold. If you have multiple keyframes for the media event, you can choose a different transition set of in-between frames.

Animate a media event

1. Create a new project.

2. Click the Media Generators window; then click Color Gradient.

3. Select the Skyscape preset; then drop it in the main window, aligning it with the beginning of the timeline.

   Vegas creates a media event, and the Video Event FX dialog box appears, displaying the parameters for the preset, as shown in Figure 7-27. Notice the timeline and controls at the bottom of the dialog box.

4. In the Video Event FX dialog box, position your cursor in the middle of the timeline. Then click the Create Keyframe button, which looks like a plus sign (+).

   Vegas adds a keyframe to the timeline. Alternatively, you can press Insert on your keyboard to create a keyframe at a selected point on the Video Event FX dialog box timeline.

5. Type a value of **-235.00** in the Aspect Ratio Angle text box.

   The gradient tilts to the right.

FIGURE 7-27
Video Event FX timeline

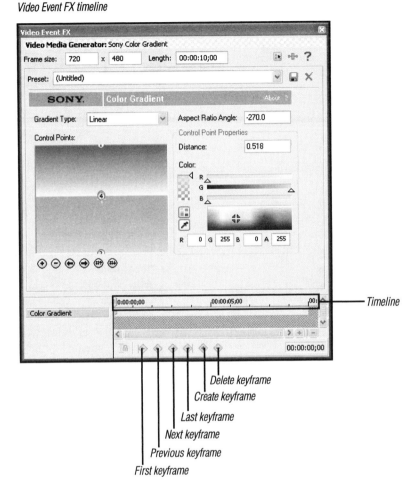

Timeline

Delete keyframe
Create keyframe
Last keyframe
Next keyframe
Previous keyframe
First keyframe

FIGURE 7-28

Selecting the interpolation mode

FIGURE 7-29

Modifying event parameters at a keyframe

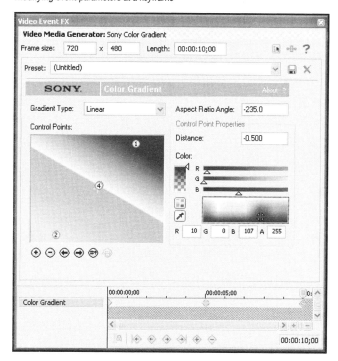

6. Position your cursor over the keyframe, and right-click. Then choose an option from the shortcut menu, shown in Figure 7-28.

   The option you choose determines how Vegas interpolates the changes between the currently selected keyframe and the next keyframe. The options are self-explanatory, with the possible exception of the Hold option. When you choose the Hold option, the change between keyframes occurs abruptly when the next keyframe is reached, much in the way a light comes on as soon as you flip the switch.

7. Position your cursor at the end of the timeline; then create another keyframe.

8. Select gradient control point number 1; then change the color to a darker blue.

   Your Video Event FX dialog box should resemble Figure 7-29.

QUICKTIP

You can use the controls at the bottom of the Video Event FX dialog box timeline (shown in Figure 7-27) to navigate from one keyframe to the next. To change the position of a selected keyframe, drag it to the desired spot on the timeline.

9. Click the Close button to exit the Video Event FX dialog box.

10. Preview the project.

    The horizon tilts to the left between the first and middle keyframe, and the sky gets darker between the middle and final keyframe. The effect is similar to a plane banking. You can use an effect like this in conjunction with animated text to introduce a video.

CREATE CUSTOM TITLES,
CREDITS, AND OTHER MEDIA

What You'll Do

In this lesson, you learn how to save a modified preset for future use.

Modifying a Generated Media Preset

If you've read this chapter from the beginning, you know that the media events you add to your projects start life as presets and then are modified to suit the project. This flexibility gives you the power to create unique events that add viewer interest to your projects. In addition to being able to modify the parameters, you can save a modified preset for future use.

Saving a Custom Preset

When you save a modified media preset, it appears in the preset category from which the custom preset was created. In other words, if you modify a Credit preset and save it as a custom preset, it appears in the Credit category. You cannot, however, save an animated preset.

FIGURE 7-30

Modifying a color gradient preset

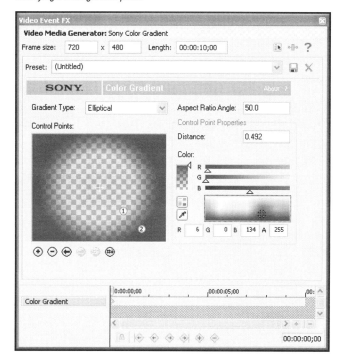

1. Create a new project.

2. Click the Media Generators window; then choose Color Gradient.

3. Select the Elliptical, Transparent to Black preset. Then drop it in the main window, aligning it with the beginning of the timeline.

   Vegas creates a media event, and the Video Event FX dialog opens, displaying the parameters for the preset.

4. Type **50** in the Aspect Ratio Angle text box.

   The ellipse in the center of the preset becomes a circle.

5. Select the second gradient control point; then change the color to a dark blue.

   Your Video Event FX dialog box should resemble Figure 7-30.

6. Select the current preset name (Untitled); then type the name with which you want the preset saved.

   Use a descriptive title, but keep it brief; otherwise, the title will be truncated when it is displayed as a category preset.

7. Click the Save Preset button that looks like a floppy disk.

   The modified preset is saved for future use, and a thumbnail image of the preset appears in the same category as the preset from which you created the custom media.

Adding Opening Credits to a Project

1. Create a new project.

2. Import a video clip into the Project Media window.

3. Click the Media Generators tab; then click Credit Roll.

4. Select the Plain Scrolling on Black preset. Then drop it in the main window, aligning the media event with the beginning of the timeline.

5. Enter the desired header text, subitem text, and one line of dual text.

6. Click the Styles tab; then change the background color to a dark blue: R=16, G=53, B=120, as shown in Figure 7-31.

7. Change the text color to an NTSC safe off-white color: R=235, B=235, G=235.

8. Close the Video Event FX dialog box.

9. Select the video clip; then add it to the project, aligning it with the end of the media event you just created.

10. Preview the title, as shown in Figure 7-32.

FIGURE 7-31

Specifying credit background color

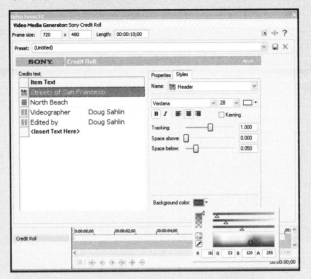

FIGURE 7-32

Sample title credit

Creating a Subtitle

1. Create a new project.

2. Import a video clip into the Project Media window.

3. Select the video clip; then drop it in the main window, aligning it with the beginning of the timeline.

4. Create a new video track.

5. Click the Media Generators window; then choose Text.

6. Select the Soft Shadow preset. Then drop it into the video track you just created, aligning it with the beginning of the timeline.

7. Select the sample text; then type Subtitle text.

8. Change the font type to Verdana, the font size to 24 points and the style to bold, as shown in Figure 7-33.

9. Click the Placement tab; then align the text to the bottom of the title safe area, as shown in Figure 7-34. Remember, you can also repeatedly press the down arrow key to nudge the text to the bottom of the title safe area.

10. Close the Video Event FX dialog box; then preview the project.

FIGURE 7-33
Changing font attributes

FIGURE 7-34
Changing text placement

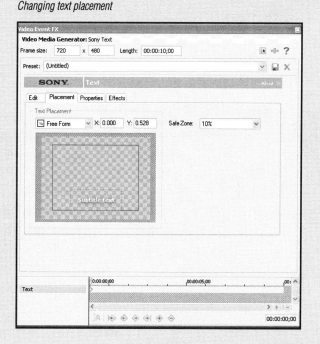

Animating Text

1. Create a new project.

2. Click the Media Generators window; then choose Text.

3. Select the Banner preset. Then drop it in the main window, aligning it with the beginning of the timeline.

4. Select the sample text; then type Animate me, as shown in Figure 7-35.

5. Create a keyframe at the end of the timeline.

6. Click the Effects tab.

7. Drag the Amount slider to the far right until a value of 1.00 appears, as shown in Figure 7-36.

8. Preview the project.

FIGURE 7-35
Editing preset text

FIGURE 7-36
Modifying preset Effect parameters

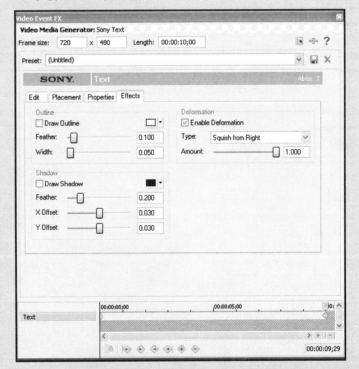

Creating a Custom Title

1. Create a new project.

2. Click the Media Generators window; then click Color Gradient.

3. Select the Soft-Blue Backdrop preset. Then drop it in the main window, aligning it with the beginning of the timeline.

4. Select the first gradient control point; then change the color to a dark blue, as shown in Figure 7-37.

5. Exit the Video Event FX dialog box.

6. Create a new video track.

7. Click the Media Generators tab, choose Text, and then select the Default Text preset.

8. Drop the preset into the video track you just created.

9. Select the default text and type **My Digital Video**.

10. Change the font size to 50 points.

11. Exit the Video Event FX dialog box.

12. Preview the project, as shown in Figure 7-38.

FIGURE 7-37
Modifying a gradient control point

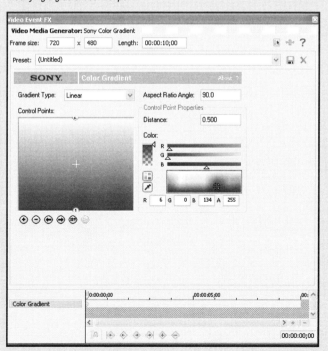

FIGURE 7-38
Previewing a custom title

You work for a production company and are creating a DVD presentation. The client wants the opening credits displayed over a static image. The opening credits display the title of the production and the name of the videographer.

1. Create a new project.

2. Import an image into the Project Media window. Make sure the image is at least 480 pixels high.

3. Drop the image into the main window, aligning it with the beginning of the timeline.

4. Create a new video track.

QUICKTIP

After you add an image to a project, select the video event, right-click, and then choose Properties from the shortcut menu. Click the Media tab, click the Pixel Aspect down arrow, and then choose the option that applies to your project to ensure that the image displays properly when the video is played back.

5. Click the Media Generators tab; then click Credit Roll.

6. Select the Scrolling on Transparent preset. Then drop it into the video track you just created, aligning the media event to the beginning of the timeline. If you have auto rippling

enabled, the video clip will ripple downstream. If so, select the video event, and align it to the beginning of the timeline.

7. Select the Title Text and type **Video Magic.**

8. Select the Subitem text; then press Delete.

9. Select the Item Left text; then type **Cinematographer.**

10. Select the Item Right text; then type **Joe Video.**

11. Select the next line of text; then press Delete.

Your Video Event FX dialog box should resemble Figure 7-39.

12. Click the Styles tab.

13. Click the Name down arrow; then choose Header from the drop-down list.

14. Change the text color to a light blue. If necessary, change the color of the Dual Item text to suit your image.

15. Preview the project.

Your Video Preview window should resemble Figure 7-40.

FIGURE 7-39
Editing credit text

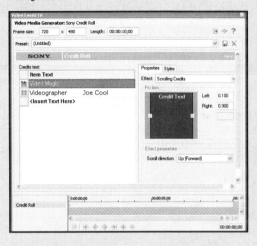

FIGURE 7-40
Previewing the project

Your product manager has left you in charge of creating opening credits for a video production. As you examine the first seconds of the project, you notice that the opening footage isn't very compelling. You decide to use animated text over the beginning video to introduce the production.

1. Create a new project.

2. Import a video clip into the Project Media window.

3. Select the video clip; then drop it in the main window, aligning it with the beginning of the timeline.

4. Create a new video track.

5. Click the Media Generators window; then choose Text.

6. Select the Curved Top preset; then drop it in the video track you just created, aligning the media event with the beginning of the timeline.

7. Select the "Sample Text" and type My Digital Video. Press Enter after you type My to create a new line.

8. Change the font size to 60 points, as shown in Figure 7-41.

9. Create a keyframe at the end of the Video Event FX timeline.

10. Select the first keyframe.

11. Click the Placement tab.

12. Drag the text to the top of the title safe area.

13. Click the Properties tab.

14. Drag the Scaling slider to set the value to 0.

15. Close the Video Event FX dialog box.

16. Preview the project.

The text will float in from the top of the frame and gradually get larger, as shown in Figure 7-42.

FIGURE 7-41
Modifying preset text

FIGURE 7-42
Previewing animated text

Your client is a rock-and-roll band. They present you with raw footage of them performing their latest hit song and want you to create a video for their Web site. After previewing the video, you determine that less is more and decide to introduce the record with classic scrolling text over a black background.

1. Create a new project.

2. Import three video clips into the Project Media window.

3. Select the clips; then drop them in the main window, aligning the first clip with the beginning of the timeline.

4. Click the Media Generators tab; then click Credit Roll.

5. Select the Plain Scrolling On Black preset; then drop it in the video track, aligning it with the beginning of the timeline.

6. Enter the following text for each text item as follows:
   - **Header text: The Grunge Boys**
   - **Subitem text: In Your Face**
   - **Item Left: Video by**
   - **Item Right: Grunge Gurl**

   Your Video Event FX dialog box should resemble Figure 7-43. If desired, click the Styles tab and change the font type to suit your taste.

7. Delete the next line of text.

8. Close the Video Event FX dialog box.

9. Preview the project.

   Your Video Preview window should resemble Figure 7-44. For a variation, overlap the title clip with the first clip; then use your favorite transition to segue from the title clip to the first clip.

FIGURE 7-43
Project Sample 1

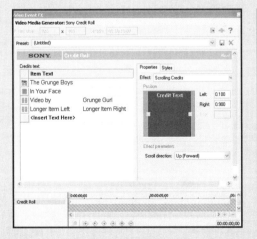

FIGURE 7-44
Project Sample 2

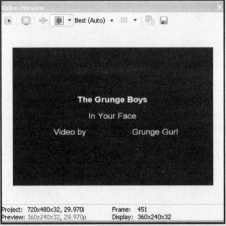

CHAPTER SUMMARY

In this chapter, you learned to add a professional touch to your projects through the use of generated media. You learned to add titles, ending credits, and text to your productions. By modifying the presets, you can create credits to suit any project. The color picker makes it possible for you to match text and background colors to other elements in your projects. Any preset you modify can be saved as a custom preset for future use.

What You Have Learned

In this chapter you:

- Learned to use the color picker.
- Learned to create generated media.
- Learned to use credit presets from the Generated Media window.
- Learned to modify presets.
- Learned to add text overlays to your projects.
- Learned to add solid color and gradient backgrounds to your projects.
- Learned to animate generated media.
- Learned to create custom titles, credits, and other media.

Key Terms from This Chapter

- Alpha. With track level, alpha determines the percentage of the underlying tracks that are visible in the rendered project. With a level of 100, the track is fully visible;

a level of 0 renders a track invisible. When used to define a color, alpha determines the opacity of the color. You can specify a color that is transparent (invisible), opaque, or partially transparent, which will let some of the underlying colors show through.

- Color picker. A device that enables you to specify color for text, backgrounds, and other media you create.
- Control point. A point in a gradient where the color changes. Vegas blends the color from one control point to the next.
- Dual item. A text item used to display text side by side. For example: Videographer...Doug Sahlin.
- Generated media. Media such as text or backgrounds that you create to augment your projects.
- Header. A bold text item used in credits and other text media.
- HSL color model. A color model where the color is determined by the hue, saturation, and luminance.
- Keyframes. A frame used to designate a change in an object parameter such as size, color, or position.
- NTSC. An acronym for National Television System Committee, which determines the characteristics of video for television sets for over 30 countries, including the US and Canada.

- NTSC safe color. A color that will display safely on an NTSC television set. The NTSC safe color range is from (R=16, G=16, B=16) to (R=235, G=235, B=235).
- Out of gamut. A color that will not display properly on a device. For example, if you specify a color of (R=0, G=0, B=0), which is true black, it will be clipped to (R=16, G=16, B=16).
- PAL. An acronym for Phase Alternating Line, the video characteristics for video for television sets in many countries around the world.
- RGB color model. A color model comprised of 256 shades of red, green, and blue.
- Single item. A text item used to display a single line of credit text.
- Title and ending credits. Title credits announce a video production displaying the title of the project and other pertinent information such as the actors, directors, and so on. Ending credits appear at the end of a production and display other pertinent information about the project such as the videographer, the locations where the production was recorded and so on.

8

CREATING SPECIAL
Effects

1. Crop and pan an event.

2. Animate video effects and transitions.

3. Zoom in on and rotate a video event.

4. Create video masks.

5. Create a collage of moving video clips.

chapter 8 CREATING SPECIAL Effects

Few video-editing applications pack as much bang for the buck as Sony Vegas. Many high-end video-editing applications give you all the tools necessary to create and render broadcast-quality video, but few feature a tool set that enables you to create special effects.

In previous chapters, you worked with titles, backgrounds, transitions, and video event FX. In this chapter, you build on your knowledge and learn how to combine different FX to create compelling video eye candy. You also learn how to crop video events, zoom in on them, and move them.

Another effect you can easily create with Vegas plug-ins is masking a video. When you create a mask, you determine which part of the underlying video clip is displayed. You can also add a mask on a single video event to reveal a portion of the video surrounded by a background. When you use this in conjunction with parent and child tracks, you can create compelling effects that rival the best Hollywood productions.

When you create special effects for video events, you work with a timeline similar to the one you worked with in Chapter 7, "Creating Generated Media." You create keyframes on the timeline, and then change plug-in parameters to alter the effect during the course of the event.

Tools You'll Use

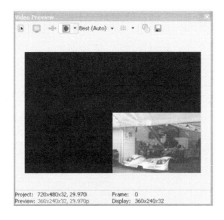

LESSON 1

CROP AND PAN
AN EVENT

What You'll Do

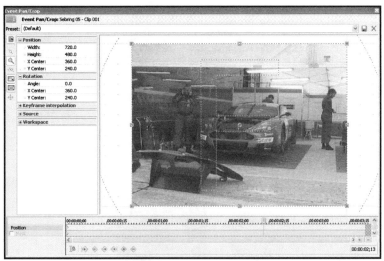

In this lesson, you learn how to crop a video event to the desired size and pan it. When you crop an event, you can shrink it, or crop the event to display a desired portion.

Cropping a Video Event

When you need to zoom in or out on a subject in a video event, you can do so by cropping to the desired portion of the video frame, and then panning to the desired subject in the clip. The end result looks as though the camera operator zoomed in on the subject. If you're working with high-quality video captures, your viewers will never know that it was your skill in Vegas, and not the deft hand of the videographer who captured the footage.

Manually Cropping and Panning

When you crop and pan a video event, you use can use tools to crop and pan to the desired area in the clip. You can resize the video event proportionately, or disproportionately.

Numerically Cropping and Panning

If you're a stickler for precision, you can type values in text boxes to numerically crop and pan an event. This enables you to precisely position the cropped video event in the desired area of the video frame.

FIGURE 8-1

Using the Event Pan/Crop icon

Event Pan/Crop icon

FIGURE 8-2

The Event Pan/Crop dialog box

Show Properties

Normal Edit tool

Zoom Edit tool

Enable Snapping

Lock Aspect Ratio

Size About Center

Move Freely
(X or Y)

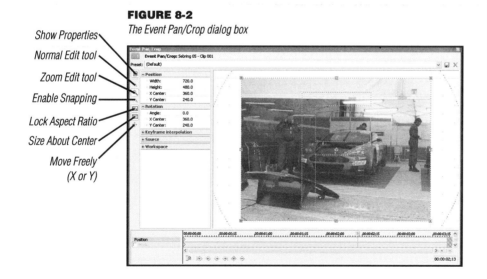

1. Create a new project.

2. Import a video clip into the Project Media window.

3. Drop the event in the main window, aligning it with the beginning of the timeline, as shown in Figure 8-1.

4. If the Video Preview window is not displayed in the workspace, choose View > Video Preview.

   When you crop and pan a video event, the results of your changes are not visible in the Event Pan/Crop dialog box. You will, however, be able to see the results of your edits in the Video Preview window.

5. Click the Event Pan/Crop icon.

   The Event Pan/Crop dialog box appears, as shown in Figure 8-2. Within this dialog box are controls that you can use to resize or pan the video event. You can resize the event proportionately or disproportionately. You can pan the event along the X, Y, or axes. Notice that there are also properties for width, height, X center, Y center, and so on.

6. Select the Normal Edit tool.

7. Click and drag any of the handles to resize the video event.

   As you move your cursor toward one of the handles, it becomes a dual-headed arrow. If you drag toward the center of the event, you zoom in on a smaller area. When you drag away from the center, you zoom out, which effectively reduces the size of the video.

TIP

To resize proportionately, click the Lock Aspect Ratio icon to select the option. Press Ctrl to momentarily override this option.

TIP

Click the Size About Center icon to resize the video clip from the center of the resizing box. When this option is deselected, the video is resized from the opposite side of the resizing box. Press Ctrl to momentarily override this option.

8. Move your cursor outside of the resizing box until it becomes a semicircle with an arrow, as shown in Figure 8-3.

   The semicircle indicates that you can manually rotate the event.

9. Click and drag to rotate the event.

   Drag right to rotate clockwise, or left to rotate counterclockwise.

QUICKTIP

Click the Show Properties button to hide property values and gain more working space in the Event Pan/Crop dialog box.

10. Move your cursor inside the resizing box until it becomes a four-headed arrow, as shown in Figure 8-4.

    The four-headed arrow indicates that you can pan the video clip. When you pan a video event, you move to the cropped area to a different part of the video clip, which in essence enables you to zoom in to a specific area within the clip.

FIGURE 8-3

Rotating an event manually

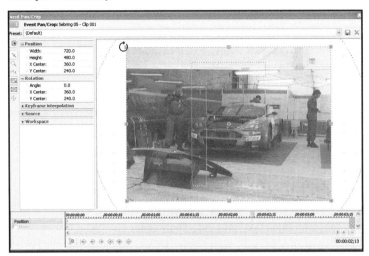

FIGURE 8-4

Panning an event manually

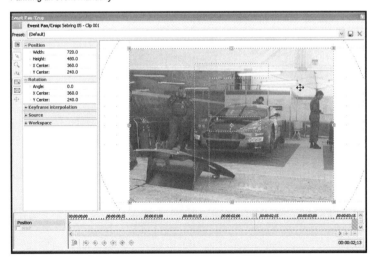

11. Click and drag to pan to the desired area of the video event.

12. Click the Move Freely (X or Y) icon in the lower-left corner of the dialog box.

    The icon becomes a dual-headed arrow pointing left and right, indicating that you can only pan the video event along the **X axis**. If you hover your cursor over the icon, the tooltip reads "Move in X Only."

13. Click the Move in X Only Icon.

    The icon becomes a dual-headed arrow pointing up and down, indicating that you can only pan the event along the **Y axis**. If you hover your cursor over the icon, the tooltip reads "Move in Y Only."

14. Click the Move in Y Only icon.

    The icon becomes a four-headed arrow, indicating you can pan freely in both axes.

15. Close the Event Pan/Crop dialog box to apply your changes.

Pan and crop an event numerically

1. Create a new project.

2. Import a video clip into the Project Media window.

3. Select the clip; then drop it in the main window, aligning it with the beginning of the timeline.

4. If the Video Preview window is not displayed in the workspace, choose View > Video Preview.

5. Click the Event Pan/Crop icon in the upper-right corner of the video event.

    The Event Pan/Crop dialog box, shown in Figure 8-5, appears. In addition to the tools discussed in the previous objective, you'll also find the properties of the video event. The video in Figure 8-5 is 720 pixels by 480 pixels. Notice that the X Center and Y Center values are exactly half of the frame size, indicating that the video event is centered in the frame. The Angle value in the Rotation section is 0, indicating that the video event has not been rotated. When you use the edit tools to manually crop and pan a video event, the property values change to reflect your modifications. In the remaining steps of this objective, you'll enter values to pan and crop the event with mathematical precision.

FIGURE 8-5

Displaying video pan/crop properties

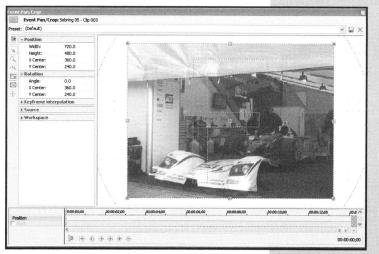

6. Make sure the Lock Aspect Ratio icon is enabled.

When this option is enabled, you can type a value for width or height, and the other value will be updated so that the video event is cropped proportionately.

7. Type a value of **1440** in the Width field.

The Height value is updated to 960, and the video is cropped to half its original size.

> **QUICKTIP**
>
> Float the Video Preview window in the workspace and align it alongside the Event Pan/Crop dialog box so that you can easily view the results of your edits.

8. Type a value of **0** in the X Center and Y Center text boxes.

The cropped video is aligned to the lower-right corner of the video frame, as shown in Figure 8-6. Note that this screenshot shows the Video Preview window. In the Event Pan/Crop dialog box, you won't be able to view the results of your modifications. All you'll see is the resized bounding box around the area of the video to which you have panned and cropped.

9. Type a value of **720** in the X Center text box.

The cropped video event is aligned to the lower-left corner of the video frame.

10. Type a value of **480** in the Y Center text box.

The cropped video event is aligned to the upper-left corner of the video frame.

11. Enter a value of **0** in the X Center text box.

The cropped video event is aligned to the upper-right corner of the video frame.

FIGURE 8-6
Panning a cropped video event

FIGURE 8-7

Selecting a pan/crop preset

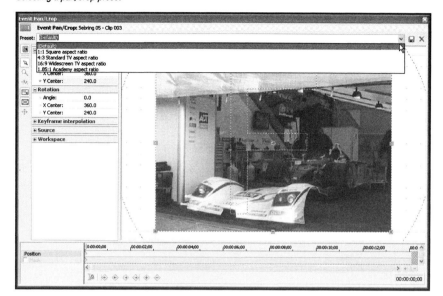

To undo a pan and crop, click the Preset down arrow and choose Default from the drop-down list.

12. Type a value of **25** in the Rotation text box.

The cropped video event is rotated 25 degrees.

TIP

To save pan and crop settings for future use, select the current name, which becomes (Untitled) as soon as you change the default settings or use one of the tools. Type a name for the modified preset, and then click the Save button. The new preset appears at the bottom of the list.

13. Experiment with different values before proceeding to the next objective.

Use pan and crop presets

1. Create a new project.

2. Import a video clip into the Project Media window.

3. Select the clip; then drop it in the main window, aligning it with the beginning of the timeline.

4. Click the Event Pan/Crop icon in the upper-right corner of the video event.

The Event Pan/Crop dialog box appears.

5. Click the Preset down arrow to reveal the drop-down list, shown in Figure 8-7.

6. Select the desired preset.

The video event is panned and cropped to the preset parameters. Figure 8-8 shows a video event as displayed in the Video Preview window that has been cropped using the 16:9 Widescreen TV Aspect Ratio preset.

FIGURE 8-8

Using a pan/crop preset

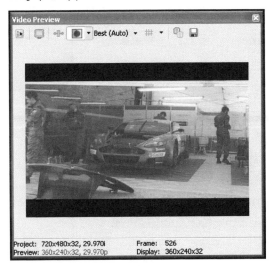

ANIMATE VIDEO EFFECTS
AND TRANSITIONS

What You'll Do

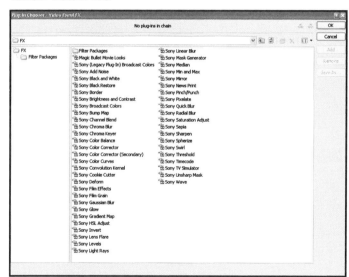

▶ *In this lesson, you learn how to animate video effects and transitions by using keyframes.*

Adding the "Wow" Factor with Animated Video FX

Video effects and transitions are like the icing on a cake. They add polish, pizzazz, and the indefinable, but instantly recognizable "wow" factor to a project. When you have compelling video, adding a plug-in is usually enough. However, if you're displaying a static image, or footage with little or no action, you can spice things up by animating a video FX plug-in, or the transition between two events.

Animating with Keyframes

When you animate a video FX plug-in or transition, you add keyframes in the same manner that you do when you animate a title or other generated media. You can add multiple keyframes to an event or transition, as well as determine how the transition between keyframes is interpolated. For example, you can choose Linear, Fast, Slow and so on to determine how the frames between keyframes are interpolated when the video is played back. If you have multiple effects applied to a video event, you can animate each effect independently.

In Chapter 5, "Adding Pizzazz with Transitions," you learned how to apply a Transition Progress envelope to a video transition that controls the manner in which the transition occurs between events. With a Transition Progress envelope, you control how the transition progresses from one event to the next. However, when you animate a transition using keyframes, you can radically change the look of the transition as it occurs by creating the desired number of keyframes, and then changing the parameters to suit your project. When it comes to animating a transition, there are no hard and fast rules. Experimentation yields the best results.

Animate video effects

1. Create a new project.

2. Import a video clip into the Project Media window.

3. Select the video clip; then drop it in the main window, aligning it with the beginning of the timeline.

4. Click the Event FX icon in the lower-right corner of the video event.

   Vegas displays the Plug-In Chooser dialog box.

5. Select the Sony Light Rays plug-in; then click Add.

6. Select the Gaussian Blur plug-in; then click Add.

   Vegas adds the plug-ins to the plug-in chain. Remember: When you add multiple plug-ins to an event, the order in which they are added determines the overall effect that is applied to the event because the plug-ins are executed in the same order they are applied.

   ### QUICKTIP

   To change the order in which a plug-in executes, click the plug-in name to select it, and then drag it to the desired position in the Video Event FX dialog box.

7. Click OK to exit the Plug-In Chooser dialog box.

   The selected plug-ins are added to the plug-in chain and displayed in the Video Event FX dialog box, shown in Figure 8-9. Notice that you have two timelines with which to work. To make changes to a timeline, you click it to select it. For example, to make changes to the Gaussian Blur timeline, click it.

8. Click the Sync Cursor button.

   This option synchronizes the position of the cursor on the Video Event FX dialog box timeline with the position of the cursor on the project timeline, enabling you to see the effects of your edits in the Video Preview window.

9. If the Video Preview window is not currently displayed in the workspace, choose View > Video Preview.

FIGURE 8-9

Adding two plug-ins to a video event

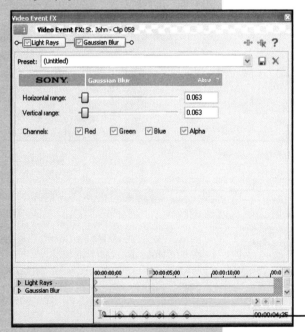

Sync Cursor button

FIGURE 8-10

Adding keyframes to a timeline

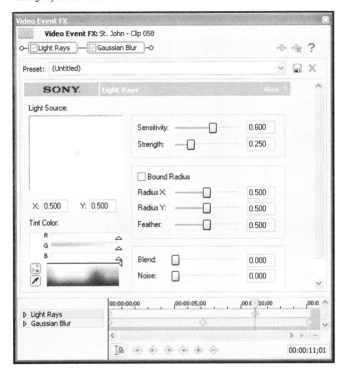

10. Click the Light Rays button in the upper-left corner of the Video Event FX dialog box.

11. Click the Preset down arrow; then choose Intense Light Rays from the drop-down list.

12. Click the Light Rays title to the left of the Light Rays timeline.

The title is highlighted in blue. You can now add keyframes to the timeline.

13. Create keyframes in the middle and end of the timeline.

To create a keyframe, click the desired point in the timeline, and then click the Create Keyframe button that looks like a plus sign.

14. Click the Gaussian Blur title to the left of the Gaussian Blur timeline.

This selects the Gaussian Blur timeline, and also displays the parameters for the Gaussian Blur plug-in in the Video Event FX dialog box.

15. Create keyframes at the question mark and the end of the timeline.

Your timeline should resemble Figure 8-10. Note that if you're adding keyframes to a long video event, the entire timeline might not be visible in the Video Event FX dialog box. If this occurs, you'll have a scroll bar at the bottom of the timeline that you can use to scroll to the hidden parts of the timeline.

16. Select the first keyframe on the Light Rays timeline.

17. Select the square icon in the middle of the Light Source window. Drag it to the left side of the window.

When you move the icon, the source of the light rays moves as well. Alternatively, you can type values in the X and Y fields under the Light Source window. For this objective, your values will be X = 0.00 and Y = .500, as shown in Figure 8-11.

18. With the first keyframe still selected, drag the Sensitivity slider until you achieve a value of approximately .200. Then drag the Strength slider until you achieve a value of approximately .500.

19. Select the last keyframe on the Light Rays timeline.

20. Select the square icon in the middle of the Light Source window; then drag it to the right side of the window.

Alternatively, you can type values in the X and Y fields. For this objective, your values will be X = 1.00 and Y = .500.

21. Select the first keyframe of the Gaussian Blur timeline. Then drag the Horizontal Range and Vertical Range sliders to achieve a value of 0.

22. Select the middle keyframe of the Gaussian Blur timeline. Then drag the Horizontal Range and Vertical Range sliders to achieve a value of 0.

At this point, you could leave the values for the Gaussian Blur plug-in at their default values for the final keyframe on the timeline. When the video is played back, the event will be in focus on the first two keyframes, and

FIGURE 8-11

Changing parameters at a keyframe

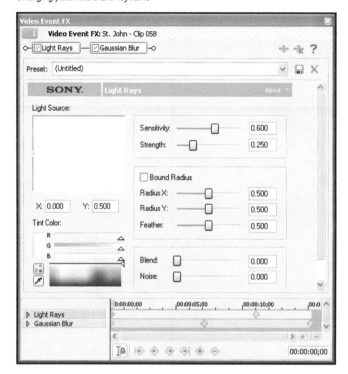

FIGURE 8-12
Modifying the Gaussian Blur timeline

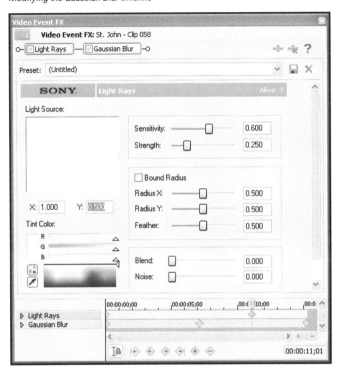

then appear to go out of focus as the Gaussian Blur values gradually increase to their default values. To give the video a dreamy, out-of-focus look, select the last keyframe, and then drag the Horizontal Range and Vertical Range sliders to achieve a value of approximately 0.50, as shown in Figure 8-12.

23. Click the Close button to exit the Video Event FX dialog box and to apply the changes to the video event.

24. Preview the project.

As the project plays back, the light rays gradually increase in strength as they move to the center of the video frame. In the last half of the project, the light rays decrease in strength and move to the right side of the video frame, and the event becomes blurrier, appearing to be out of focus. For a variation on this effect, you can change the color of the light rays on the middle keyframe.

> **NOTE**
>
> Remember, you can click the Split Screen down arrow in the Video Preview window to choose one of the presets to view the video without the plug-in applied in one half of Video Preview window, and with the plug-in applied in the other half. To see the plug-in as it will appear in your rendered video, click the Preview Quality down arrow, and choose Best from the drop-down list.

Animate a video transition

1. Create a new project.

2. Import two video clips into the Project Media window.

3. Select the video clips; then drop them in the main window, aligning them with the beginning of the timeline.

4. Overlap the video events to create a crossfade.

   As discussed in Chapter 5, the crossfade is the place to start when you want to apply a video transition to segue from one event to the next. Create a crossfade of at least three seconds in duration; otherwise, your animated transition will fly by so fast, viewers will barely be able to see it.

5. Click the Transitions tab; then choose Flash.

   The Flash transition presets appear in the Transitions window.

6. Select the Hard Flash preset; then drop it on the transition.

   Vegas displays the Video Event FX dialog box.

7. Create three keyframes on the timeline, one at the start, one at the end, and one in the middle.

8. Select the middle keyframe; then change the color to a dark red, as shown in Figure 8-13.

9. Click the Close button to exit the Video Event FX dialog box and apply your changes.

10. Preview the project.

    When the transition is encountered, the color of the flash changes from bright white to red before changing to white at the end of the transition. This short objective is just one example of what is possible when animating transitions. Experiment with some of the other transition presets to see what effects you can create by changing parameters at keyframes. Remember that this technique works best with transitions that are three seconds or longer in duration.

FIGURE 8-13

Animating a transition

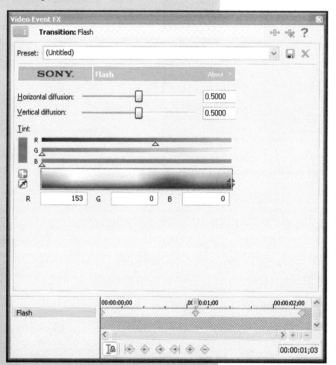

ZOOM IN ON AND
ROTATE A VIDEO EVENT

What You'll Do

▶ *In this lesson, you learn to zoom in on a specific portion of a video event, as well as rotate it.*

Zooming In on a Subject

The beauty of digital video is in the myriad of things you can do with it after you get it inside a stout video editing application, such as Vegas. When you assemble a project and begin previewing it, you might notice some video events that would look good zoomed in. When this is the case, you can click the Event Pan/Crop icon, and then add keyframes inside the Event Pan/Crop dialog box. At each keyframe, you crop to select the desired portion of the video and, if needed, pan to the desired subject. When the event is played back, it appears as though a cameraman zoomed and panned to focus on a subject.

Rotating a Subject

Zooming and panning is just one part of the equation. If you've watched your fair share of video productions, you've probably noticed clips where the cameraman zoomed in on a subject while rotating the camcorder. When you see videos of this nature, the camera operator probably had an expensive boom setup. Or maybe the effect was done post-production in a video-editing application. You can create the same effect in Vegas using a pan/crop envelope.

When you want to rotate a video event, you also work with keyframes in the Event Pan/Crop dialog box. You can rotate the event manually, as outlined previously in this chapter, or you can enter a value in the Angle text box. If you rotate an event without zooming in on it, at some point you'll see black, because the video frame is wider than it is tall.

Zoom in on an event

1. Create a new project.

2. Import a video clip that contains a faraway subject into the Project Media window.

3. Select the video clip; then drop it in the main window, aligning it with the beginning of the timeline.

4. If the Video Preview window isn't displayed in the workspace, choose View > Video Preview.

5. Click the Event Pan/Crop icon.

   Vegas displays the Event Pan/Crop dialog box.

6. Click the Sync Cursor icon at the bottom of the timeline in the Event Pan/Crop window.

   This synchronizes the cursor position in the Event Pan/Crop dialog box with the cursor position on the event timeline. In other words, when you navigate along the timeline in the Event Pan/Crop window, the identical frame is selected on the event video timeline, which enables you to view the effects of your edits in the Video Preview window.

   QUICKTIP

   Undock the Video Preview window and position it alongside the Event Pan/Crop window to make it easier to see the results of your edits.

7. Use the right and left arrow keys to navigate the timeline in the Event Pan/Crop dialog box.

8. When you reach a frame on which you want to zoom in on your subject, click and drag one of the corner handles on the pan/crop bounding box.

Vegas adds a keyframe to the timeline.

9. Continue navigating the Event Pan/Crop dialog box timeline. Use the crop handles to zoom in or out on the subject.

   Remember: You can also pan while zooming, as outlined previously in this chapter. Figure 8-14 shows a video event with three keyframes on the timeline. Notice that the Event Pan/Crop dialog box shows the entire video frame, whereas the Video Preview window shows the cropped and panned video.

   QUICKTIP

   Press Alt+0(zero) to change focus from the Event Pan/Crop window to the timeline.

10. Close the Event Pan/Crop dialog box and preview the project.

FIGURE 8-14

Zooming in on a subject

Rotate an event

1. Create a new project.

2. Import a video clip into the Project Media window.

3. Select the video clip; then drop it in the main window, aligning it with the beginning of the timeline.

4. If the Video Preview window is not currently displayed in the workspace, choose View > Video Preview.

QUICKTIP

To display or hide the Video Preview window, press Alt+4.

5. Click the Event Pan/Crop icon.

   The Event Pan/Crop dialog box appears.

6. Click the Sync Cursor button.

7. Navigate the timeline until you reach the frame where you want to rotate the video event.

8. Zoom in and pan to your subject matter, as outlined previously.

If you don't zoom in on your subject, you'll see the edge of the video when you rotate the event.

9. Manually rotate the event using the Normal Edit tool, as outlined previously.

If you rotate counterclockwise in the Event Pan/Crop dialog box, the video event actually rotates clockwise. Alternatively, you can type a value in the Angle field in the Rotation section of the dialog box. Type a negative value to rotate the event clockwise or a positive value to rotate the event clockwise, as shown in Figure 8-15.

10. Navigate to other points on the timeline; then pan, crop, and rotate as desired.

When you have the Sync Cursor option enabled, Vegas creates a keyframe whenever you navigate to a different point on the timeline, and make a change in the Event Pan/Crop dialog box.

NOTE

You can right-click the keyframe and choose the manner in which Vegas interpolates the frames between keyframes by selecting an option from the shortcut menu. Your choices are Linear, Fast, Slow, Smooth, Sharp, and Hold.

11. Click the Close button to exit the Event Pan/Crop dialog box.

12. Preview the project.

If you panned and cropped the video event, the subject matter is magnified as if the videographer zoomed in on the subject. The event rotates in the desired direction.

FIGURE 8-15

Rotating an event

CREATE VIDEO
MASKS

What You'll Do

In this lesson, you use the Cookie Cutter plug-in to mask underlying video tracks.

Using the Cookie Cutter Plug-In

When you create a project with multiple tracks, you can do some truly wonderful things. One compelling technique is creating a mask. When you create a mask on one track, you reveal a portion of the underlying, or masked track. You can manually create a mask by creating points. This technique is covered in Chapter 9, "Creating Video Eye Candy." The focus of this lesson is the Cookie Cutter plug-in. As the name implies, this plug-in creates a shape, which in essence is a mask cutout, to reveal the video on the underlying track.

Using Preset Shapes as Masks

When you add the Cookie Cutter plug-in to a video event, you can choose from a wide variety of shapes. You can use a circle, diamond, rectangle, or triangle as a mask to the underlying track. If desired,

you can have multiple shapes as a mask. The plug-in also has other interesting presets, such as Grate, Picture in Picture, and Top Left Portrait.

Animating the Cookie Cutter Plug-In

As with other video plug-ins, you can animate the Cookie Cutter plug-in by adding keyframes to the timeline in the Video Event FX dialog box. You then modify the plug-in parameters on each keyframe to achieve the desired result. In addition to animating the plug-in, you can pan and crop the underlying video track or the top video track. Vegas gives you the artistic license to mix and match plug-ins and other techniques to create your own unique eye-catching productions.

FIGURE 8-16

Modifying Cookie Cutter plug-in parameters

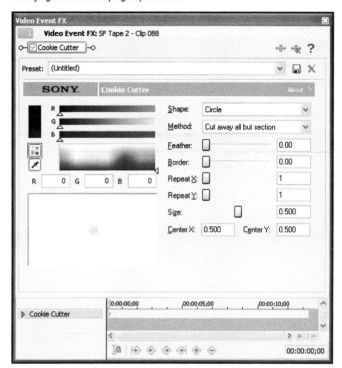

1. Create a new project.

2. Import two video clips into the Project Media window.

3. Select the video clips and right-click. Then drop the video clips into the main window, aligning them with the beginning of the timeline.

4. Release the mouse button; then choose Add Across Tracks from the shortcut menu.

   Vegas creates two video tracks, and if the video has embedded audio, it creates two audio tracks as well.

5. Click the Event FX icon on the top video track.

   Vegas displays the Plug-In Chooser-Video Event FX dialog box.

6. Select the Cookie Cutter plug-in; then click Add.

   Vegas adds the plug-in to the video event.

7. Click OK to exit the Plug-In Chooser-Video Event FX dialog box.

   Vegas displays the plug-in parameters in the Video Event FX dialog box, shown in Figure 8-16.

8. Click the Preset down arrow; then choose Circle, Center from the drop-down list.

   The preset you choose serves as the basis for the final effect. As with other Vegas plug-ins, you can modify the parameters to get the desired results.

9. Click the Shape down arrow; then choose an option from the drop-down list. For the purpose of this objective, choose the Arrowhead Right shape.

The shape you choose determines the shape of the mask used to reveal the underlying track.

10. Click the Method down arrow; then choose an option from the drop-down list.

This option determines what parts of the underlying video are visible. Choose Cut Away All But Selection to reveal the underlying track directly under the shape, or choose Cut Away Selection to reveal everything on the underlying track except the shape itself.

11. Drag the Feather slider to determine how the shape border blends into the background.

The default value of 0 doesn't apply feathering. Alternatively, you can type a value between 0 and 1 in the Feather field. A higher value causes smoother blending of the shape border into the background.

12. Drag the Border slider to determine the thickness of the shape's border.

Alternatively, you can type a value between 0.00 (no border) and 1.0 (the border fills the shape, occluding the underlying track) in the Border field.

13. Drag the Repeat X and Repeat Y sliders to determine how many instances of the shape mask the underlying track.

Alternatively, you can type a value between 1 and 10. The Size value determines the number of shapes that are visible in the video frame.

14. Drag the Size slider to determine the size of the shape(s) masking the underlying track.

Alternatively, you can enter a value between 0.00 and 1.00. If you specify a large value and many shapes, you might not be able to see all the shapes in the video frame.

15. Enter a value in the Center X and Center Y fields to determine the center of the shape(s) within the video frame.

The default values place the shape(s) in the center of the video frame. You can enter a value between Center X = 0 (right side of the video frame), Center Y = 0 (top of the video frame), and Center X = 1.0 (left side of the video frame), and Center Y = 1.0 (bottom of the video frame). Alternatively, you can click and drag the small square in the center of the window to the left of these fields to manually move the shape(s).

FIGURE 8-17

Masking with the Cookie Cutter plug-in

16. Choose a color from the color picker.

   This determines the color of the shape border. Alternatively, you can click the Pick Color from Screen button (it looks like an eyedropper), and sample a color from a video track, the Video Preview window, or anywhere else in the workspace.

17. Click the Close button to exit the dialog box and preview the video.

   Figure 8-17 shows a preview of the Cookie Cutter plug-in at work.

CREATE A COLLAGE
OF MOVING VIDEO CLIPS

What You'll Do

In this lesson, you create a compelling introduction with a collage of four moving video clips. The clips are cropped to a fourth of their original size and stacked in the center of the video frame. When the project plays, the clips move from the center outward, eventually filling the frame.

Creating a Video Collage

When you want to announce your video production with a bang, consider creating a collage of moving video clips. The combination of small videos clips floating across the video frame, combined with compelling video clips, creates the type of visual eye candy that will leave your viewing audience wondering what you'll do to top the introduction.

Animating the Collage

When you use this technique, you combine several of the skills you've already learned. You begin by adding four video clips to your project across tracks. Next, you'll crop each video clip to a fourth of its original size. Then you'll add keyframes and move each video clip to the corner of the video frame. During this lesson, you'll learn a couple of shortcuts to speed up your production.

Create a collage of video clips

1. Create a new project.

2. Import four video clips into the Project Media window.

3. Select the video clips and right-click. Then drag the video clips into the main window, aligning them with the beginning of the timeline.

4. Release the mouse button; then choose Add Across Tracks from the shortcut menu.

5. Trim the video clips so they're of equal duration.

6. Click the Event Pan/Crop icon for the video event in the first track.

   Vegas displays the Event Pan/Crop dialog box. Make sure you have clicked the Lock Aspect option button.

7. Type a value of **1440** in the Width text box.

   Vegas resizes the height to 960. These dimensions crop the video to a fourth of its original size.

8. Click the Close button to exit the Event Pan/Crop dialog box and apply your changes.

9. Right-click the video event in the first track; then choose Copy from the shortcut menu.

10. Select the video events in tracks 3, 5, and 7.

    Click the first video event in track 3 to select it. Then Ctrl+click the video events in tracks 5 and 7.

11. Right-click; then choose Paste Event Attributes from the shortcut menu.

    Vegas crops the selected events to the same size as the event you copied.

12. Use the playhead to navigate to the middle of your production.

13. Click the Event Pan/Crop icon for the video clip in the first track.

    Vegas displays the Event Pan/Crop dialog box.

14. Click the Sync Cursor icon to the left and below the Event Pan/Crop timeline.

    When you click the Synch Cursor icon, Vegas synchronizes the position of the playhead on the timeline, with the position of the playhead in the Event Pan/Crop dialog box.

15. Type a value of **0** in the X Center text box and a value of **0** in the Y Center text box, as shown in Figure 8-18. Then click the Close button.

    Vegas creates a keyframe in the Event Pan/Crop dialog box. The values you typed position the video event at the lower-right corner of the video frame.

16. Click the Event Pan/Crop icon for the video event on track 3.

FIGURE 8-18

Changing the video event position

17. Position your cursor in the middle of the timeline, and then type a value of **720** in the X Center dialog box and a value of **480** in the Y Center text box. Click the Close button.

Vegas creates a keyframe on the Event Pan/Crop timeline. These values position the video event at the upper-left corner of the video frame.

18. Click the Event Pan/Crop icon for the video event on track 5.

19. Type a value of **0** in the X Center text box and a value of **480** in the Y Center text box. Then click the Close button.

Vegas creates a keyframe on the Event Pan/Crop timeline. These values position the video event in the upper-right corner of the video frame.

20. Click the Event Pan/Crop icon for the video event on track 7.

21. Type a value of **720** in the X Center text box and a value of **0** in the Y Center text box. Then click the Close button.

Vegas creates a keyframe on the Event Pan/Crop timeline. These values place the video event in the lower-left corner of the video frame.

22. Preview the project.

As the project plays back, the video events move from the center of the video frame to the four corners, as shown in Figure 8-19. The video events continue playing but are stationary for the last half of the project. You can augment this effect by creating a new video track at the top of the track list, and then using transparent text to create a title to

display an introduction for the video. Position the media event so that the title is displayed after the video events have moved to the perimeter of the video frame. Another possibility is to stagger the times so that the events don't move at the same time.

FIGURE 8-19
Previewing the collage project

Cropping an Event

1. Create a new project.

2. Import a video clip into the Project Media window.

3. Select the clip; then drop it in the main window, aligning it with the beginning of the timeline.

4. If the Video Preview window is not displayed in the workspace, choose View > Video Preview.

5. Click the Event Pan/Crop icon to open the Event Pan Crop dialog box.

6. Select the Video Preview window; then float it in the workspace, positioning it alongside the Event Pan/Crop dialog box.

7. Use the Normal Edit tool or type a value in the Width text box to resize the video event so that it occupies less of the video frame, as shown in Figure 8-20.

8. Click the Close button to exit the Event Pan/Crop dialog box.

9. Keep the project open. You'll be using it for the next skills review.

Panning an Event

1. Click the Event Pan/Crop icon in the lower-right corner of the video event.

2. Use the Normal Edit tool to pan the video event to a different location.

3. Type a value of 0 in the X Center text box and a value of 0 in the Y center text box.

   Doing so positions the cropped video event near the lower-left corner of the video frame, as shown in Figure 8-21. Note that the actual position will vary depending on the size to which you have cropped the video.

FIGURE 8-20

Cropping a video event

FIGURE 8-21

Panning an event

4. Create a keyframe at the end of the Event Pan/Crop timeline.

5. Type a value of 720 in the X Center text box and a value of 480 in the Y Center text box.

   This positions the video event near the upper-right corner of the video frame.

6. Click the Close button to exit the Event Pan/Crop dialog box.

FIGURE 8-22
Animating a cropped event

7. Preview the video, as shown in Figure 8-22.

Using the Cookie Cutter Plug-In

1. Create a new project.

2. Import two video clips into the Project Media window.

3. Select the clips and right-click. Then drop the clips in the main window, aligning them with the beginning of the timeline.

FIGURE 8-23
Modifying a plug-in preset

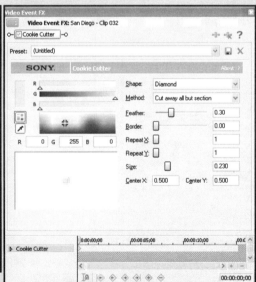

4. Release the mouse button and then choose Add Across Tracks from the shortcut menu.

5. Click the Event FX icon on the top track video event.

6. Select Sony Cookie Cutter; then click Add to add the plug-in to the chain.

7. Click OK to exit the Plug-In Chooser-Video Event FX dialog box.

8. Click the triangle to the right of the Preset field; then choose Diamond, Center, Blurred.

9. Drag the Feather slider to achieve a value of .10, and then size the diamond as shown in Figure 8-23.

10. Click the Close button to exit the Video Event FX dialog box.

11. Preview the project, as shown in Figure 8-24.

12. Keep the project open. You'll be using it in the next skills review.

Animating the Cookie Cutter Plug-In

1. If the Video Preview window is not currently displayed in the workspace, choose View > Video Preview.

2. Click the Event FX icon for the video event to which you just applied the Cookie Cutter plug-in.

3. Click the Sync Cursor icon below the timeline.

4. Float the Video Preview window; then align it next to the Video Event FX dialog box so that you can preview your changes.

5. Click the center of the Video Event FX timeline to navigate to the middle of the event.

6. Drag the Feather slider to .50 to modify the parameter and create a keyframe, as shown in Figure 8-25.

7. Position your cursor at the end of the Video Event FX timeline.

8. Drag the Size slider to achieve a value of .50 and create a keyframe.

9. Click the Close button to exit the Video Event FX dialog box.

10. Preview the video, as shown in Figure 8-26.

FIGURE 8-24
Creating a mask with the Cookie Cutter plug-in

FIGURE 8-25
Creating a keyframe while modifying a parameter

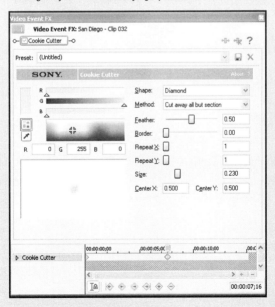

FIGURE 8-26
Previewing an animated plug-in

You work in the production department for a local TV station. Your supervisor presents you with a miniDV cassette of amateur videographer's footage of a historic motor race, which has a scene not recorded by your staff. The footage, although in focus, was shot from a spectator area; therefore, the cars appear distant. You decide to crop the event and zoom in on the action.

1. Create a new project.

2. Import a video clip into the Project Media window. Preferably, choose a clip in which the subject is far away and not centered in the video frame.

3. Select the clip; then drop it in the main window, aligning it with the beginning of the timeline.

4. Click the Event Pan/Crop icon.

5. Navigate the timeline until you arrive at a frame where you'd like to zoom in on the subject.

6. Use the Normal Edit tool to crop the video event, as shown in Figure 8-27. Your objective is to zoom in on the subject.

7. If necessary, pan to center the subject in the frame.

8. Click the Close button to exit the Event Pan/Crop dialog box.

9. Preview the video, as shown in Figure 8-28.

FIGURE 8-27
Cropping a video event

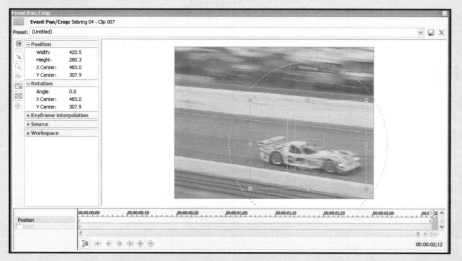

FIGURE 8-28
Previewing a cropped video

You're previewing video for a project you've been assigned to produce. Your boss has told you she wants an impressive introduction to the video. As you preview the video clips, you decide to start the project with a bang by displaying a still image that gradually increases in size and expands beyond the boundary of the video frame.

1. Create a new project.

2. Import a still image into the Project Media window. You'll get better results if you choose an image that is larger than the video frame.

3. If the Video Preview window is not displayed in the workspace, choose View > Video Preview.

4. Select the Event Pan/Crop icon.

5. Use the Normal Edit tool to shrink the video event to a fraction of its original size. As you make your changes, preview your work in the Video Preview window, as shown in Figure 8-29.

6. Create a keyframe at the end of the Event Pan/Crop timeline.

7. Because the cropping handles are probably beyond the boundary of the dialog box, crop the image numerically so that it exceeds the boundary of the video frame, as shown in Figure 8-30.

8. Click the Close button to exit the Event Pan/Crop dialog box.

9. Preview the video.

FIGURE 8-29

Cropping an image

FIGURE 8-30

Cropping with the Normal Edit tool

DESIGN PROJECT

You run an independent production company. A new client contacts you to create a video portfolio to vault her modeling career. After meeting with the client, you realize that a thing of beauty is a joy forever, so you decide to use a still image from her portfolio as an introduction to the video. You decide to use a mask to reveal the client's beauty during the first few seconds of the video production.

FIGURE 8-31
Design Project sample 1

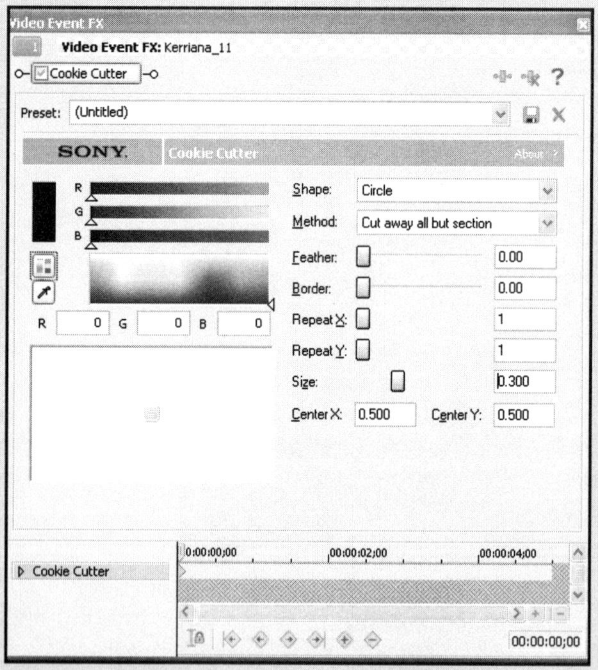

1. Create a new project.

2. Import an image of a person into the Project Media window. A head and shoulders shot is preferable.

3. Select the image and drop it in the main window, aligning it with the beginning of the timeline.

4. If the Video Preview window is not displayed in the workspace, choose View > Video Preview.

5. Click the Event FX icon on the video event you just created.

6. Choose the Sony Cookie Cutter plug-in. Then click the Add button.

7. Accept the default preset. Then drag the Size slider to achieve a value of about .030, as shown in Figure 8-31.

8. Click the Synch Cursor icon

9. Navigate to the middle of the timeline.

10. Drag the Size slider to achieve a value of .30.

11. Navigate to the end of the timeline.

12. Drag the Size slider to achieve a value of 1.00.

13. Preview the project, as shown in Figure 8-32.

FIGURE 8-32
Design Project sample 2

CHAPTER SUMMARY

In this chapter, you learned to create special effects for your video productions. Cropping and panning an event is a way to zoom in on a portion of a video clip. If you animate cropping and panning, it's equivalent to zooming in on an object. Video masks are an ideal way to add special effects to a project. When you add a video mask to a multi track project, you let portions of the underlying track appear when the video is played.

What You Have Learned

In this chapter you:

- Learned to crop and pan a video event manually.
- Learned to crop and pan an event numerically.
- Learned to rotate a video event.

- Learned to add pizzazz to your productions by animating effects and video transitions.
- Learned to animate with timeline keyframes.
- Learned to create video masks with the Cookie Cutter plug-in.
- Learned to create a collage of moving video clips.

Key Terms From this Chapter

- Collage. In video, a collection of video clips arranged within the video frame.
- Crop. To specify which part of a video clip is shown. You can crop to zoom in on a small area of a clip or to resize a clip.
- Mask. A device that designates which part of an event is hidden or displayed.

- Pan. To move a video clip within the video frame.
- Video frame. The boundaries of a video clip.
- X axis. From left to right in the video frame (horizontal).
- Y axis. From top to bottom in the video frame (vertical).

9

CREATING VIDEO
Eye Candy

1. Create a *Star Wars* intro.

2. Create a split frame video title.

3. Add pizzazz with 3D track motion.

4. Create fly-through text.

5. Create a Bezier mask.

6. Create handwritten text.

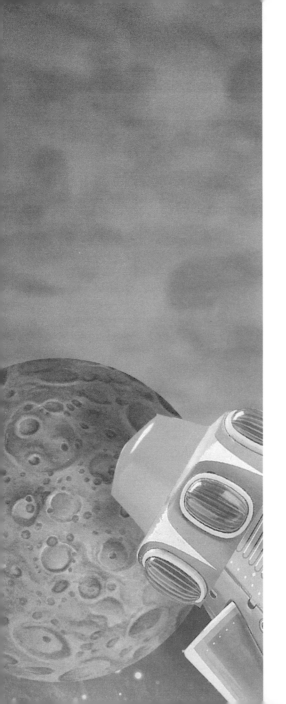

9 CREATING VIDEO
Eye Candy

In the last chapter, you had an introduction to creating special effects with Vegas plug-ins. To quote an old rock-n-roll song, "You ain't seen nuthin' yet." In this chapter, you learn some more recipes for creating compelling videos. Many of the effects you learn can be mixed and matched. Remember, you can create multiple tracks and composite them to combine effects.

If you thought the Cookie Cutter plug-in was cool, what 'til you see what you can do with a **Bezier** mask. That's right, you can draw a mask with a tool that functions identically to a pen tool in an illustration application. You can even animate a Bezier mask by adding keyframes and then moving the points that comprise that mask.

Rotating Video Clips and Other Delights

Panning and cropping an event can create some wonderful effects as you learned in the last chapter. But there's more lurking under the hood of this wonderful application called Vegas. There's a composite method known as 3D Source Alpha that I alluded to in an earlier chapter. Using this composite method with 3D track motion, you can make a video event appear as though it's a playing card being flipped through space. You can move the video track on any axis, rotate the track, and so on. You have views that enable you to manipulate the video track position from the top, left, or front. If you've ever worked with a 3D application, manipulating the position of a video track in three dimensions will seem familiar to you.

Creating Compelling Intros

Vegas ships with a plethora of compelling credits. In the lessons that follow, you'll learn how to combine credits with some of the special effects from the last chapter, to create some truly wonderful introductions for your videos. If you loved *Star Wars*, you'll learn how to create the same type of intro for your productions. You'll also learn how to create a title that displays in one half of the video frame, alongside a video in the other half of the frame.

Animating Text

Scrolling credits are just one way to announce a production. You can also create compelling introductions by moving text in 3D space. With this technique, you can simulate an airplane flying through a text cloud, or create an effect that looks like the text is being written letter by letter.

As with any tool, experimentation is the key. Take the effects you learned in the last two chapters and think of ways you can augment them to suit your own productions. When you see something really special in a Hollywood movie, ask yourself how you can replicate the effect in Vegas. Let your mind drift, experiment and play in Vegas and in no time you'll be creating video productions that will dazzle your audiences.

Tools You'll Use

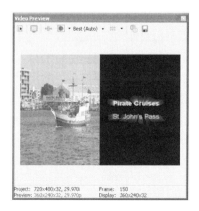

CREATE A STAR WARS
INTRO

What You'll Do

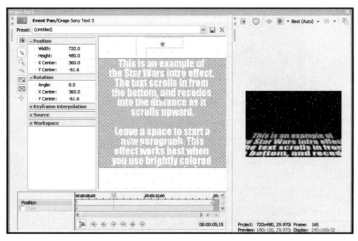

 In this lesson, you learn how to create an intro similar to the one in the legendary Star Wars *movie. Scrolling text with perspective is an interesting way to begin a production, especially when you have a back story to tell.*

Creating a Text Mask

The first step is to create a mask for the text. You create a mask that makes the text appear to fade into deep space. You achieve this effect by using a linear gradient media

for the top track. You then assign the Mask Generator plug-in to the track. This plug-in uses the colors from the gradient to mask the text. When the text first appears onscreen, it is razor sharp and then gradually blurs into oblivion. The blending of the gradient colors from white to black is what achieves this effect, combined with the composite method for the track.

Creating the Scrolling Text

If you've seen the movie, you know that *Star Wars* begins with text that appears at the bottom of the screen and scrolls to the top. As you'll remember from the chapter on titles, there is a scrolling credits preset.

However, this preset offers no perspective, therefore it cannot be used for this technique. You can however introduce perspective through the use of a plug-in and get the text to scroll with a bit of judicious panning. The text is on its own track. In fact, this lesson will be your introduction to parent/child compositing.

Adding Perspective to the Text

You add the element of perspective to the text by using the Deform plug-in. You set the parameters for this plug-in to expand the text at the bottom and compress it at the top, which makes it narrower as it exits the frame.

Generating the Star Field

You complete the effect by creating a star field in the background. This appears on a different track, which is not a child of the text mask track. Therefore, the stars appear behind the text, but are not affected by the mask layer.

FIGURE 9-1

Creating the video mask

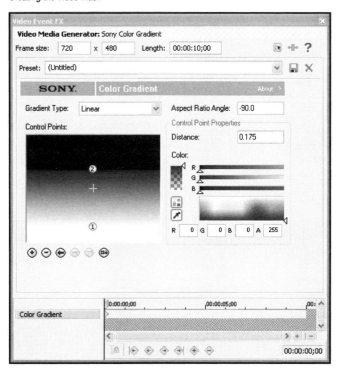

1. Create a new project.

2. Click the Media Generators tab. Then choose Color Gradient

3. Select the Gradient, White to Black preset and drop it in the main window, aligning it to the beginning of the timeline.

   The Video Event FX dialog box appears.

4. Type a value of **−90** in the Aspect Ratio Angle field.

   This value rotates the gradient 90 degrees in a clockwise direction.

5. Select gradient control point number 1. Then type a value of **−.350** in the Distance field.

6. Select gradient control point number 2. Then type a value of **.175** in the Distance field.

   Your dialog box should look like Figure 9-1. These values determine where the text is not masked, partially masked, and fully masked. At the bottom of the frame, where the gradient is pure white, the text will be completely visible. As the gradient changes from white to black, the text will get more opaque, creating the illusion of distance. At the top of the frame, where the gradient is pure black, the text is not visible.

7. Type a value of **00:00:20;00** in the Length text box near the top of the dialog box.

This changes the duration of the media to 20 seconds. When you use this technique in your own productions, select a length that doesn't cause the text to fly past too quickly. After all, you want your viewers to be able to read it.

> **NOTE**
>
> Even though you change the duration in the Video Event FX dialog box, the media is still the default length on the timeline. Move your cursor to the tail of the clip, and then click and drag to extend the duration of the media event to what you specified in the Video Event FX dialog box.

8. Click the Close button to exit the Video Event FX dialog box.

Vegas creates the media event. In order to complete the mask, you're going to add a plug-in to the media event, as well as the track.

9. Click the Track FX icon directly above the Level slider in Track 1.

Vegas displays the Plug-in Chooser-Video Track FX dialog box.

10. Select the Sony Mask Generator plug-in. Then click Add, and click OK to exit the dialog box.

The Video Event FX dialog box appears with the default parameters for the Sony Mask Generator plug-in.

11. Accept the default parameters and click the Close button to exit the dialog box.

Vegas adds the plug-in to the track. This plug-in converts the track into a mask.

12. On the video track, click the Compositing Mode button to the right of the Level slider. Then choose Multiply (Mask) from the drop-down list.

Now that you've created a mask, your next step is to create the text that will scroll from the bottom to the top of the video frame.

Create the text

1. Click the Media Generators tab. Then choose Text.

2. Select the Default Text preset. Then drop it in the main window, below the track you just created, aligning the media with the beginning of the timeline.

Vegas creates a new track below the mask track you just created. The Video Event FX dialog box appears displaying the parameters for the preset.

3. Choose a blocky font such as Arial Black or Impact. Then specify a font size of 34 points or more.

Your goal is to create text that stands out against the star-field background you'll create in the next objective. If desired, you can apply the Bold style to the text.

4. Select the sample text and type the desired text.

As you type your text, remember to press Enter to create a new line. This effect works best when you type several lines of text. If you're telling a story to introduce your

FIGURE 9-2

Aligning the text

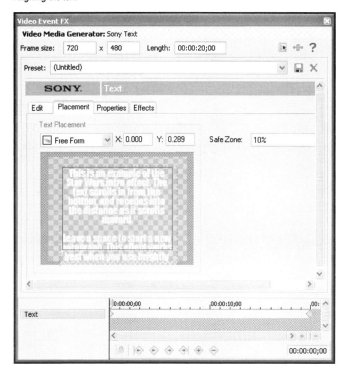

production, you can create a blank line to introduce the next paragraph.

5. Click the Properties tab. Then accept the default text color, or choose a different color.

This effect works best when you use bright colors that stand out from the background. Experiment with different text colors to suit the background for your project. Remember, you can always edit the generated media and change the text color after previewing the intro.

6. Click the Placement tab. Then manually align the text so that it appears at the top of the safe area, as shown in Figure 9-2.

To center the text, you may have to type **0** in the X text field. The text should not exceed the title safe boundary. If it does not, click the Edit tab and adjust the length of each line so that it is just inside the title safe boundary.

> **NOTE**
>
> If your text exceeds the boundary of the video frame, position your cursor at the end of the timeline, and then move your text so that the last line of the text is above the bottom of the video frame.

7. Click the Properties tab. Then drag the Leading slider to achieve a value of approximately .76. Alternatively, you can type **.76** in the Leading text box.

This narrows the space between each line. If you leave this parameter at its default setting, each line of text will be far apart because of the perspective you're going to introduce with the Deform plug-in.

8. Type a value of **00:00:20:00** in the Length text box.

9. Click the Close button to exit the dialog box.

Vegas creates the media event, as shown in Figure 9-3.

10. Click the Make Compositing Child button on video track 2.

Vegas indents the track, your indication that it is a child of the track above. When you create a child track and the parent track has a mask, the mask is applied to the child track. Additional children of the parent track will be masked as well. However, if you add a regular track underneath a child track, it is not masked.

11. Click the Event FX icon on the lower-right corner of the media event you just created.

Vegas opens the Plug-in Chooser-Video Event FX dialog box.

12. Select the Sony Deform plug-in. Then click Add.

13. Click OK to exit the dialog box.

Vegas displays the Video Event FX dialog box.

FIGURE 9-3

Creating the text

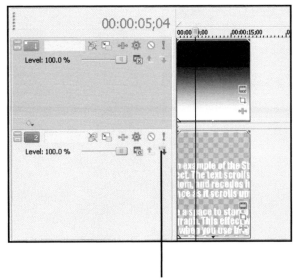

Make Compositing Child button

FIGURE 9-4

Applying the Deformer plug-in

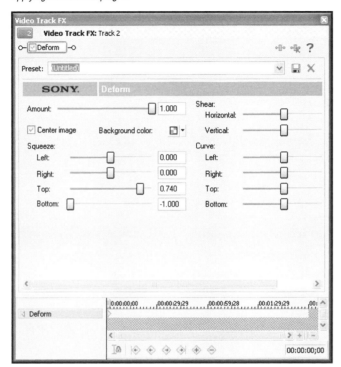

14. Drag the Amount slider to achieve a value of 1. Then in the Squeeze section, drag the Top slider to achieve a value of .74 and the Bottom slider to achieve a value of –1.000, as shown in Figure 9-4. Alternatively, you can type these values in the applicable text fields.

15. Click the Close button to exit the dialog box.

Now that you've distorted the text to add perspective, your next step is to scroll the text during the course of the introduction. You achieve this result by panning the text media event.

Scroll the text

1. Click the Event Pan/Crop icon for the text media event you just created.

Vegas displays the Event Pan/Crop dialog box.

2. Select the first keyframe on the Position timeline. Then type a value of **–240** in the Y Center text box.

3. Move your cursor to the end of the time-line. Then type a value of **720** in the Y Center text box to create a keyframe, as shown in Figure 9-5.

   These values will scroll the text from the bottom of the frame to the top of the frame during the course of the intro.

4. Click the Close button to exit the dialog box.

   Vegas applies the pan parameters to the media event. Now that you've got the text scrolling, it's time to create the star-field background.

Create a star-field background

1. Click the Media Generators tab. Then choose Solid Color.

2. Select the Black preset. Then drop it in the main window; below the track you just cre-ated, making sure you align the event with the beginning of the timeline.

   Vegas creates a new track for the event and displays the Video Event FX dialog box.

3. Type a value of **00:00:20;00** in the Length field.

4. Accept the other parameters. Then click the Close button.

   Vegas adds the media event to the project. Remember to extend the length of the event to match the value you entered in the Length field.

5. Click the Event FX icon in the lower-right corner of the event you just created.

FIGURE 9-5

Scrolling the text

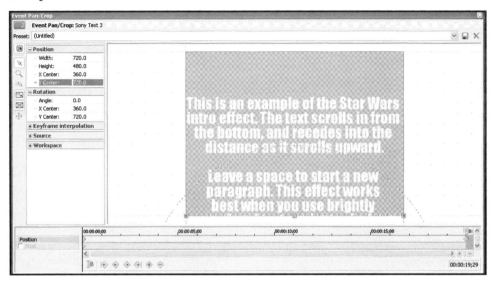

352   VEGAS 6 REVEALED

Creating Video Eye Candy   Chapter 9

FIGURE 9-6

Previewing the Star Wars title effect

Vegas displays the Plug-in Chooser-Video Event FX dialog box.

6. Select the Sony Add Noise plug-in and click Add. Then select the Sony Black Restore plug-in and click Add.

7. Click OK to exit the dialog box.

   Vegas adds the plug-ins to the event and displays the Video Event FX dialog box.

8. Click the Add Noise button ⬚Add Noise. Then drag the Noise Level slider to achieve a value of about .820 and click the Animate check box.

   This plug-in adds noise to the video. If you accept the default animate parameter, the noise is animated. High values generate lots of noise. By clicking the Animate check box, the plug-in generates static noise in the background.

9. Click the Black Restore ⬚Black Restore button. Then drag the Amount slider to achieve a value of approximately .370.

   The values in Step 8 and 9 are a matter of personal taste. The Add Noise plug-in gives you lots of white stars while the Black Restore plug-in restores some of the black in the background. Feel free to experiment with these values to suit your own taste. It's helpful if you have the Video Preview window open while doing this so you can see the effect of your edits.

10. Click the Close button. Then preview the project.

    Your project should resemble Figure 9-6.

CREATE A SPLIT
FRAME VIDEO TITLE

What You'll Do

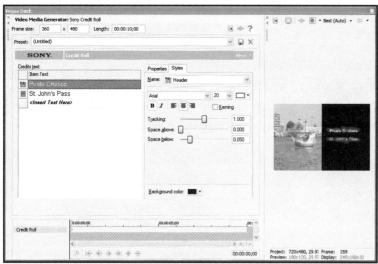

In this lesson, you create an introduction where scrolling text is displayed in the right half of the video frame, and the first video event is played in the left half of the frame. The video is cropped to half its width. After the title is displayed, the video is restored to its normal width.

Creating the Opening Credits

In this lesson, you'll see how combining several techniques can take a run-of-the-mill introduction and turn it into something special. Don't get me wrong; the Vegas presets are wonderful. But you can truly make them your own with a bit of experimentation and some mixing and matching.

This effect begins with the Scrolling Credits preset. But instead of filling up the full video frame with scrolling text, you're going to display it in the right half of the video frame. You do so by creating a media event that's half the width of the video frame, and then panning it to the right side of the video frame.

Adding Panache to the Opening Credits

Displaying opening credits alongside a video is compelling in and of its own right. In this lesson, you're going to take the effect over the top by adding the Light Rays plug-in. Remember, you can animate a Video FX plug-in. If you like the effect you create in this lesson, feel free to animate the light rays after the last objective.

Cropping the Video Event

The opening video event for this project resides in the first track. When you recreate this technique with your own footage, remember to choose a video clip that's longer in duration than your opening credits. In this lesson, our opening credits use the default duration of 10 seconds while the video clip is approximately 15 seconds in duration. After the credits play, the video gradually increases to its original size.

FIGURE 9-7
Adding the first video event

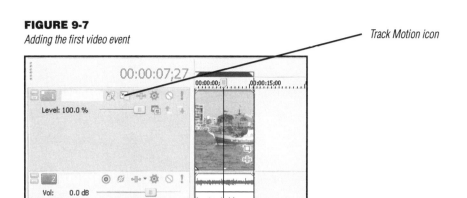

Track Motion icon

FIGURE 9-8
Cropping and moving the video event

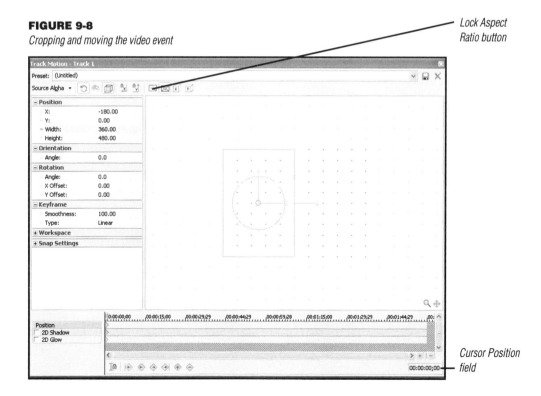

Lock Aspect
Ratio button

Cursor Position
field

1. Create a new project.
2. Select a video clip that's at least 15 seconds in duration and import it into the Project Media window.
3. Select the video clip. Then drop it in the main window, aligning it to the beginning of the timeline, as shown in Figure 9-7.
4. Click the Track Motion icon at the lower-right corner of the video event you just created.

   Vegas displays the Track Motion dialog box.
5. Select the first keyframe. Then click the Lock Aspect Ratio button.

   This deselects the option, making it possible for you to change the width of the video track without altering the height.
6. Then enter a value of **–180** in the X text box and a value of **360** in the Width text box, as shown in Figure 9-8.

   These values position the video on the left side of the video frame, displaying the video at half size.
7. Create a keyframe at the 10-second mark on the Position timeline.

   You're not changing any values here. Creating the keyframe holds constant the values from the first keyframe. Remember, you can navigate to a frame by entering the desired timecode in the text box at the lower-right corner of the dialog box.

Lesson 2   Create a Split Frame Video Title

TIP

The Track Motion timeline is two hours long, making it difficult to manually position a keyframe with precision. Click inside Cursor Position field in the lower-right corner of the dialog box, and then type the desired time-code to position the cursor.

8. Create a keyframe at the 12-second mark on the timeline.

9. Type a value of **0** in the X text box and a value of **720** in the Width text box, as shown in Figure 9-9.

10. Click the Close button to exit the dialog box.

Create the opening credits

1. Click the Media Generators tab. Then choose Credit Roll.

2. Select the Plain, Scrolling on Black preset. Drop the preset in the main window, below the track you just created, aligning the media event to the beginning of the timeline.

   Vegas creates a new video track and displays the Video Event FX dialog box.

3. Enter a value of 360 in the first Frame Size field. Then type the desired credit text, as shown in Figure 9-10.

4. Click the Styles tab and choose the desired font style, size, and color, and specify the other text parameters to achieve the desired look.

5. Click the Close button.

   Vegas adds the generated media to the project.

FIGURE 9-9

Restoring the video to normal width

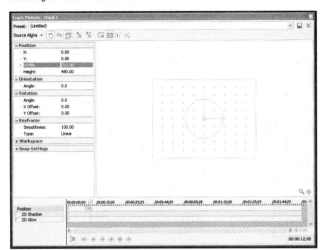

FIGURE 9-10

Creating the opening credits

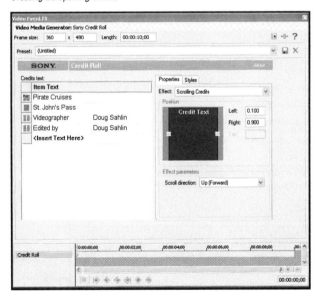

FIGURE 9-11

Panning the opening credits

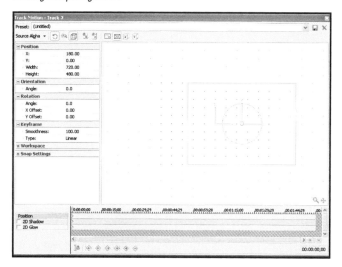

FIGURE 9-12

Previewing the project

1. Click the Video FX icon in the lower-right corner of the opening credit event you just created.

   Vegas displays the Plug-in Chooser-Video Event FX dialog box.

2. Select the Sony Light Rays plug-in and click Add. Then click OK.

   Vegas displays the Video Event FX dialog box.

3. Accept the default parameters for the plug-in. Then click the Close button.

4. Click the Track Motion icon in the lower-right corner of the opening credits track.

   Vegas displays the Track Motion dialog box.

5. Enter a value of 180 in the X Center text box, as shown in Figure 9-11.

   This value moves the opening credits to the right side of the video frame.

6. Preview the project, as shown in Figure 9-12.

ADD PIZZAZZ WITH
3D TRACK MOTION

What You'll Do

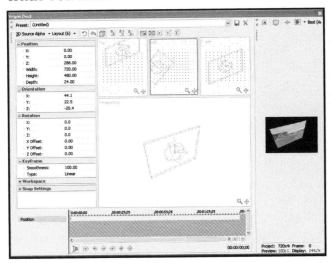

In this lesson, you learn to use the new Vegas 3D Track Motion to make a video clip appear as though it's rotating and moving in 3D space.

Adding 3D Track Motion to a Video Track

Vegas 6 has a ton of goodies you can use to create professional quality video. One of them is 3D Track Motion, which was introduced with Vegas 5.0. With this powerful feature, you can make it appear as though a video event, or for that matter, a media event, is flying and tumbling through space. With 3D track motion, you can spin or move a video event up or down, forward or backward, or from left to right. If you want to add the ultimate eye candy to a video production, this is the tool to use.

Using 3D Source Alpha Compositing

When you want to apply 3D Track Motion, you don't apply it to a single event, you apply it to the whole track. Of course, if you only want to apply 3D Track Motion to a few events, you can create additional tracks for the video events that will not have 3D Track Motion applied. You use the 3D Source Alpha compositing method for any track to which you want to apply 3D Track Motion.

Applying 3D Track Motion

After choosing 3D Source Alpha as the track composite method, you apply track motion, which opens this daunting dialog box with more controls than you'll find in the cockpit of a Boeing 757. Well, not really, but there are controls that you use to move, resize, and rotate the video clips on the video track. There are also a plethora of icons at the top of the 3D Track Motion dialog box that you use to constrain motion, sizing, and rotation to a specific axis.

TIP

If you're not familiar with working in 3D, you have three axes: X, which is from left to right; Y, which is from top to bottom, and Z, which is from front to back. It may help to visualize a shoebox without a lid, laid on its side. The right wall of the box is the intersection of the Z and Y axes, the bottom wall is the intersection of the X and Z axes, while the back wall is the intersection of the Y and X axes.

When you work with a track to which you've assigned the 3D Source Alpha compositing method, you'll find four windows in the Track Motion dialog box. Three windows display a facsimile of a video clip from the front, top, and left side. The fourth window displays a visual representation of how the video clip looks in 3D space. You use the controls to manipulate the clip in any of the windows. You can use the Video Preview window to preview the results of your edits on the video clips in the track.

Animating 3D Track Motion

The Track Motion dialog box also has a timeline. You navigate along the timeline, and then work with the controls in the dialog box to achieve the desired result. When you play back the project, Vegas **interpolates** the position of the video clip on the frames between keyframes. If you have multiple events on a 3D motion track, the effect is seamless and the 3D motion is smoothly transferred from one event to the next.

Apply 3D motion to a track

1. Create a new project.
2. Import a video clip into the Project Media window. Then select the video clip and drop it in the main window, aligning it with the beginning of the timeline, as shown in Figure 9-13.
3. Click the track's Composite Mode button and choose 3D Source Alpha from the drop-down list.
4. Click the Track Motion icon.

   Vegas displays the Track Motion dialog box shown in Figure 9-14.

Move a track in 3D space

1. If the Video Preview window is not displayed in the workspace, choose View > Video Preview.
2. In the Perspective window, position your cursor over the icon that represents the video frame.

   Vegas highlights the icon, indicating you can move the video clip.
3. Click and drag the video frame to move it to a new location.

FIGURE 9-13

Beginning a 3D track motion project

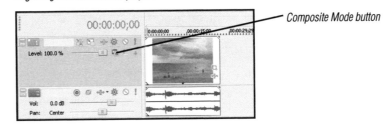

Composite Mode button

FIGURE 9-14

Track Motion dialog box

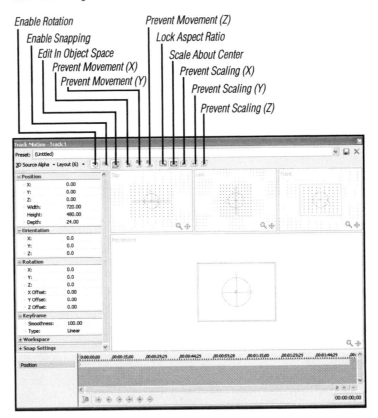

Enable Rotation
Enable Snapping
Edit In Object Space
Prevent Movement (X)
Prevent Movement (Y)
Prevent Movement (Z)
Lock Aspect Ratio
Scale About Center
Prevent Scaling (X)
Prevent Scaling (Y)
Prevent Scaling (Z)

FIGURE 9-15

Moving the track

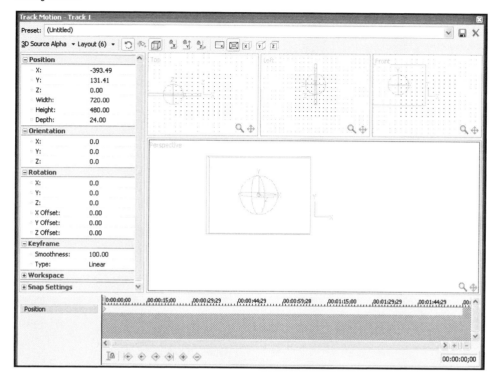

As you drag the icon, the icons that represent the video frames in the other windows are updated, as does the Video Preview window, as shown in Figure 9-15. Notice that there is an icon that indicates the center of the video frame.

TIP

To prevent motion along a particular axis, click the Prevent Movement icon (shown previously in Figure 9-14) for the desired axis.

4. In the Perspective window, position your cursor over the circular icon in the center of the video frame icon.

   Vegas highlights one of the circular icons indicating you can rotate the object along that axis. Notice that there are three rings in the video frame icon, one for each axis.

5. Position your cursor over the desired icon. Then click and drag to rotate freely along that axis.

6. Release the mouse button when the video is in the desired position.

   Experiment with the other two icons to rotate the clip in the other axes.

TIP

To prevent rotation along a particular axis, click the Prevent Rotation icon (shown previously in Figure 9-14) for the desired axis.

7. Position your cursor at any corner of the video frame icon.

Your cursor becomes a circle, as shown in Figure 9-16.

8. Click and drag to resize the video.

Drag toward the center of the video frame to reduce the size of the video frame, or away from the center to increase the size of the video frame. The video frame is resized proportionately, unless you click the Lock Aspect Ratio icon to deselect the option.

> **NOTE**
>
> Scaling is relative to the center of the video frame, unless you click the Scale About Center icon to deselect the option. When you disable scaling from the center, the video frame is scaled from the corner opposite the corner from which you are scaling.

9. Position your cursor in the video frame in the Left window.

The video frame is highlighted, indicating you can change its position from the Left plane. From this plane you can move the frame from front to back, and from top to bottom.

10. Click and drag the video frame to the desired position.

You constrain motion and rotation relative to a particular plane when you work in the Left, Top, or Front windows.

11. Position your cursor inside the circular icons. Then click and drag to rotate the video frame.

When you rotate in the Left window, rotation is relative to that plane. You can rotate the video frame on a particular axis from within the Left, Top, or Front windows.

FIGURE 9-16

Scaling the video

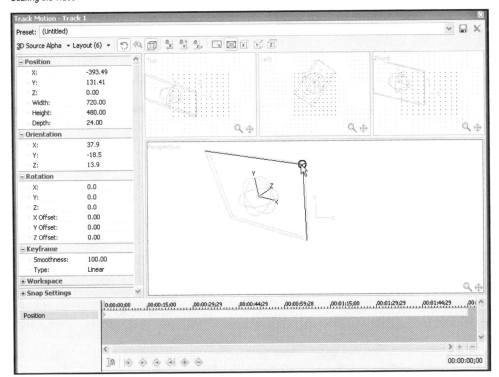

You can also move the video frame in 3D space by typing values in the text boxes in the left window. As you manually move the video frame in any of the four windows, notice the change in values. This will give you an indication of the values you need to enter to get a desired result.

Animate 3D track motion

1. Click the Sync Cursor icon.

   This synchronizes the cursor position in the Track Motion dialog box timeline, with the cursor position on the track timeline.

2. Click the desired frame on the track timeline.

   The timeline in the Track Motion dialog box is two hours in duration, which makes it hard to navigate to an individual frame when you've got a production that's less than two hours. When you have the Sync Cursor icon enabled, the proper frame is selected in the Track Motion dialog box as you select it on the track timeline. You can also type the desired timecode in the Cursor Position field in the lower-right corner of the Track Motion dialog box.

3. Scale, rotate, or move the video frame within any of the windows.

   Vegas creates a keyframe on the Track Motion dialog box timeline.

4. Navigate to a different frame on the track timeline. Then, in the Track Motion dialog box, rotate, scale, or move the video frame in any of the windows.

Vegas creates an additional keyframe on the Track Motion timeline.

NOTE

You can change the manner in which Vegas interpolates the frames in-between keyframes by right-clicking the keyframe, and then choosing an option from the drop-down list. Your choices are Linear, Fast, Slow, Smooth, Sharp, and Hold. This functions identically to the other timelines you've worked with in previous chapters.

5. Click the Close button to exit the Track Motion dialog box.

   Notice there are keyframes on timeline below the video event (as shown in Figure 9-17) that signify where you've changed the position, size, or rotation of the video frame. You can double-click a keyframe to open the Track Motion dialog box and edit any of the parameters at that keyframe. You can also select a keyframe on the track timeline and drag it to a different position on the timeline.

6. Preview the project.

CAUTION

Never preview a 3D motion project with your cat in your lap. The frenetic motion may cause the poor feline to cough up a hairball on your keyboard.

FIGURE 9-17
Track motion keyframes

CREATE FLY-THROUGH
TEXT

What You'll Do

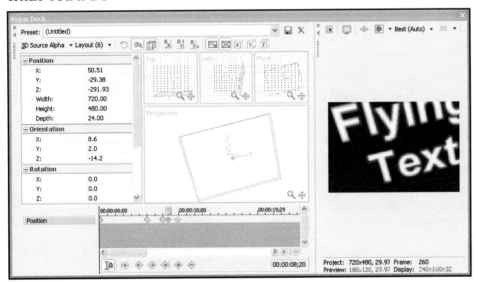

 In this lesson, you use 3D Track Motion to create an effect similar to an airplane flying through text. This technique can be used to good effect when you want to start off a production with a bang.

Creating Scintillating Text

This chapter's all about video eye candy. What could be cooler than flying through the title of your production? If that doesn't get your audience to stand up and take notice, make sure they're still breathing. To achieve this effect, you begin with one of the text presets from the Media Generators window. After you've finished creating and formatting the text, you choose the 3D Alpha compositing mode and you're ready to begin.

Flying Text Through 3D Space

You apply 3D Track Motion to the track on which the text appears. You use the methods discussed in the previous lesson to fly the text in from the distance, perhaps adding a bit of rotation to spice things up. You can then hold the text stationary so your audience can read it and catch their breath, before flying the text right through them.

Create the text

1. Create a new project.
2. Click the Media Generators tab. Then choose Text.
3. Select the Default preset and drop it in the main window, aligning it to the beginning of the timeline.

   The Video Event FX dialog box appears, showing the parameters for the Default text preset.
4. Select the Sample Text and type **Flying Text**. Press Enter after you type **Flying** so the text is on two lines.
5. Accept the default parameters and then click the Close button.

   When you use this technique for your own productions, feel free to use whatever font type you choose. The effect works best when you use a large font size.

Add 3D track motion

1. If the Video Preview window is not displayed in the workspace, choose View > Video Preview.
2. Click the Compositing Mode icon on the video track on which you created the text and choose 3D Source Alpha from the drop-down list.

3. Click the Track Motion icon on the text video track.
4. Click the Sync Cursor icon.
5. In the Cursor Position text box in the lower-right corner of the Track Motion dialog box, type **00:00:06:00** and press Enter.

   You can navigate to a desired frame by typing the desired timecode in the textbox in the lower-right corner of the window. Be sure to enter the timecode in the proper format: hh:mm:ss;ff.
6. Press Insert to create a keyframe.
7. In the Cursor Position text box in the lower-left corner of the Track Motion dialog box, type **00:00:08;00** and press Enter.

   Press Insert to create a keyframe.

   The reason for creating two keyframes is so that legible text is onscreen for two seconds before flying out of the frame. Creating your keyframes before rotating, scaling, or moving the video frame ensures that the text is readable.
9. Select the first keyframe.
10. From the Top view, select the video frame and move it to the back of the window.

11. From the Perspective view, scale the video frame, rotate it, and move it to the upper-right corner of the window, as shown in Figure 9-18.

12. On the track timeline, position your cursor on the last frame of the text media event.

13. In the Track Motion dialog box Perspective window, rotate the video frame.

14. In the Top window, drag the video frame beyond the boundary of the window.

Vegas adds a keyframe on the Track Motion dialog box timeline.

15. Click the Close button to exit the Track Motion dialog box.

16. Preview the project.

Viola! You've got flying text. Your results should look similar to Figure 9-19.

> **TIP**
>
> To spice up this effect, add one keyframe between the first keyframe and the keyframe where the text is stationary. Rotate the video frame, and if desired, drag it to a different position for the ultimate in frenetic flying text.

FIGURE 9-18

Text on the move

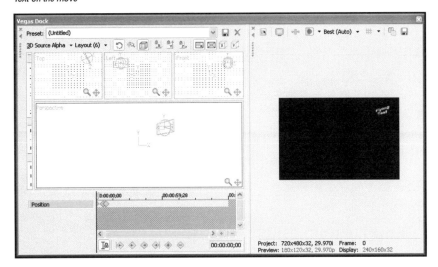

FIGURE 9-19

Flying text

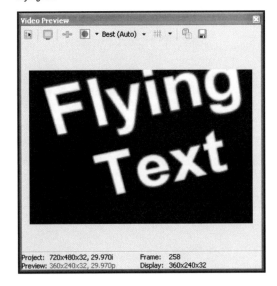

CREATE A
BEZIER MASK

What You'll Do

In this lesson, you learn how to create a mask using drawing tools similar to those used in illustration programs. This enables you to accurately trace a shape or area that you want to mask.

Using the Event Pan/Crop Mask Option

When you're compositing videos on multiple tracks, it's often desirable to create a mask on one video track to display a particular area of the underlying video track. You already learned how to accomplish this task using the Sony Cookie Cutter plug-in in a previous chapter. However, this plug-in limits you to preset shapes.

If you want to display an intricate area of a video track, for example a shape or object in a still image, and want to reveal the inverse on an underlying video track, you can do so by using the Event Pan/Crop dialog box. Within this dialog box there's an option to create a mask. When you select this option, you can draw an intricate mask to select the area of the video track you want to display. As an added bonus, you can add keyframes to the timeline to animate the mask, a technique you'll learn in the next lesson.

Drawing the Mask

You draw the mask by using a tool that looks like a pen. Inside the Event Pan/Crop dialog box preview window, you click the tool wherever you want to add a point. Then it's a matter of adding enough points to define the shape you want to mask. In essence, you're creating points to trace the area you want to mask. Each point is connected to create the path that defines the mask. You can create straight points or curve points to define the mask. This gives you the capability to draw straight lines, or curved lines between points, or as illustrators refer to them, **paths**. You complete the mask by clicking the first point you created to close the path. After creating the mask, you can fine-tune your work by moving individual points, or moving the **tangent** handles on curve points.

Set up the project

1. Create a new project.

2. Import two video clips into the Project Media window.

   One of the video clips should have a stationary object such as a building, a coffee cup, or a flashlight for which you can easily create a mask. Alternatively, you can mask a still image such as the one being used in this lesson to reveal underlying video clip. After you gain some experience with drawing masks, you can branch out to video clips with more complex shapes.

3. Select the clips, and then right-click and drop the clips in the main window, aligning them with the beginning of the timeline.

4. Release the mouse button and choose Add Across Tracks from the shortcut menu.

   Vegas creates a video track for each clip, as well as an audio track if the video has embedded audio.

5. If necessary, move the track that you are going to mask to the top of the list. If necessary, trim the longer event so that the events are of equal duration.

   Your timeline should resemble Figure 9-20.

6. Click the Event Pan/Crop icon on the video event on the top track.

   Vegas displays the Event Pan/Crop dialog box.

FIGURE 9-20

Setting up the project

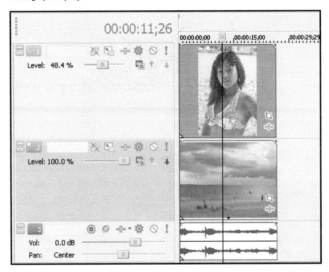

FIGURE 9-21

Mask creation tools

Normal Edit tool —
Anchor Creation tool —

Anchor Deletion tool —

Split Tangent tool ⌐
Zoom Edit tool ⌐
Enable Snapping —

Move Freely (X or Y) —

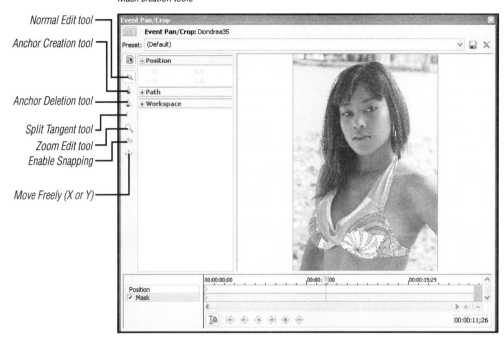

7. Click the Mask check box at the bottom of the dialog box.

Vegas displays the mask creation tools shown in Figure 9-21.

Create the mask

1. Select the Anchor Creation tool. Then click inside the Event Pan/Crop preview window to create the first anchor point of the mask.

A yellow square appears indicating the position of the anchor point.

2. Click inside the Event Pan/Crop preview window to create the second point of the mask.

A straight line connects the two points. If the shape you're masking contains a curved line between points, click and drag to create tangent handles. As you drag, you can move the mouse to define the tangents, which determines the shape of the curve between anchor points.

> **TIP**
>
> When you create a mask, don't be too concerned about getting it perfect. You can go back and edit the mask after you've created all the anchor points. When you edit the mask, you can zoom in on the mask, move the points, adjust the tangent handles, and so on.

3. Continue adding anchor points to define the shape of the mask.

4. Click the first anchor point to close the path and finish creating the mask.

As you move your cursor towards the first anchor point, all of the points in the mask are highlighted, indicating that you can close the path. Figure 9-22 shows a mask before fine-tuning.

Fine-tune the mask

1. Select the Zoom Edit tool.

2. Click and drag around an area where the anchor points need to be edited.

Vegas zooms in on the area you selected with the Zoom Edit tool.

3. Edit the mask using the following tools:

- **Normal Edit tool**—Move your cursor over the path between two points, click the path, and then drag it to a new location; or, move your cursor over an anchor point, click the point, and drag it to a new location; or, move your cursor over a tangent handle, click the handle, and drag to redefine the curve point and the path between the selected point and the next or previous point, depending on which handle you select.

> **TIP**
>
> Select the Normal Edit tool and move your cursor outside of the path until it becomes a hand. You can then click and drag to pan to a different location. This comes in handy when you're zoomed in on the path.

FIGURE 9-22

Mask before editing

FIGURE 9-23
Completed mask

TIP

To zoom out, click the plus sign to the left of the Workspace title. Type a lower value in the Zoom (%) text box to zoom out and see more of the video event.

- Anchor Creation tool—Click at any point on the path where you need to add an additional anchor point.

QUICKTIP

You can also use the Anchor Creation tool to create an additional mask within the video event.

- Anchor Deletion tool—Click an anchor point to remove it from the path.

- Split Tangent tool—Click a straight point to add tangent handles, thereby converting it to a curve point. Click a curve point to remove tangent handles, thereby converting it to a straight point.

- Zoom Edit tool—Click inside the Event Pan/Crop preview window to zoom in to the next-highest magnification level. Click and drag around an area you want to zoom in on.

4. Continue editing anchor points to define the mask area. Figure 9-23 shows a completed mask.

5. Click the Close button to exit the Event Pan/Crop dialog box.

6. Preview the project. Figure 9-24 shows an example of this technique. Notice how the skyline masked from the top video track is displayed over the contents of the underlying video track. Track Motion was also used to align the masked image to the right side of the video frame.

Preserving a Person's Anonymity

If you interview a person on video who wants to remain anonymous, duplicate the track, then apply the Sony Pixelate plug-in to the top track and adjust the parameters so that the person's face is not recognizable. Create a mask on this track and use the techniques from the previous lesson to mask out the person's face. If your subject was moving during the interview, you'll have to add keyframes to the Mask timeline and adjust the mask anchor points so that the person's face is masked as he or she moves. Figure 9-25 shows an example of this technique.

FIGURE 9-24
A masked track displayed over an underlying track

FIGURE 9-25
Preserving a person's anonymity

CREATE
HANDWRITTEN TEXT

What You'll Do

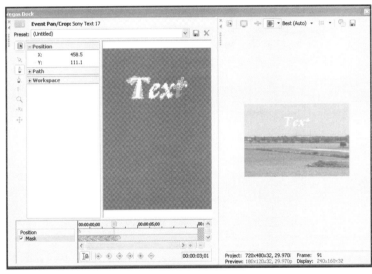

▶ *In this lesson, you learn how to create an intriguing introduction that appears as though an invisible hand is writing the title for a production.*

Creating a Handwritten Text Intro

Diversity is the key to creating professional-quality productions. Vegas 6 is a powerful tool in that regard. There are enough tools for you to create widely diverse productions. One of those tools is masking that you learned in the previous lesson. When you combine the default text preset with a mask and keyframe animation, you can create an introduction where the text is revealed bit by bit as if the introduction is being written in longhand by an invisible hand.

Creating the Text

You use the Default text preset to achieve this effect. You choose a font style that looks like script and position the text as desired. Because the Default text preset is over a transparent background, it's relatively easy to create a mask for the text. Although this can be a tedious process, the results are well worth it.

Masking the Text

You mask the text using the techniques presented in the last lesson. You begin by creating a small mask that doesn't select any of the text. Due to the fact that the Default text preset is over a transparent background, the mask has no affect. You then navigate along the Mask timeline and modify the mask to reveal part of the text. You continue navigating along the mask timeline in small increments, modifying the mask as you go to reveal the first letter in its entirety. You navigate further along the timeline and create a new mask for the second letter. You continue this process until the second letter is totally revealed; create a new mask for the third letter, and so on, until the entire intro text is revealed. When the project is played back, the effect is seamless and the intro is handwritten a letter at a time.

Begin the project

1. Create a new project.

2. Import a video clip into the Project Media window. Then select the video clip and drop it in the main window, aligning the text to the beginning of the timeline.

3. Right-click video track 1 and choose Insert Video track from the shortcut menu.

4. Click the Media Generators tab and choose Text. Then select the Default preset and drop it into the video track you just created, aligning it to the beginning of the timeline.

   Vegas displays the Video Event FX dialog box showing the parameters for the Default text preset.

5. Select the Sample Text and type **Text**. Then select a font that looks like script from the Font drop-down list, as shown in Figure 9-26.

   > **NOTE**
   >
   > When you use this technique for your own projects, you may have to increase the default length to properly display the intro if you're displaying several words.

6. Click the Placement tab. Then select the text and align it to the top of the video frame, making sure the text is within the title safe area.

7. If necessary, click the Properties tab and change the text color to one that suits your video production.

8. Click the Close button to apply your changes to the generated media event.

FIGURE 9-26

Formatting the title text

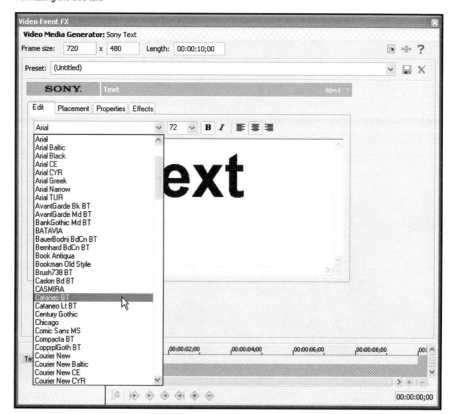

FIGURE 9-27

Creating the first keyframe

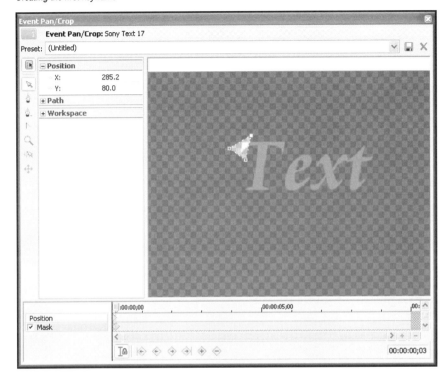

1. Click the Event Pan/Crop icon.
2. Click the Mask check box as outlined in the previous lesson.
3. Select the Anchor Creation tool and create a mask with three anchor points. Do not select any of the text at this time.
4. Click the Sync Cursor icon.
5. Click the Mask timeline. Then press the right arrow key three times.
6. Select the Normal Edit tool and move two of the anchor points to reveal a bit of the first letter, as shown in Figure 9-27.

   Vegas creates a keyframe on the Mask timeline. When you're masking text, you may find it helpful to have the Video Preview window displayed so you can view the masked text as it will appear in the finished project.
7. On the Mask timeline, select the last keyframe you created. Then press the right arrow key three times.
8. Select the Normal Edit tool and move the points to reveal more of the letter.

9. Continue navigating along the timeline, adding keyframes and moving points until you've revealed the first letter, as shown in Figure 9-28.

You may have to add additional anchor points when revealing the letter. Notice the additional anchor points in Figure 9-28 to reveal the stem of the letter *T*.

10. On the Mask timeline, select the last keyframe. Then click the right arrow key three times.

11. Select the Anchor Creation tool and begin creating a mask for the letter *E*.

12. Continue navigating along the timeline, moving and adding points as needed to create a mask for the letter *E*.

13. Create new masks and keyframes for the remaining letters.

You'll end up with many keyframes and four masks, as shown in Figure 9-29.

14. Click the Close button to exit the Event Pan/Crop dialog box.

15. Preview the project.

The text will gradually appear. The project will simulate text being handwritten. Experiment with this technique on different script fonts. You can vary the speed of the handwriting by creating a bigger gap between keyframes. As you gain more experience with creating the letter masks, you'll instinctively know when you need to add anchor points. This technique will take some time when you're masking several words, but the results are well worth it.

FIGURE 9-28
Revealing the first letter

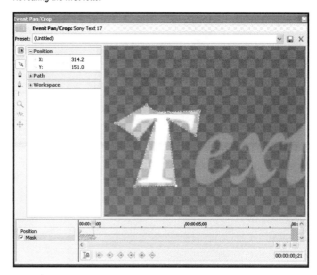

FIGURE 9-29
The completed mask

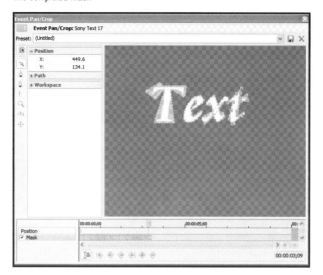

Creating a 3D Motion Track

1. Create a new project.

2. Import a video clip into the Project Media window.

3. Select the video clip and drop it in the main window, aligning it to the beginning of the timeline.

4. Click the Compositing Mode icon and choose 3D Source Alpha from the drop-down menu, as shown in Figure 9-30.

5. Click the Track Motion icon for Track 1.

6. Use the 3D Track Motion tools to change the video frame position and size in 3D space, as shown in Figure 9-31.

7. Keep the project open; you'll be using it in the next review.

FIGURE 9-30

Choosing the composite mode

FIGURE 9-31

Moving the video frame in 3D space

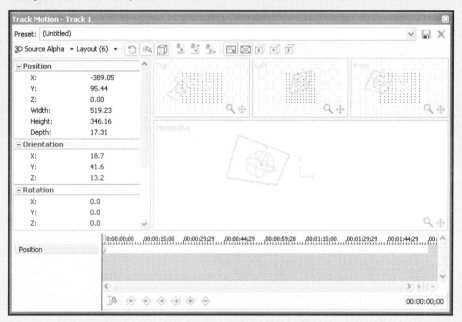

Adding Keyframes to the Motion Track

1. Click the Sync Cursor icon.

2. On the track timeline, navigate to a different frame.

3. In the Motion Track dialog box, change the position, rotation, and size of the video frame, as shown in Figure 9-32.

4. On the track timeline, navigate to the last frame of the video event.

5. In the top window of the Motion Track dialog box, select the video frame icon and drag it so that it appears to fly towards the viewer.

6. Click the Close button.

7. Preview the project, as shown in Figure 9-33.

FIGURE 9-32

Adding keyframes

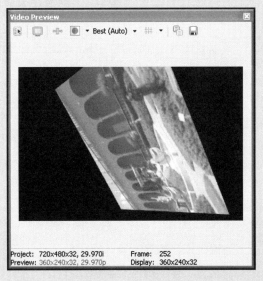

FIGURE 9-33

Previewing a 3D track motion project

Creating a Mask

1. Create a new project.

2. Select an image and a video clip and import them into the Project Media window. Choose one video clip that has an element that can be masked for display over another video track.

3. Right-click the clips and drop them in the main window, aligning them to the beginning of the timeline.

4. Release the mouse button and then choose Add Across Tracks from the shortcut menu.

5. If necessary, move the video track with the image to the top of the track list, as shown in Figure 9-34.

6. Click the Track Motion icon for the track with the image. Then resize the image and move it to one of the corners of the video frame.

7. Click the Event Pan/Crop icon on the video event on the uppermost track.

8. Click the Mask check box.

9. Use the Mask creation tools to draw a mask, as shown in Figure 9-35.

10. Preview the project.

FIGURE 9-34

Creating a project with multiple tracks

FIGURE 9-35

Creating a mask

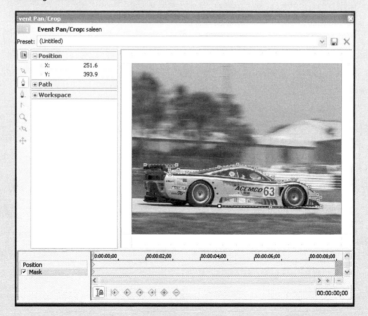

You edit video for an independent film-maker. You're producing an entertainment video and the director of the production has asked you to deliver some information to the audience before the first scene plays. Before making a hasty exit to direct his next masterpiece, he mumbles "*Star Wars*, but without the stars."

1. Create a new project.

2. Click the Media Generators tab and choose Text.

3. Select the Solid Background default and drop it in the main window, aligning it to the beginning of the timeline.

4. Select the Sample Text, and then type the information the director wants you to display. Type several lines of text, pressing Enter when you need to create a new line.

5. Choose the desired font size, color, and other font parameters. Remember: This technique works best with bold, blocky text. Remember to adjust the placement of the text on the first and last keyframe if your text exceeds the video frame.

6. Click the Event Pan/Crop icon.

7. Select the first keyframe and type a value of –240 in the Y Center text box.

8. Navigate to the end of the Event Pan/Crop Position timeline. Then type a value of **720** in the Y Center text box, as shown in Figure 9-36.

9. Click the Close button.

10. Click the Event FX icon at the lower-right corner of the media event you just created.

11. Select the Sony Deform plug-in and click Add. Then click OK.

12. In the Video Event FX dialog box, drag the Amount slider to achieve a value of 1.00.

13. Drag the Top slider to achieve a value of .725.

14. Drag the Bottom slider to achieve a value of –1.000.

Click the Close button.

Preview the project, as shown in Figure 9-37.

FIGURE 9-36

Project Builder 1, Sample 1

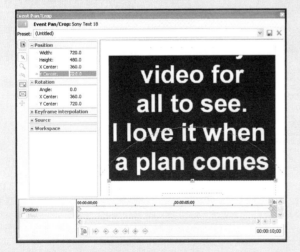

FIGURE 9-37

Project Builder 1, Sample 2

Your production supervisor leaves you in charge of creating a video project. Her parting words are, "Start the thing off with a bang." After viewing the clips, you decide to create two tracks of video clips spinning in 3D space before the opening credits.

1. Create a new project.

2. Import two video clips into the Project Media window.

3. Right-click the video clips and drop them in the main window, aligning them to the beginning of the timeline.

4. Release the mouse button, and choose Add Across Tracks from the shortcut menu.

5. Click the Compositing Mode icon for each track and choose 3D Source Alpha.

6. Click the Track Motion button in the first track.

7. In the Track motion window, type 360 in the Width text box and 240 in the Height Text box.

8. Drag the video frame to a different position, as shown in Figure 9-38. Remember to open the Video Preview window so you can see the effects of your edits.

9. Click the Sync Cursor button.

10. On the track timeline, position your cursor in the middle of the video event.

11. In the Track Motion dialog box, move and rotate the clip as desired.

12. On the track timeline, position your cursor near the end of the video event.

13. In the Track Motion dialog box, move and rotate the clip as desired.

14. Repeat steps 6 through 13 for the second video track.

15. Preview the project, as shown in Figure 9-39.

FIGURE 9-38
Project Builder 2, Sample 1

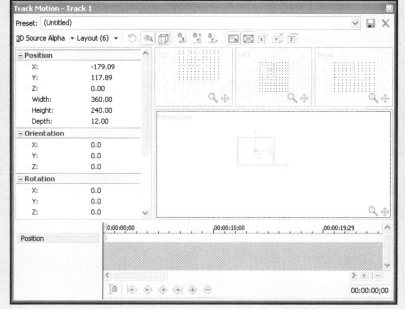

FIGURE 9-39
Project Builder 2, Sample 2

DESIGN PROJECT

You're creating a video for a travel agency. Your client supplies clips of fantastic scenery. After previewing the clips, you decide to use something special to introduce the video: handwritten text.

1. Create a new project.

2. Import a video clip into the Project Media window.

3. Select the video clip and drop it in the main window, aligning it to the beginning of the timeline.

FIGURE 9-40

Design Project Sample 1

4. Right-click the video track in the track list and choose Insert Video Track from the shortcut menu.

5. Click the Media Generators tab and choose Text.

6. Select Default text and drop it into the video track you just created, aligning the media to the beginning of the timeline.

7. Select the sample text and type a title for your production.

8. Choose a font that looks like script.

9. If necessary, set other font attributes such as color and font size.

10. Click the Close button to exit the Video Event FX dialog box.

11. Click the Event Pan/Crop icon to open the Event Pan/Crop dialog box.

12. Click the Mask check box.

13. Create masks and keyframes for each letter, as outlined earlier in this chapter. See Figure 9-40 for an example of a mask for a letter under construction.

14. Click the Close button.

15. Preview the video, as shown in Figure 9-41.

FIGURE 9-41

Design Project Sample 2

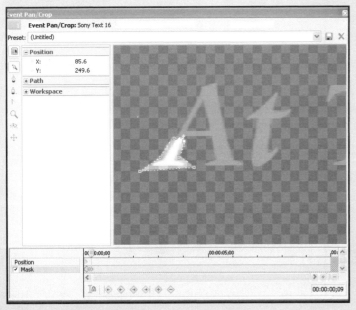

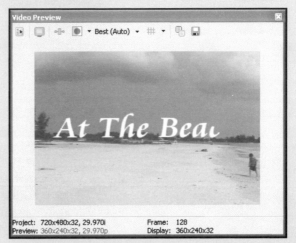

Creating Video Eye Candy   Chapter 9

In this chapter, you learned to take your video productions to the next level with the judicious implementation of video eye candy. The addition of a mask to a video track enables you to display portions of the underlying track. Adding a *Star Wars* type intro is also a great way to start off any production with a bang. As if that isn't enough, 3D Track Motion lets you send video clips flying through 3D space.

What You Have Learned

In this chapter, you:
- Learned to create a realistic star field.
- Learned to create a scrolling introduction similar to the one used in *Star Wars*.
- Created a Bezier mask.
- Learned to animate text.
- Simulated handwritten text with multiple keyframes and masks.

Key Terms from This Chapter

- **Back story.** Events that happened before the beginning of a story or video. Onscreen text or narration are commonly used to tell a back story.

- **Bezier.** A method used to create curves in paths. In Vegas, Bezier curves are used to describe the paths used to create masks.

- **Interpolates.** Using a mathematical algorithm, Vegas determines which position or state an object is in between keyframes. For example, if Vegas is interpolating an event's position between keyframes on a 3D motion track, it compares the event's position and rotation from one keyframe to the next, and uses that information to determine where the event should be positioned on each frame between keyframes.

- **Path.** Interconnected lines and curves that define a shape. In Vegas, a path determines the boundary of a mask.

- **Perspective.** The ability to view objects that vanish into the distance. For example, the edges of a road are parallel, but appear to converge to a single point in the distance.

- **Tangent handles.** A handle that appears tangentially to a point that defines the end of a curve. A dot at each end of the handle can be clicked and dragged to change the curve to which the point is attached.

10

RENDERING YOUR
Project

1. Choose a template.

2. Render for the Web.

3. Render for CD-ROM.

4. Render high-quality video for DVD projects.

5. Create a custom template.

chapter 10 RENDERING YOUR Project

After you create a project, you preview the project to make sure it plays as desired. If your project has extensive video effects, you can preview your production with the project frame rate by building a dynamic RAM preview, as outlined in Chapter 11, "Vegas Tricks and Tips,"(found on the Web site). The next step is to choose a file format. There are many file formats from which to choose. Sometimes the actual choice can be quite daunting. In this chapter, you begin by getting an overview of the rendering process.

The file format you choose depends on the destination of your rendered video. The lessons in this chapter show you how to render files for use on the Web and CDs, and how to render high-quality video DVD projects. You'll learn which file formats are applicable for each destination.

However, choosing the file format is only one piece of the puzzle. Then you have to decide which template to use. You can use the same template as the project settings or choose a different template. When you capture video from a camcorder, the

resulting video is usually the proper frame size and frame rate for broadcast-quality video and the pixels are rectangular. When you render a video for display on a computer monitor, you need to choose the proper template to render the video as square pixels.

Another factor in the rendering equation is **data rate**. Data rate is measured as kilobytes per second. When you render video for display on a Web site, you choose a data rate that enables Web site visitors to view the video as it streams into their Web browser. If the video data rate exceeds the maximum data rate of the viewer's Internet connection, the video will stop playing until enough additional data has streamed into the viewer's browser to resume playback. And of course, you must use different data rates on the Internet, depending on whether users access the Internet with dial-up, DSL, or cable modems.

Vegas provides you with a wide variety of templates you can use to cover just about any eventuality. However, when you need to deviate from a template, you can do so by specifying different settings. If you need to use the same settings on a regular basis, you can save the settings as a custom template.

Tools You'll Use

Custom Template - QuickTime 6

Template: 56 Kbps Video

Description: Audio: 11,025 Hz, 16 Bit, Mono, IMA 4:1 compression.
Video: 15 fps,160x120, Sorenson 3 compression.
Use this setting for streaming over 56 Kbps modems.

☑ Include video

Frame size: (Custom frame size)
Width: 160   Height: 120

Frame rate: 15.000 (Multimedia)

Field order: None (progressive scan)

Pixel aspect ratio: 1.000

Video format: Sorenson Video 3   Configure...

Compressed depth: 24 bpp color

Quality: Low — High   75.4 %

Data rate: Basic

Target rate, KBps (Kbytes/second): 5

☐ Peak rate, KBps (Kbytes/second):

☑ Keyframe every (frames): 15   ☐ Natural only

Project | **Video** | Audio | Streaming

OK   Cancel

Rendering complete: Chapter 11.wmv

100 %

Approximate time left   00:00:00
Elapsed time (hh:mm:ss):   00:00:04

☐ Close this dialog box when rendering completes

Open   Open Folder   Close

Default Template
SVCD NTSC
SVCD PAL
DVD NTSC
DVD PAL
DVD NTSC video stream
DVD PAL separate streams
DVD Architect NTSC video stream
DVD Architect NTSC Widescreen video stream
DVD Architect 24p NTSC video stream
DVD Architect 24p NTSC Widescreen video stream
DVD Architect PAL video stream
DVD Architect PAL Widescreen video stream
HD 720-24p
HD 720-30p
HD 720-60p
HD 1080-24p
HD 1080-30p
HD 1080-60i
HDV 720-25p
HDV 720-30p
HDV 1080-50i
HDV 1080-60i

Custom Template - Windows Media Video V9

Template: 3 Mbps Video

Description: Audio: 96 Kbps, 44,100 Hz, 16 Bit, Stereo.
Video: 30 fps, 640x480, WMV V9 Compression.
Use this setting for high-quality video playback from a CD-ROM.

Video rendering quality: Good
Draft
Preview
Good
Best

Project | Audio | Video | Bit rate | Index/Summary

OK   Cancel

Audio Interchange File Format (AIFF) (*.aif)
Dolby Digital AC-3 (*.ac3)
MainConcept MPEG-1 (*.mpg)
MainConcept MPEG-2 (*.mpg)
MP3 Audio (*.mp3)
OggVorbis (*.ogg)
QuickTime 6 (*.mov)
RealMedia 9 (*.rm)
Scott Studios Wave (*.wav)
Sony Perfect Clarity Audio (*.pca)
Sony Wave64 (*.w64)
Video for Windows (*.avi)
Wave (Microsoft) (*.wav)
Windows Media Audio V9 (*.wma)
Windows Media Video V9 (*.wmv)

CHOOSE A TEMPLATE

What You'll Do

In this lesson, you get an introduction to rendering a project in Vegas.

Choosing a File Format

After you create a production, you preview the production to make sure it's up to snuff. If all is well, your next step is to render the project. You can render the project using the project settings, or you can use different settings. Your first step is to choose the file format. Each file format has several templates from which to choose. You can also create a custom template, a task that's covered in an upcoming lesson.

Choosing a Template

After selecting the file format, you choose a template. The template you choose depends on the destination for the rendered video. Each preset template contains specific settings for an intended destination. For example, if your production will be part of an NTSC DVD, you choose the NTSC DVD template.

Rendering the File

After specifying the file format and template, you name the video and choose a folder in which to save the rendered file. After you click Save, Vegas 6 begins rendering your project to the desired file format. It may take a considerable amount of time to render a lengthy project. Render time is also dependent upon your processor speed and available memory.

FIGURE 10-1

Render As dialog box

FIGURE 10-2

Choosing a file format

```
Audio Interchange File Format (AIFF) (*.aif)
Dolby Digital AC-3 (*.ac3)
MainConcept MPEG-1 (*.mpg)
MainConcept MPEG-2 (*.mpg)
MP3 Audio (*.mp3)
OggVorbis (*.ogg)
QuickTime 6 (*.mov)
RealMedia 9 (*.rm)
Scott Studios Wave (*.wav)
Sony Perfect Clarity Audio (*.pca)
Sony Wave64 (*.w64)
Video for Windows (*.avi)
Wave (Microsoft) (*.wav)
Windows Media Audio V9 (*.wma)
Windows Media Video V9 (*.wmv)
```

Choose a file format

1. Open an existing project that you want to render.

2. Choose File > Render As.

   The Render As dialog box shown in Figure 10-1 appears.

3. Type a name for the file in the File Name field.

4. Click the Save As Type down arrow, and choose a file format from the drop-down list shown in Figure 10-2.

   Note that there are formats for both audio and video. You can render project audio as an independent file. In the upcoming lessons, you'll gain an understanding of the most popular file types for videos you'll display on the Web, on CD-ROM, or on DVD.

Choose a template and render the project

1. Click the template down arrow, and choose the desired template from the drop-down list shown in Figure 10-3.

   The available templates differ depending on the file format you choose. The templates shown in Figure 10-3 are for the MainConcept **MPEG**-2 (*mpg) format that is commonly used for broadcast-quality video.

2. Click the Save button.

   Vegas renders the file and displays a dialog box showing the percentage completed, elapsed time, and remaining time.

   > **CAUTION**
   >
   > Rendering is processor-intensive. It's not advisable to multi-task when you're rendering a project.

FIGURE 10-3

Choosing a template

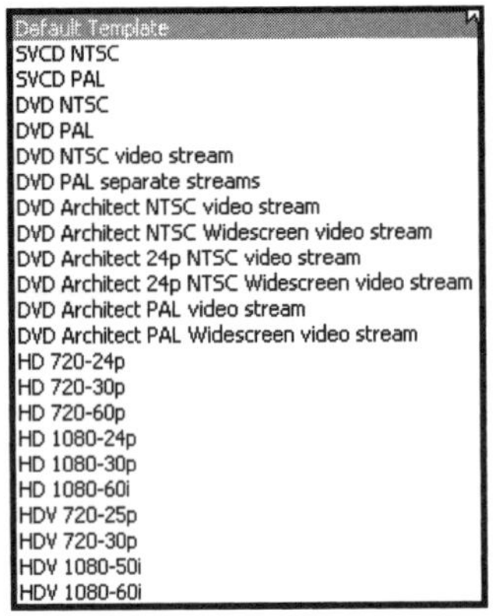

Default Template
SVCD NTSC
SVCD PAL
DVD NTSC
DVD PAL
DVD NTSC video stream
DVD PAL separate streams
DVD Architect NTSC video stream
DVD Architect NTSC Widescreen video stream
DVD Architect 24p NTSC video stream
DVD Architect 24p NTSC Widescreen video stream
DVD Architect PAL video stream
DVD Architect PAL Widescreen video stream
HD 720-24p
HD 720-30p
HD 720-60p
HD 1080-24p
HD 1080-30p
HD 1080-60i
HDV 720-25p
HDV 720-30p
HDV 1080-50i
HDV 1080-60i

RENDER FOR
THE WEB

What You'll Do

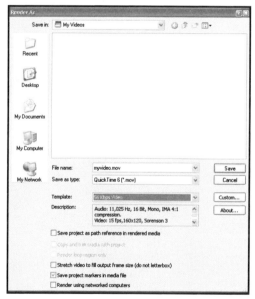

In this lesson, you learn to render two versions of a project for Web site display.

Choosing a Web-Friendly Format

When you create a project that you want to display on a Web site, you're concerned with a couple of things. First, you want a format whereby the video streams into the associated player. When video streams into a player, the video begins playing as soon as enough data has downloaded. There are three formats to consider that stream the video information into the applicable player:

- **MOV** streams into the Apple Quick-Time player
- **WMV** streams into the Windows Media Player
- **RM** streams into the Real Player

There are pros and cons to each player. Many Webmasters give visitors a choice by posting videos in each format.

QUICKTIP

When you post a video in a certain file format, include a link to the Web site where visitors can download the applicable player.

Understanding Data Rate

When you render a video, you specify a data rate, or choose a template that renders a video that will be delivered at a given data rate. Broadcast-quality video for DVD is delivered at a data rate of **8Mbps**, whereas video for the Web ranges anywhere from **28Kbps** for the slowest dial-up connections to 450Kbps for a high-speed DSL or cable modem.

In this regard, you have to know how your visitors will access the Web site. If they're visiting the Web site using a 56Kbps dial-up modem, they won't be able to watch a video with a high data rate without the video pausing playback while additional data downloads. This is situation where a Webmaster should post multiple versions of a video file: one for dial-up, one for medium speed DSL or cable, and one for high-speed DSL or cable.

Choosing the Proper Template

When you render a project for Web delivery, it's not a matter of choosing the right template; it's more a matter of deciding how many versions of the file you will need to post to accommodate all visitors to the site. For a dial-up modem, you should consider posting a smaller frame size (160 pixels by 120 pixels or 176 pixels by 144 pixels), with a frame rate of 15 fps (frames per second), and a data rate of no more than 34Kbps for both audio and video, whereas for a high-speed cable modem you can post a video with a frame size of 320 pixels by 240 pixels, with a frame rate of 30 fps and a data rate of 450Kbps for both audio and video. The higher data rate of the cable setting enables you to deliver stereo sound to your audience and smooth full-motion video, as compared to choppy video and monophonic music for the dial-up settings.

The upcoming lessons assume your viewing audience uses the Windows Media Player and accesses the Internet using dial-up and high-speed cable modems. You'll render two files and compare them for quality.

FIGURE 10-4

Choosing a template for a dial-up connection

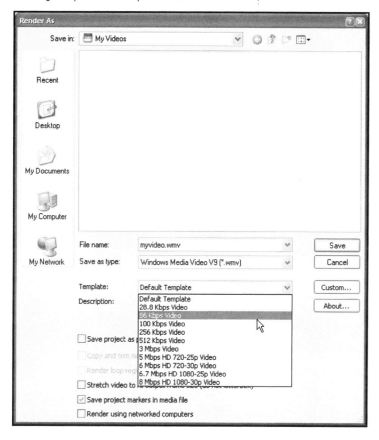

Choose a file format

1. Create a new project.
2. Import a video file into the Project Media window.

   Import a video file that's at least 10 seconds in duration.
3. Click the Media Generators tab, choose your favorite opening credit, and drop it in the main window, aligning it to the beginning of the timeline.

   Change the text if desired. Your main goal in this lesson is to compare the quality of the text between the dial-up and cable versions of the rendered project.
4. Select the video clip and drop it in the video track, overlapping it with the media event you just created.

   This creates a crossfade from the opening credits to the first event. You'll be able to compare the quality of the crossfade in the two versions you render.
5. Choose File > Render As to open the Render As dialog box.
6. Click the Save As Type down arrow and choose Windows Media Video V9 (*wmv).

Choose the templates

1. Click the template down arrow. Then choose 56 Kbps Video, as shown in Figure 10-4.

   Notice the description for the template: the video is only 15 fps with a miniscule frame size and the audio is monophonic with a very low data rate.

2. Name the file **test_dial_up** and specify the folder to which you want the file saved.

3. Click the Save button to render the file.

The file should render out fairly quickly. While rendering, Vegas displays the Rendering dialog box and a progress bar indicates how much of the project has been rendered. After the render is complete, the progress bar in the dialog box reads 100% and the Open button becomes available, as shown in Figure 10-5.

4. Click the Open button.

The rendered video opens in the Windows Media Player. Notice how small the credit text is, almost illegible. When the video plays, the image quality is poor and the sound is garbled. But for people with a dial-up modem, viewing any video is exciting.

5. Click Close.

6. Choose File Render As.

The Render As dialog box appears with the previously used file format and template selected.

7. Click the triangle to the right of the template field. Then choose 512 Kbps Video, as shown in Figure 10-6.

Notice the difference in the description of this template compared to the description in Figure 10-4. These settings result in much higher quality, as you'll soon see.

FIGURE 10-5

Rendering completed

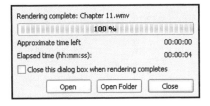

FIGURE 10-6

Choosing a template for high-speed cable access

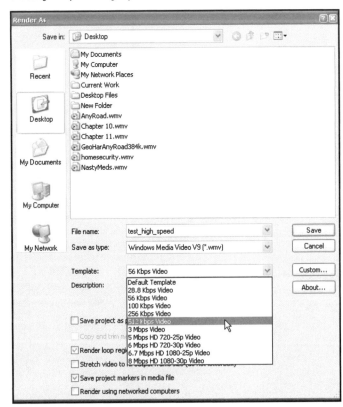

8. Name the file **test_high_speed**. Then click the Save button.

   Vegas begins rendering the file. Notice that it takes a while longer to render at these settings. That's because Vegas is creating twice as many frames using this template, and the data rate is higher.

9. When the video finishes rendering, click the Open button.

   The rendered file opens in the Windows Media Player. Notice how much clearer the title text is. The video and audio quality are vastly improved as well.

10. Minimize Vegas and navigate to the folder in which you stored the rendered video files.

11. Right-click the file you rendered for dial-up, choose Properties from the shortcut menu, and note the file size of the video.

12. Right-click the file you rendered for high-speed cable, choose Properties from the shortcut menu, and note the file size of the video.

    The file size is significantly larger than the dial-up render version of the project.

13. Keep the project open; you'll be using it in the next lesson.

    Save the file if you won't be reading the next lesson immediately. The object is to compare the quality of the different versions of the rendered project, as well as file size.

RENDER FOR
CD-ROM

What You'll Do

In this lesson, you render a high-quality video suitable for computer viewing from a CD-ROM.

Creating Video for CDs

When you render video for distribution on CDs, you can use a much higher data rate. Modern CD players are capable of getting the data from disc to computer quickly, which enables you to render higher-quality video, with a larger frame size, a higher frame rate, and a higher data rate. The difference in quality is amazing. The quality almost rivals that of VHS video.

Choosing the Proper Format

When you render a project for distribution on CDs, the MOV, WMV, and RM video formats will yield excellent quality. However, the Real Media Player isn't universally accepted. If your intended audience doesn't have the player installed on their machines, they may not be willing to download it. In this regard, your best bet is MOV or WMV, because both players are in widespread use.

Choosing the Proper Template

When you render a project for distribution on CD, you choose a template that specifies a frame size of 640 pixels x 480 pixels, a frame rate of 30 fps, and a data rate of 3Mbps, six times the data rate you specify for high-speed cable modem delivery. This combination yields high-quality video that plays back smoothly on modern computers.

In this lesson, you'll be rendering using the WMV file format for a direct comparison to the last lesson. When you're finished with the lesson, try rendering the file using the QuickTime 6 (*mov) for a comparison of the two formats and try to familiarize yourself with this popular format. If you don't have the Apple QuickTime player installed on your machine, you can download it here: http://www.apple.com/quicktime/products/qt/.

NOTE

You can also choose a template to render a file for a VCD (Video CD). This renders an MPEG-1 file suitable for use on a VCD. VCD discs can be viewed on set-top DVD players that support the format. You cannot create a VCD in Vegas. You'll need third-party software, such as Sonic MY DVD, to create a VCD.

Choose a format for CD video

1. Choose File > Render As to open the Render As dialog box.

    If you still have the project open from the last lesson, the previously used settings appear in the dialog box. If you saved the project, open it and perform Step 1, you'll see the previously used settings as well.

2. Click the Save As Type down arrow and choose Windows Media Video V9 (*wmv) from the drop-down list.

3. Click the Template down arrow and choose 3 Mbps Video from the drop-down list, as shown in Figure 10-7.

Compare these settings with the previous settings you used to render the file. Your video has a larger frame size and stereo-quality audio. The frame rate is 30 fps, just the ticket for CD video.

4. Type **test_CD** in the File Name field. Then navigate to the same folder in which the other renders of this project are stored.

Render and preview the file

1. Click the Save button.

    Vegas renders the file and the Rendering dialog box appears. Notice how much longer it takes to render this file. After Vegas renders the video, the Open button appears.

2. Click the Open button.

    The file opens in the Windows Media Player. Notice how much better the quality of the video is compared with the other files you've rendered.

3. Minimize Vegas and navigate to the folder in which you saved the file.

4. Navigate to the folder in which you stored the file, right-click the file, and choose Properties from the shortcut menu.

    Compare the file size to the other renders of this project.

5. Keep the project open; you'll be using it in the next lesson.

FIGURE 10-7

Choosing a template for CD-quality video

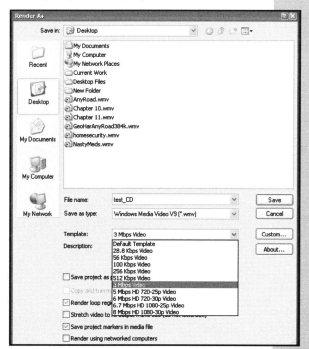

RENDER HIGH-QUALITY VIDEO
FOR DVD PROJECTS

What You'll Do

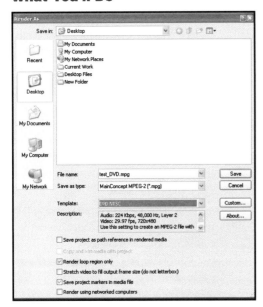

 In this lesson, you learn to render broadcast quality video for distribution on DVD and playback on set-top DVD players.

Choosing the Correct Format

When you create video for distribution on DVD, the standard file format is MainConcept MPEG-2. Many DVD authoring applications support the Windows Video AVI format. However, this format must be transcoded to MPEG-2 format when the DVD is built. Therefore, your best bet is to render the project as an MPEG-2 file. Vegas does a wonderful job of rendering high-quality MPEG-2 video. After you render the file in Vegas, you use an application such as Sony DVD Architect to author the DVD.

If you own Sony DVD Architect, you have a license that enables you to render audio tracks as Dolby Digital AC-3 files. This option is convenient if your DVD authoring application supports alternate audio tracks, as Sony DVD Architect does.

Understanding Broadcast Standard and Frame Rates

When you render video for playback on a television set, you must choose the proper broadcast standard. Your choices are NTSC (National Television System Committee), PAL (Phase Alternating Line), and HD (High Definition). The HD format is not an option unless you have one of the new camcorders capable of recording in that format.

Choosing the Correct Template

After choosing the MPEG-2 file format, it's a matter of finding the template that matches your video and the television broadcast standard. The title of each template tells you all you need to know; for example, DVD NTSC.

FIGURE 10-8

Rendering completed

```
Default Template
SVCD NTSC
SVCD PAL
DVD NTSC
DVD PAL
DVD NTSC video stream
DVD PAL separate streams
DVD Architect NTSC video stream
DVD Architect NTSC Widescreen video stream
DVD Architect 24p NTSC video stream
DVD Architect 24p NTSC Widescreen video stream
DVD Architect PAL video stream
DVD Architect PAL Widescreen video stream
HD 720-24p
HD 720-30p
HD 720-60p
HD 1080-24p
HD 1080-30p
HD 1080-60i
HDV 720-25p
HDV 720-30p
HDV 1080-50i
HDV 1080-60i
```

Choose a file format for broadcast-quality video

1. Choose File > Render As to open the Render As dialog box.

2. Click the triangle to the right of the Save As Type field and choose MainConcept MPEG-2 (*mpg) from the drop-down list.

3. Click the triangle to the right of the Template field and choose DVD NTSC from the drop-down list, as shown in Figure 10-8.

   If your project is PAL video, choose the DVD PAL template. Note there are also templates for widescreen and HD video.

   ### TIP

   If your DVD authoring application has the option to create **VCDs** or **SVCDs**, you can create video discs on CD-R discs that are close to VHS quality. Render the files using MainConcept MPEG-1 (*mpg) format and choose the VCD option for the desired broadcast standard. The VCD can be played back on most modern set-top DVD players.

4. Type **test_DVD** in the File Name field. Then navigate to the same folder in which you stored the previous renders.

Render and preview the file

1. Click the Save button.

   Vegas renders the file and the Rendering dialog box appears. Notice how much longer it takes to render this file. After Vegas renders the video, the Open button appears.

2. Click the Open button.

The file opens in the Windows Media Player. Notice how much better the quality of the video is compared with the other files you've rendered.

NOTE

When you preview the video, you may see something that looks like scan lines. That is because broadcast quality DVD is usually interlaced for television display. When the video is played back on a television, the interlaced fields are blended and the resulting playback is high-quality video.

3. Minimize Vegas and navigate to the folder in which you saved the file.

4. Right-click the file and choose Properties from the shortcut menu.

   Compare the file size to the other renders of this project.

5. Keep the project open; you'll be using it in the next lesson.

CREATE A
CUSTOM TEMPLATE

What You'll Do

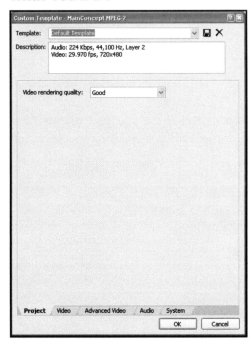

In this lesson, you learn how to modify one of the preset templates and save it as a custom template for future use.

Choosing a Template That's Almost Perfect

When you need to create a custom template, there's no need to reinvent the wheel. Start with a template that's almost perfect for your needs, and then modify the parameters to suit your projects. After you open the Render As dialog box, click the Custom button and you can begin modifying the template.

Modifying the Template

When you modify a template, you can change rendering quality, video frame and data rates, audio data rates, and more, depending on the template you are modifying. Each set of parameters is neatly nestled within a tab.

Saving the Template

After modifying a template, you give it a unique name. You can also type a description of the template that appears in the Description field when you select the template.

In this lesson, you modify one of the Windows Media Video templates for use with projects rendered for CD-ROM.

FIGURE 10-9

Project tab

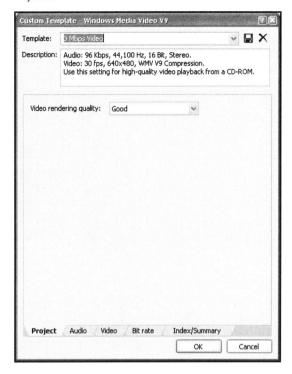

1. If the project from the last lesson is not open, choose File > Open, select the project and then click the Open button.

2. Choose File > Render As to open the Render As dialog box.

3. Click the Save As Type down arrow and choose Windows Media Video V9 (*wmv).

4. Click the triangle to the right of the Template field and choose 3 Mbps Video from the drop-down list.

5. Click the Custom button.

   Vegas displays the Project tab shown in Figure 10-9.

Modify the template

6. Click the Video Rendering Quality down arrow and choose Best from the drop-down list.

   Note that you also have the options of: Good (the default), Preview, and Draft. Best takes the longest to render, but delivers the highest quality video. For test renders, Preview and Draft will speed up the render.

7. Click the Audio tab.

The Custom Template dialog box reconfigures to show the available audio options, as
shown in Figure 10-10. Note that these differ
depending on the file format you choose.

8. Click the Mode down arrow and choose
Quality VBR from the drop-down list.

This setting delivers the best possible audio
using **VBR** encoding. Variable bit rate
increases the data rate when the encoder
encounters complex audio passages such as
music, and lowers the data rate when
encountering background noise or silence.
Note that the Attributes field changed when
you changed quality. You can modify the
attributes by choosing a different option
from the drop-down list.

9. Click the Video tab.

The Custom Template reconfigures to show
the options for video, as shown in Figure
10-11.

10. Click the Mode down arrow. Then choose
CBR (2 Pass) from the drop-down menu.

This encoding method makes two passes to
determine the optimum bit rate for the
video file being rendered. The first pass
examines the video and determines what bit
rate to use, while the second pass com-
presses the video.

11. Click the Image Size down arrow. Then
choose Custom from the drop-down list.

FIGURE 10-10
Audio tab

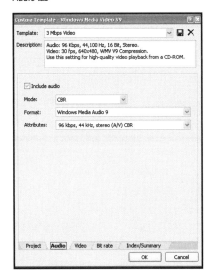

FIGURE 10-11
Video tab

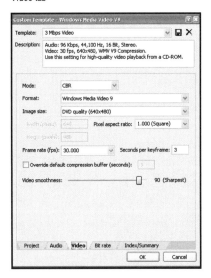

FIGURE 10-12

Bit Rate tab

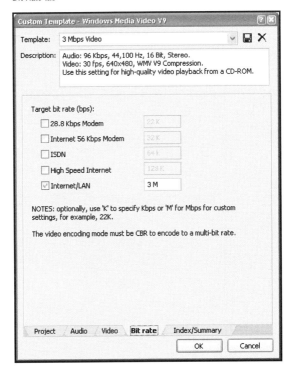

Notice there are also preset sizes. Custom enables you to specify the video frame size. When you create a custom frame size, make sure it's the same aspect ratio as the device on which the video will be played. If you're playing it back on a computer monitor, use a 4:3 aspect ratio.

12. Type **480** in the Width field and **320** in the Height field.

Notice there are other options you can modify such as Video smoothness, frame rate, and seconds per keyframe.

13. Click the Bit Rate tab.

The Custom Template dialog box reconfigures to show the Bit rate options, as shown in Figure 10-12. Notice you can choose from presets or specify a custom value.

14. Accept the current bit rate settings. Then click the Index/Summary tab.

The Custom Template dialog box reconfigures to show the index and summary options, as shown in Figure 10-13.

15. Enter the desired information by typing it into a field.

You can enter information identifying yourself or your company as the author of the video, the title of the video, copyright information, and so on. The information you enter shows up as a property of the file, and may be displayed in the associated video player.

16. Select the text in the Description field and type a new description.

This information appears when you select the template. Enter a description that tells you what type of video you're using the template for and gives a brief description of the settings.

17. Select the template name and then type a new name.

You cannot save a modified template using the default preset name.

18. Click the Save button (the floppy disk icon next to the Template field).

The custom template is saved and appears on the drop-down list of templates for the applicable file format type. In this case it would appear as one of the Windows Media Player v9 (*wmv) templates.

19. Click OK to exit the Custom Template dialog box.

FIGURE 10-13

Index/Summary tab

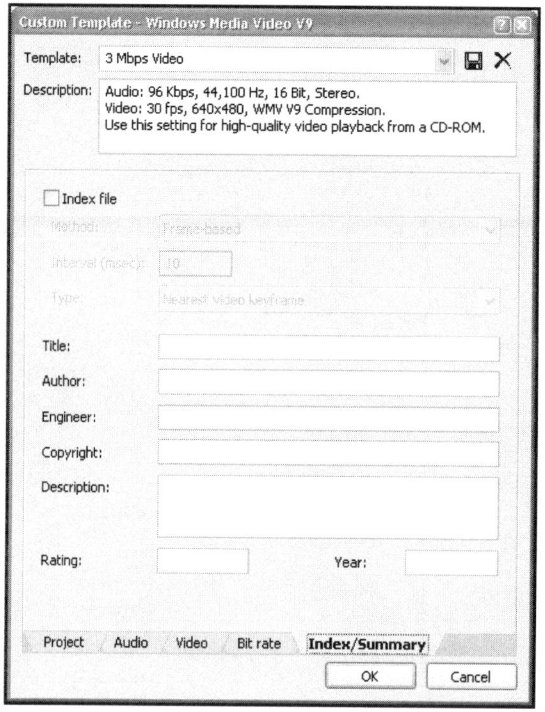

Rendering a Video for the Web

1. Create a new project.

2. Import two video clips into the Project Media window.

3. Select the video clips and drop them in main window, aligning them with the beginning of the timeline.

4. Choose File Render As to display the Render As dialog box shown in Figure 10-14.

   When opened, the Render As dialog box defaults to the previous format used.

5. Type a name for the rendered file. Then click the Save as Type down arrow and choose QuickTime 6 (*mov) from the drop-down list.

6. Click the Template down arrow and choose 56 Kbps Video, as shown in Figure 10-15.

7. Specify the folder in which to save the file, and then click Save.

8. After the video renders, click Open to preview the file.

9. Save the project; you'll be using it in the next skills review.

FIGURE 10-14
Render As dialog box

FIGURE 10-15
Choosing a template

SKILLS REVIEW

Modifying a Template

1. Choose File > Render As.
2. Click Custom.
3. Click the Quality down arrow. Then choose Best from the drop-down list.
4. Click the Video tab.
5. Drag the Quality slider to achieve a value of approximately 75, as shown in Figure 10-16.
6. For the template name, type High Quality Web in front of 56 Kbps Video, as shown in Figure 10-17.
7. Click the floppy disk icon next to the Template field to save the template.

FIGURE 10-16
Modifying video quality

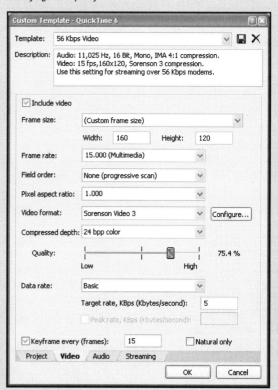

FIGURE 10-17
Naming a custom template

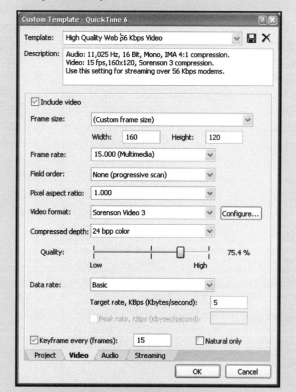

Render a File with a Custom Template

1. Create a new project.

2. Import three video clips into the Project Media window.

3. Select the video clips and drop them in the main window, aligning them to the beginning of the timeline.

4. Choose File > Render As.

5. Click the Save As Type down arrow and choose QuickTime 6 (*mov).

6. Click the Template down arrow and choose High Quality Web 56 Kbps Video from the drop-down list, as shown in Figure 10-18.

7. Type a name for the file in the File Name field. Then click the Save button to render the file.

FIGURE 10-18

Choosing a custom template

You work in the production department for a company that creates educational CD-ROMs. Your boss rushes in and says she needs a sample of the project you're working on ASAP for a board meeting in an hour. You tell her it won't be perfect, but it will give the staff a rough idea of what the final project will look like.

1. Open an existing project.

2. Choose File > Render As.

3. Type a name for the file and specify the folder in which to save the file.

FIGURE 10-19

Project Builder 1, Sample 1

4. Click the Save As Type down arrow. Then choose Windows Media Video V9 (*wmv) from the drop-down list.

5. Click the triangle to the right of the Template field. Then choose 3 Mbps Video.

6. Click the Custom button.

FIGURE 10-20

Project Builder 1, Sample 2

7. Click the Video rendering quality down arrow and choose Draft from the drop-down list shown in Figure 10-19.

8. Click the Bit Rate tab.

9. Select the 3 M value in the Internet/LAN field.

10. Type a value of 512 K, as shown in Figure 10-20.

11. Click OK to exit the dialog box without saving the modified template.

12. Click Save to render the file.

PROJECT BUILDER 2

Your boss returns and tells you your video was a big hit at the staff meeting. The sales staff wants a high-quality version with a frame size of 480 x 320 in the QuickTime format.

1. Open the project you rendered in the last lesson.

2. Choose File > Render As.

FIGURE 10-21
Project Builder 2, Sample 1

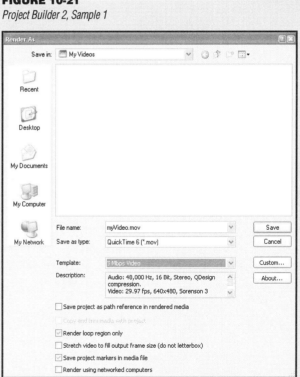

3. Click the Save As Type down arrow and choose QuickTime 6 (*mov) from the drop-down list.

4. Click the template down arrow and choose 3 Mbps.

5. Click the Custom button shown in Figure 10-21.

6. Click the Video Quality down arrow and choose Best from the drop-down list.

FIGURE 10-22
Project Builder 2, Sample 2

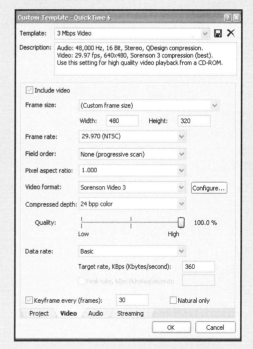

7. Click the Video tab.

8. Click the Frame Size down arrow, and choose Custom from the drop-down list.

9. Type a value of 480 in the Width text box, and 320 in the Height text box, as shown in Figure 10-22.

10. Click OK to exit the dialog box.

11. Type a name for the file and specify the folder to which the rendered file is to be saved. Then click Save to render the project.

The head of the sales staff sees the high-quality version of your project a few minutes before quitting time. He rushes into your office and says he'd like three versions of the file: one for dial-up modem customers, one for high-speed cable customers, and another version for a DVD that you'll author in Sony DVD Architect. He says he'd really appreciate it if you'd have the files ready by morning and would be willing to pay overtime. You frown, and then you remember the Vegas script for batch rendering. You tell him no problem. As he leaves the room, you wonder how you're going to account for your time while Vegas does all the heavy work.

1. Open the project you rendered in the last lesson.

2. Choose Tools > Scripting > Batch Render.

3. Click the plus sign (+) next to the Windows Media Video V9 title.

4. Choose 56 Kbps Video and 512 Kbps Video, as shown in Figure 10-23.

5. Click the minus sign (-) to collapse the group.

6. Click the plus sign (+) to the left of the MainConcept MPEG-2 title.

7. Choose DVD NTSC, as shown in Figure 10-24.

8. Type a name in the Base File Name field.

9. Click the Browse button to navigate to the folder in which you want the rendered files saved.

FIGURE 10-23
Design Project, Sample 1

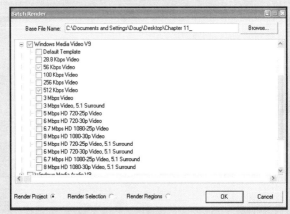

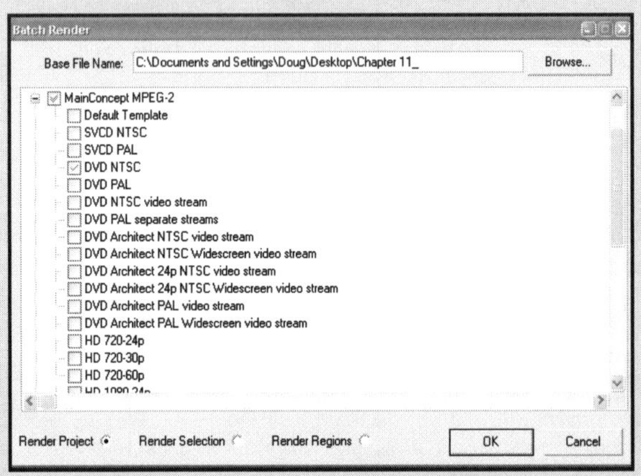

10. Click OK to render the files.

FIGURE 10-24
Design Project, Sample 2

CHAPTER SUMMARY

After editing a video project, you render the project for the intended destination. When you render a project, you can choose the file format for the intended player. Vegas has a wide variety of preset templates for each supported video file format. When you choose a preset, you determine the quality, frame size, and frame rate of the video, as well as the audio characteristics of the rendered video. If the specifications of the preset don't suit your needs, you can modify the preset and save it as a custom preset.

What You Have Learned

In this chapter you:
- Learned to render your projects for their intended destination.
- Learned to render projects for Internet viewing.
- Learned to render video for distribution on CDs.
- Learned to render broadcast-quality video.
- Learned to choose the proper file formats to display the video in popular video players.

- Learned to create custom templates to suit your projects.

Key Terms From this Chapter
- **CBR.** Constant Bit Rate, a method of encoding video and audio at a constant bit rate. You specify the bit rate to which Vegas encodes the file.
- **Data rate.** The amount of data transferred when a video is broadcast. Higher data rates result in better-quality video.
- **Kbps.** Kilobits per second, a unit of measure for data transfer. One kilobit equals one thousand bits. This unit of measure is used to measure data transfer on modems.
- **Mbps.** Megabits per second, a unit of measure for data transfer. One megabit equals one million bits. This unit of measure is used to measure data transfer on network and high-speed connections.
- **MOV.** MOVie, an Apple video format for viewing in the Apple QuickTime Player.

- **MPEG.** Acronym for Motion Picture Experts Group, a consortium that specifies parameters for video and audio. You can find more information about MPEG at www.mpeg.org.
- **RM.** Real Media, a video format for viewing in the Real Player.
- **SVCD.** Super Video Compact Disc, video discs created on CD-R discs. SVCD video is higher quality than VCD video.
- **VBR.** Variable Bit Rate, a method of encoding video and audio at varying bit rates. You specify the maximum allowable bit rate. When the file is rendered, Vegas varies the bit rate used to encode the file, using lower bit rates for simple passages and higher bit rates for complex passages.
- **VCD.** Video Compact Disc, video discs created on CD-Rs. VCD video quality is close to the quality of VHS video.
- **WMV.** Windows Media Video, a Windows video format for viewing in the Windows Media Player.

A

GLOSSARY

Acid Pro. A Sony application that enables you to create music by assembling sampled music loops on a timeline that is similar to that used by Vegas.

Alpha. With track level, alpha determines the percentage of the underlying tracks that are visible in the rendered project. With a level of 100, the track is fully visible; a level of 0 renders a track invisible. When used to define a color, alpha determines the opacity of the color. You can specify a color that is transparent (invisible), opaque, or partially transparent, which will let some of the underlying colors show through.

Audio bit depth. The number of bits used to represent a single sample. Higher bit depths ensure cleaner audio. 8-bit samples use less memory and disk space, but are inherently noisier.

Audio Busses. Devices that you use to control the audio output in your projects. You can add up to 26 audio busses to a project, which in theory works like a sound mixing board.

Audio sampling rate. The number of samples per second used to store a sound. Higher sampling rates ensure better fidelity at the expense of a larger file size.

Back story. Events that happened before the beginning of a story or video. Onscreen text or narration are commonly used to tell a back story.

Bezier. A method used to create curves in paths. In Vegas, Bezier curves are used to describe the paths used to create masks.

Cache. Items stored in computer memory.

CBR. Constant Bit Rate, a method of encoding video and audio at a constant bit rate. You specify the bit rate to which Vegas encodes the file.

Clock Wipe transitions. A transition group with presets that look like the hour hand of a clock revealing the next scene.

Collage. In video, a collection of video clips arranged within the video frame.

Color picker. A device that enables you to specify color for text, backgrounds, and other media you create.

Complementary color. A color from the opposite side of the color wheel.

Composite blend modes. Determines how multiple tracks are blended.

Control point. A point in a gradient where the color changes. Vegas blends the color from one control point to the next.

Crop. To specify which part of a video clip is shown. You can crop to zoom in on a small area of a clip or to resize a clip.

Crossfade. A video transition for events that are overlapped, where one event fades into the next. Vegas gradually decreases the opacity of the first event while increasing the opacity of the second event.

Data rate. The amount of data transferred when a video is broadcast. Higher data rates result in better-quality video.

Decibel. A unit of measure to determine the level of a sound. A decibel level above 100 is a very loud sound, whereas a decibel level of 130 is painful for humans.

Dissolve transitions. A group of transitions that dissolves the video from the previous scene into the next scene.

Dual item. A text item used to display text side by side. For example: Videographer…Doug Sahlin.

DV (Digital Video)-compliant media. Media such as miniDV and microDV tapes that are used to digitally record video.

Event FX. A filter that is applied to an event.

Event group. A group of events that acts as a single entity on the timeline. You can reposition an event group, but you cannot apply Event FX to an event group.

Events. Media you add to the Vegas timeline. You can change the duration of events and then enhance them with Event FX.

FireWire. An external device for transmitting data from devices to a computer. FireWire supports data transfer rates of 400 Mbps (1394a) or 800 Mbps (1394b).

Flash transitions. A group of transitions that uses a flash of light to reveal the next scene.

Frame rate. The number of frames played per second.

Generated media. Media such as text or backgrounds that you create to augment your projects.

HDV. An acronym for High Definition Video. HDV video format has a 16:9 (widescreen) aspect ratio MPEG-2 compliant transport stream that is captured on digital videotape. Supported frame rates are 60i (frames-per-second interlaced), 30p (progressive), 50i, and 25p.

Header. A bold text item used in credits and other text media.

Histogram. A graph that measures the levels from 0 (black) to 255 (white).

HSL color model. A color model where the color is determined by the hue, saturation, and luminance.

In point. The point at which an event begins playing, as compared to the original media. By specifying a different In point, you can prevent unwanted footage at the beginning of a media clip from playing, without altering the original media.

Interpolates. Using a mathematical algorithm, Vegas determines which position or state an object is in between keyframes. For example, if Vegas is interpolating an event's position between keyframes on a 3D motion track, it compares the event's position and rotation from one keyframe to the next, and uses that information to determine where the event should be positioned on each frame between keyframes.

Jscript. A programming language used to create instructions to be executed by a computer. Jscript can be used to create Vegas scripts.

Kbps. Kilobits per second, a unit of measure for data transfer. One kilobit equals one thousand bits. This unit of measure is used to measure data transfer on modems.

Keyframes. A frame used to designate a change in an object parameter such as size, color, or position.

Markers. Visual indications of specific areas in a project as created by the Vegas user. Each marker is noted numerically, and can be named.

Mask. A device that designates which part of an event is hidden or displayed.

Master Mixer. A device used to adjust the combined level of all audio tracks and busses in your project.

Mbps. Megabits per second, a unit of measure for data transfer. One megabit equals one million bits. This unit of measure is used to measure data transfer on network and high-speed connections.

Media Manager. A new feature in Vegas 6 that enables you to manage the media you use in your projects. You can add tags to media. Tags can be used when searching the Media Manager.

Mixer window. A device in the Window Docking area that is used to mix project audio.

MOV. MOVie, an Apple video format for viewing in the Apple QuickTime Player.

MPEG. Acronym for Motion Picture Experts Group, a consortium that specifies parameters for video and audio. You can find more information about MPEG at www.mpeg.org.

Non-destructive editing. The capability to edit events without modifying the original media.

Non-Real-Time Event FX. Plug-ins that are applied to audio events, and cannot be pre-

viewed in real time. When you apply a Non-Real-Time Event FX to an audio event, Vegas makes a copy of the event with the plug-in applied and adds it as a take.

NTSC safe color. A color that will display safely on an NTSC television set. The NTSC safe color range is from (R=16, G=16, B=16) to (R=235, G=235, B=235).

NTSC. An acronym for National Television System Committee, which determines the characteristics of video for television sets in the following countries: USA, Antigua, Bahamas, Barbados, Belize, Bermuda, Bolivia, Burma, Canada, Chile, Colombia, Costa Rica, Cuba, Dominican Republic, Ecuador, El Salvador, Greenland, Guam, Guatemala, Guyana, Honduras, Jamaica, Japan, South Korea, Mexico, Netherlands Antilles, Nicaragua, Panama, Peru, Philippines, Puerto Rico, St. Vincent & the Grenadines, St. Kitts, Saipan, Samoa, Surinam, Taiwan, Tobago, Trinidad, Venezuela, and the Virgin Islands.

Out of gamut. A color that will not display properly on a device. For example, if you specify a color of (R=0, G=0, B=0), which is true black, it will be clipped to (R=16, G=16, B=16).

Out point. The point at which an event stops playing, as compared to the original media. By specifying a different Out point, you can prevent unwanted footage at the end of a media clip from playing, without altering the original media.

Page Curl transition. A group of transitions that curls the video from one scene into the next, much like the pages of a book being turned.

PAL. An acronym for Phase Alternating Line, the video characteristics for video for television sets in the following countries: Afghanistan, Algeria, Argentina (PAL-N), Australia, Austria, Bahrain, Bangladesh, Belgium, Brunei, Cameroon, Canary Islands, China, Cyprus, Denmark, Finland, Germany, Ghana, Gibraltar, Greece, Hong Kong, Iceland, India, Indonesia, Ireland, Israel, Italy, Jordan, Kenya, North Korea, Kuwait, Liberia, Luxembourg, Madeira, New Zealand, Nigeria, Norway, Oman, Pakistan, Paraguay (PAL-N), Portugal, Qatar, Saudi Arabia, Sierra Leone, Singapore, South Africa, Spain, Sri Lanka, Sudan, Swaziland, Tanzania, Thailand, Turkey, Uganda, United Arab Emirates, United Kingdom, Uruguay (PAL-N), Yemen (the former Yemen Arab Republic was PAL), and the former People's Democratic Republic of Yemen, Yugoslavia, Zambia, and Zimbabwe.

Pan. To move a video clip within the video frame.

Path. Interconnected lines and curves that define a shape. In Vegas, a path determines the boundary of a mask.

Perspective. The ability to view objects that vanish into the distance. For example, the edges of a road are parallel, but appear to converge to a single point in the distance.

Plug-in Chain. Multiple Event FX applied to an event.

Punch-in point. A point on the timeline where you begin recording.

Punch-out point. A point on the timeline where you stop recording.

Push transition. A group of transitions that appears to push in the next scene.

RAM. Random Access Memory; computer memory that programs can access randomly to store information. The Dynamic RAM Preview command renders video to RAM so that it can be previewed in real time.

Regions. An area of the timeline in the project specified by the Vegas user. Visual markers denote the beginning and ending frame of each region. Each region is noted numerically, and can be named.

RGB color model. A color model comprised of 256 shades of red, green, and blue.

Ripple editing. Changing the position of events on the timeline that are downstream from events you add to a timeline. In essence, ripple editing makes room for the newly inserted events.

RM. Real Media, a video format for viewing in the Real Player.

Script. A set of instructions used to automate tasks in Vegas. For example, you can run a script to render a video in multiple formats.

Scrub control. A slider used to rapidly navigate (scrub) through a project. You can scrub forward or backward.

Semitones. An interval equal to a half tone in the standard diatonic scale.

Single item. A text item used to display a single line of credit text.

Sliding. When you slide an event that is a smaller than the original clip, the media file maintains its position in the timeline, but the event moves in the direction you drag.

Slipping. When working with an event that is smaller than the original media, you can slip the event to determine which portion of the original footage is displayed in the event.

Slip-trimming. When you slip-trim an event, the opposite edge of the event is unaffected and the event is trimmed from the direction you drag.

Smart Resampling. Vegas uses Smart Resampling to synchronize a stretched or compressed event with the project frame rate.

Sony DV codec. The codec used by Vegas when compressing video during capture, and decompressing video for playback within Sony Vegas.

Sony DVD Architect. An application used to author a DVD project.

Sony Sound Forge. A Sony application used to edit sound clips. Sony Sound Forge works interactively with Sony Vegas, enabling you to use Sound Forge to edit audio events.

Sony Video Capture. An application installed with Vegas that is used to capture video from camcorders and other video playback devices such as video decks, that you connect to a computer via an IEEE 1394 port of an OHCI-compliant video capture card.

Splitting an event. Using a menu command to split an event into two events.

Stretching an event. Increasing the duration of an event without changing or repeating the contents.

Subclip. A portion of the original media that is created in the Trimmer. Subclips are added to the Project Media window.

SVCD. Super Video Compact Disc, video discs created on CD-R discs. SVCD video is higher quality than VCD video.

Tangent handles. A handle that appears tangentially to a point that defines the end of a curve. A dot at each end of the handle can be clicked and dragged to change the curve to which the point is attached.

The Explorer. A device in the Window Docking area that is used to navigate to system folders. The Vegas Explorer is similar to the Windows Explorer.

Timecode. A method of measuring time in a video project. Timecode is measured as hh:mm:ss:ff, where hh is hours, mm is minutes, ss is seconds, and ff is frames. For example, 01:20:05:10 is 1 hour, 20 minutes, 5 seconds, and 10 frames into the project.

Title and ending credits. Title credits announce a video production displaying the title of the project and other pertinent information such as the actors, directors, and so on. Ending credits appear at the end of a production and display other pertinent information about the project, such as the

videographer, the locations where the production was recorded, and so on.

Track Compressor. A plug-in used to limit the dynamic range of an audio track.

Track EQ. A plug-in used to equalize an audio track.

Track Noise Gate. A plug-in that is used to correct deficiencies in audio tracks, such as background noise and hiss.

Trimmer. A device used to precisely trim a clip to the desired length.

VB. Visual Basic, a programming language used to create instructions to be executed by a computer. VB can be used to create Vegas scripts.

VBR. Variable Bit Rate, a method of encoding video and audio at varying bit rates. You specify the maximum allowable bit rate. When the file is rendered, Vegas varies the bit rate used to encode the file, using lower bit rates for simple passages and higher bit rates for complex passages.

VCD. Video Compact Disc, video discs created on CD-Rs. VCD video quality is close to the quality of VHS video.

Velocity envelope. Used to change the speed of an event. A velocity envelope can speed up, slow down, or play an event in reverse.

Video Bus. A track that enables you to add and animate event FX to the entire production. You animate effects applied to a track through the use of keyframes. You can also

add envelopes to the video bus track to modify the entire production device.

Video frame. The boundaries of a video clip.

Video Preview Window. Displays a project's video output at the current cusor position during editing and playback.

Video Supersampling. An envelope you can add to the Video Bus Track. Supersampling can improve the appearance of animation effects you've added, such as 3D Track Motion and animated plug-ins.

Voice-over recordings. Audio recordings that can be used to narrate videos.

Window Docking Area. The bottom of the Vegas workspace, which is used to dock windows. You can drag windows from the Window Docking area and float them in the workspace.

Wipe transition. A group of transitions that appears to wipe the video of one scene into the next.

WMV. Windows Media Video, a Windows video format for viewing in the Windows Media Player.

X axis. From left to right in the video frame (horizontal).

Y axis. From top to bottom in the video frame (vertical).

D

W-Z